NEW WORLD™

POCKET BOOK
of
FACTS

Edited by Laura J. Reed

MACMILLAN • USA

Macmillan General Reference
A Simon & Schuster Macmillan Company
1633 Broadway
New York, NY 10019-3785

A Webster's New World book

MACMILLAN is a registered trademark
of Macmillan, Inc.

Manufactured in the United States of America

02 01 00 99 98 - 5 4 3 2 1

ISBN: 0-02-862750-4

Contents

12. Sports, Continued

13. Science & Technology 305

14. Environment 335

14. Environment, Continued

15. Weather 361

16. Time Zones & Area Codes 373

17. Holidays, Measurements & Miscellaneous 387

Acknowledgments

The author gratefully acknowledges data from the following sources for use in preparing charts, lists, and tables:

The Wellness Encyclopedia, UCLA

American Academy of Pediatrics

American Academy of Family Physicians

The Parents Guide to Alternatives in Education, Koetsch, Ph.D.

National Home Education Research Institute

Market Data Retrieval

The College Entrance Examination Board

The Higher Education Research Institute

U.S. News & World Report

Fortune Magazine

American Federation of Labor & Congress of Industrial Organizations

National Employment Weekly

International Monetary Fund

Entrepreneur

American Automobile Manufacturers Association

Eno Transportation Foundation, Inc.

National Credit Union Association

U.S. National Science Foundation

Paul Kagan Association

Nielsen Media Research

Warren Publishing

Corporation for Public Broadcasting

Veronis, Schuler & Associates

Louis Harris & Associates

M Street Corporation

Electronic Industries Association

Recording Industry of America

Pollstar

Book Industry Study Group

Editor & Publisher

Audit Bureau of Circulations & Magazine Publishers of America

Publishers Information Bureau

League of American Theaters & Producers

Variety

Theater Communications Group

Opera America

American Symphony Orchestra League

Amusement Business

National Sporting Goods Association

Bowling Headquarters, Greendale, WI

Amateur Softball Association

The Worth Book of Softball

National Golf Foundation

Experimental Aircraft Association

Soaring Society of America

National Marine Manufacturers Association

National League of Professional Baseball Clubs

American League of Professional Baseball Clubs

National Basketball Association

Association of Racing Commissioners International

Academy of Television Arts & Sciences

National Collegiate Athletic Association

Professional Bowlers Association

Federation Internationale de Eschecs

U.S. Chess Federation

National Greyhound Association

Westminster Kennel Club

The American Kennel Club

Cat Fanciers Association

International Game Fish Association

National Hockey League

U.S. Golf Association

PGA Tour

U.S. Trotting Association

The Indianapolis Motor Speedway

American Motorcycle Association

Federation Internationale Morotcycliste

International Amateur Athletic Federation

The New York Public Library Desk Reference

The World Almanac & Book of Facts

The Top 10 of Everything

The Practical Guide to Practically Everything

The Wall Street Journal Almanac

The Joy of Cooking

Some of the art included in this book was provided by Corel Corporation.

Introduction

Today, we have access to many sources of information. There are comfortable, traditional ones like newspapers, books, radio, and TV, and a growing collection of new ones like internet newsgroups, web sites, and on-line searches. Sometimes, finding ourselves knee-deep in all these options -- wonderful as they are -- can be confusing. And sometimes, it can be ridiculously difficult to get an answer to a simple question!

For that reason, Webster's New World™ has developed *The Pocket Book of Facts*. It is easy to use and provides answers to thousands of everyday questions. We've included hundreds of charts, graphs, tables, and lists to give you the facts you need at a glance. Where possible, we've also provided source information, including web addresses, to help you find more information on topics of interest to you.

What This Book Is and What It Isn't

A book of facts is an ambitious undertaking -- especially one small enough to fit in your pocket, backpack, or briefcase. So we carefully sifted through mountains of data, choosing only the most interesting, entertaining, and useful facts.

Obviously, we had to leave out some things. What we left out, though interesting, was so technical or specialized as to be useless to most people. You won't find, for example, the Julian calendar, or the melting point of copper. You will, however, find the driving time between Boston and New York, the fastest growing jobs, tips on sites to see in Utah, and 30 years' worth of Super Bowl winners.

A Word About Statistical Information

In our effort to cover a wide variety of topics, we have included some which are mostly statistical in nature.

Realizing that statistics soon become out-of-date, and that some take so long to collect that they seem somewhat dated when first released, we have attempted to present several years' worth, in order to show any trends. In the *Entertainment* section, for example, you can see how much more popular golf and softball are becoming as leisure activities, along with the ups and downs of scouting and bowling participation.

How to Find What You're Looking for

The table of contents helps you search for things by category. The index helps you search for individual items alphabetically.

For example, if you need to settle a bet about who won the 1975 World Series, you could look up *Sports* in the table of contents, and find the *Baseball* section.

Use the index for things that are not so obvious. To find out the crime rate for Alaska, for example, look up *crime* or *Alaska* in the index. Either one will direct you to the *Comparative Statistics* section of the chapter titled *These United States*.

With Webster's New World™ Pocket Book of Facts, you always have instant access to the facts you need.

1. Nations of the World

See also 'Weather' and 'Travel.'

People of the World

Capitals & Governments

Most Populous Nations

People of the World

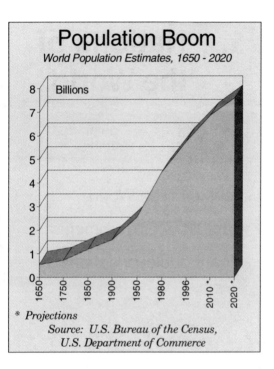

Population Boom
World Population Estimates, 1650 - 2020

Billions

8
7
6
5
4
3
2
1
0

1650 1750 1850 1900 1950 1980 1996 2010* 2020*

* Projections
Source: U.S. Bureau of the Census,
U.S. Department of Commerce

The population of the world did not reach the 1 billion mark until the early 1800s. By 1980, it had topped 4 billion. Then, swelling by another 1.3 billion in just 16 years, world population topped 5.7 billion in 1996.

Where the People Live

Population by Continent, in Millions, 1650 - 1900

Continent or Region	1650	1750	1850	1900
North America	5	5	39	106
South America	8	7	20	38
Europe	100	140	265	400
Asia	335	476	754	932
Africa	100	95	95	118
Oceania, Australia	2	2	2	6
Antarctica		Uninhabited		
World	550	725	1,175	1,600

Population by Continent, in Millions, 1950 - 1996

Continent or Region	1950	1980	1996	% of World
North America	166	252	295	5.1
Latin Am., Caribb.	166	362	489	8.5
Europe	392	484	507	8.8
Asia	1,411	2,601	3,428	59.4
Africa	229	470	732	12.7
Former USSR	180	266	293	5.2
Oceania, Australia	12	23	29	0.5
World	2,556	4,458	5,772	100%

Population Projections by Continent, in Millions

Continent or Region	2010	2020
Africa	1,009	1,230
Asia	4,075	4,495
Latin Am., Caribb.	583	643
North America	331	358
Europe	523	521
Former USSR	307	318
Oceania, Australia	34	37
World	6,863	7,602

Changing Populations

Population by Nation with Projections, in Thousands

Nation	1996	2010	2020
Afghanistan	22,664	34,098	43,050
Albania	3,249	3,858	4,257
Algeria	29,183	38,479	44,783
Andorra	73	92	97
Angola	10,343	14,982	19,272
Antigua/Barbuda	66	74	80
Argentina	34,673	39,947	43,190
Armenia	3,464	3,577	3,665
Australia	18,261	20,434	21,696
Austria	8,023	8,223	8,262
Azerbaijan	7,677	8,410	9,007
Bahamas	259	293	314
Bahrain	590	759	870
Bangladesh	123,063	153,195	172,041
Barbados	257	272	284
Belarus	10,416	10,924	11,059
Belgium	10,170	10,358	10,271
Belize	219	299	356
Benin	5,710	8,955	11,920
Bhutan	1,823	2,474	3,035
Bolivia	7,165	8,941	10,246
Bosnia/Herzegovina	2,656	2,892	2,966
Botswana	1,478	1,598	1,553
Brazil	162,661	183,747	194,246
Brunei	300	410	490
Bulgaria	8,613	8,928	8,777
Burkina Faso	10,623	14,150	16,569
Burundi	5,943	8,229	10,197
Cambodia	10,861	15,679	20,208
Cameroon	14,262	20,630	25,896
Canada	28,821	32,534	34,753
Cape Verde	449	646	812
Central African Rep.	3,274	4,177	4,780

Population by Nation, in Thousands, Continued

Nation	1996	2010	2020
Chad	6,977	10,055	12,831
Chile	14,333	16,382	17,535
China	1,210,005	1,340,357	1,413,251
Colombia	36,813	44,504	49,266
Comoros	569	919	1,249
Congo	2,528	3,298	3,817
Costa Rica	3,463	4,416	5,044
Côte d'Ivoire	14,762	20,261	24,634
Croatia	5,004	4,986	4,821
Cuba	10,951	11,481	11,699
Cyprus	745	858	936
Czech Republic	10,321	10,445	10,271
Denmark	5,250	5,417	5,458
Djibouti	428	588	751
Dominica	83	89	96
Dominican Republic	8,089	9,928	11,152
Ecuador	11,466	14,534	16,546
Egypt	63,575	80,689	92,350
El Salvador	5,829	7,332	8,473
Equatorial Guinea	431	615	783
Eritrea	3,910	6,018	7,674
Estonia	1,459	1,401	1,370
Ethiopia	57,172	81,169	100,813
Fiji	782	933	1,037
Finland	5,105	5,109	5,075
France	58,041	60,562	61,087
Gabon	1,173	1,445	1,675
Gambia, The	1,205	1,864	2,399
Georgia	5,220	5,188	5,205
Germany	83,536	88,975	88,870
Ghana	17,698	22,929	26,516
Greece	10,539	11,135	11,076
Grenada	95	115	141
Guatemala	11,278	15,284	18,131
Guinea	7,412	9,450	11,849

Population by Nation, in Thousands, Continued

Nation	1996	2010	2020
Guinea-Bissau	1,151	1,579	1,925
Guyana	712	695	685
Haiti	6,732	8,681	10,252
Honduras	5,605	7,643	9,042
Hungary	10,003	9,456	9,103
Iceland	270	303	325
India	952,108	1,155,830	1,289,473
Indonesia	206,612	249,679	276,017
Iran	66,094	88,231	104,282
Iraq	21,422	34,545	46,260
Ireland	3,567	3,452	3,570
Israel	5,422	6,696	7,439
Italy	57,460	57,660	55,665
Jamaica	2,595	2,900	3,213
Japan	125,450	127,548	123,620
Jordan	4,212	6,112	7,529
Kazakstan	16,916	17,564	18,408
Kenya	28,177	33,920	35,236
Kiribati	81	95	98
Korea, North	23,904	28,491	30,969
Korea, South	45,482	51,235	53,451
Kuwait	1,950	3,160	3,560
Kyrgyzstan	4,530	5,403	6,257
Laos	4,976	7,168	8,923
Latvia	2,469	2,293	2,212
Lebanon	3,776	4,973	5,748
Lesotho	1,971	2,428	2,693
Liberia	2,110	4,540	5,991
Libya	5,445	8,913	12,391
Liechtenstein	31	35	36
Lithuania	3,646	3,650	3,646
Luxembourg	416	495	523
Macedonia	2,104	2,261	2,296
Madagascar	13,671	20,096	25,988
Malawi	9,453	10,662	10,719

Population by Nation, in Thousands, Continued

Nation	1996	2010	2020
Malaysia	19,963	25,691	29,830
Maldives	271	423	554
Mali	9,653	14,966	20,427
Malta	376	425	450
Marshall Islands	58	100	144
Mauritania	2,336	3,630	4,859
Mauritius	1,140	1,328	1,440
Mexico	95,772	120,115	136,096
Micronesia	125	141	143
Moldova	4,464	4,818	5,000
Monaco	32	33	34
Mongolia	2,497	3,018	3,393
Morocco	29,779	38,442	44,519
Mozambique	17,878	25,116	30,810
Myanmar	45,976	58,236	67,501
Namibia	1,677	2,513	3,267
Nauru	10	11	12
Nepal	22,094	30,783	37,767
Netherlands	15,568	16,382	16,490
New Zealand	3,548	4,029	4,326
Nicaragua	4,272	5,863	6,973
Niger	9,113	13,678	17,983
Nigeria	103,912	157,375	205,160
Norway	4,384	4,577	4,632
Oman	2,187	3,516	4,731
Pakistan	129,276	170,750	198,722
Palau	17	20	21
Panama	2,655	3,238	3,625
Papua New Guinea	4,395	5,925	7,044
Paraguay	5,504	7,730	9,474
Peru	24,523	29,988	33,226
Philippines	74,481	97,119	112,963
Poland	38,643	40,342	40,833
Portugal	9,865	10,080	10,005
Qatar	548	660	735

Population by Nation, in Thousands, Continued

Nation	1996	2010	2020
Romania	21,657	20,741	20,135
Russia	148,178	149,978	149,632
Rwanda	6,853	10,080	11,040
Saint Kitts and Nevis	41	50	57
Saint Lucia	158	183	202
Saint Vincent and the Grenadines	118	132	146
San Marino	25	26	27
São Tomé and Príncipe	144	196	232
Saudi Arabia	19,409	31,198	43,255
Senegal	9,093	14,362	19,497
Seychelles	78	84	89
Sierra Leone	4,793	7,399	9,716
Singapore	3,397	4,026	4,330
Slovakia	5,374	5,735	5,837
Slovenia	1,951	1,926	1,856
Solomon Islands	413	620	767
Somalia	9,639	14,524	18,955
South Africa	41,743	49,200	52,264
Spain	39,181	40,398	39,758
Sri Lanka	18,553	21,331	22,877
Sudan	31,065	47,512	58,545
Suriname	436	534	598
Swaziland	999	1,566	2,128
Sweden	8,901	9,322	9,515
Switzerland	7,207	7,674	7,802
Syria	15,609	23,329	28,926
Taiwan	21,466	23,966	25,155
Tajikistan	5,916	8,019	10,019
Tanzania	29,058	36,076	40,102
Thailand	58,851	66,092	69,298
Togo	4,571	7,401	10,146
Tonga	106	119	128
Trinidad and Tobago	1,272	1,323	1,409
Tunisia	9,020	11,280	12,751

Population by Nation, in Thousands, Continued

Nation	1996	2010	2020
Turkey	62,484	76,570	85,643
Turkmenistan	4,149	5,362	6,380
Tuvalu	10	12	15
Uganda	20,158	26,355	30,872
Ukraine	50,864	49,915	49,038
United Arab Emirates	3,057	4,873	6,080
United Kingdom	58,490	59,159	59,289
United States	265,563	298,026	323,052
Uruguay	3,239	3,582	3,811
Uzbekistan	23,418	30,536	36,628
Vanuatu	178	230	266
Venezuela	21,983	27,345	30,876
Vietnam	73,977	88,602	99,153
Western Samoa	214	288	341
Yemen	13,483	21,841	29,469
Yugoslavia	10,615	11,062	11,067
Zaire	46,499	69,293	91,548
Zambia	9,159	11,471	13,022
Zimbabwe	11,271	11,905	11,344

Countries with Largest Populations	Countries with Smallest Populations
1. China	1. Nauru
2. India	2. Tuvalu
3. United States	3. Palau
4. Indonesia	4. San Marino
5. Brazil	5. Liechtenstein
6. Russia	6. Monaco
7. Pakistan	7. St. Kitts, St. Nevis
8. Japan	8. Marshall Islands
9. Bangladesh	9. Antigua/Barbuda
10. Nigeria	10. Andorra

Countries with the Best Life Expectancy for Men

1. San Marino
2. Iceland
3. Japan
4. Andorra
5. Hong Kong
6. Israel
7. Canada
8. Sweden
9. Martinique
10. Switzerland

Countries with the Best Life Expectancy for Women

1. San Marino
2. Japan
3. Andorra
4. Switzerland
5. France
6. Canada
7. Hong Kong
8. Martinique
9. Australia
10. Iceland

Countries with the Highest Marriage Rates

1. Cuba
2. Bermuda
3. Philippines
4. Liechtenstein
5. Benin
6. Seychelles
7. Puerto Rico
8. Maldives
9. Bangladesh
10. Turkmenistan

Countries with the Highest Divorce Rates

1. Latvia
2. Russia
3. Belarus
4. Cuba
5. Ukraine
6. United States
7. Puerto Rico
8. Estonia
9. Lithuania
10. Moldova

Capitals & Governments

Capitals & Governments

Capitals & Governments of Nations of the World

Nation	Capital	Government
Afghanistan	Kabul	In transition
Albania	Tirana	In transition
Algeria	Algiers	Republic
Andorra	Andorra la Vella	Co-principality of France & Spain
Angola	Luanda	In transition
Antigua/Barbuda	Saint John's	Parliamentary dem. [1]
Argentina	Buenos Aires	Republic
Armenia	Yerevan	In transition
Australia	Canberra	Fed. parliamentary [1]
Austria	Vienna	Federal republic
Azerbaijan	Baku	In transition
Bahamas	Nassau	Ind. commonwealth [1]
Bahrain	Manama	Monarchy
Bangladesh	Dhaka	Republic
Barbados	Bridgetown	Parliamentary dem. [1]
Belarus	Minsk	In transition
Belgium	Brussels	Const. monarchy
Belize	Belmopan	Parliamentary dem. [1]
Benin	Porto-Novo	Mulitparty democracy
Bhutan	Thimphu	Monarchy
Bolivia	La Paz and Sucre	Republic
Bosnia/Herzegovina	Sarajevo	Republic
Botswana	Gaborone	Parliamentary republic
Brazil	Brasilia	Federal republic
Brunei	Bandar Seri Begawan	Const. sultanate
Bulgaria	Sofia	In transition
Burkina Faso	Ouagadougou	Military
Burundi	Bujumbura	Republic
Cambodia	Phnom Penh	Disputed
Cameroon	Yaounde	Unitary republic
Canada	Ottawa	Confederation [1]

Capitals & Governments, Continued

Nation	Capital	Government
Cape Verde	Praia	Republic
Central African Rep.	Bangui	Military republic
Chad	N'Djamena	Republic
Chile	Santiago	Republic
China	Beijing	Communist
Colombia	Bogota	Republic
Comoros	Moroni	Independent republic
Congo	Brazzaville	Republic
Costa Rica	San Jose	Democratic republic
Côte d'Ivoire	Abidjan	Republic
Croatia	Zagreb	Republic
Cuba	Havana	Communist
Cyprus	Nicosia	Administered by Turkey
Czech Republic	Prague	Parliamentary dem.
Denmark	Copenhagen	Const. monarchy
Djibouti	Djibouti	Republic
Dominica	Roseau	Parliamentary dem.
Dominican Rep.	Santo Domingo	Republic
Ecuador	Quito	Republic
Egypt	Cairo	Republic
El Salvador	San Salvador	Republic
Equatorial Guinea	Malabo	Republic
Eritrea	Asmara	In transition
Estonia	Tallinn	Republic
Ethiopia	Addis Ababa	Republic
Fiji	Suva	Military republic
Finland	Helsinki	Republic
France	Paris	Republic
Gabon	Libreville	Republic
Gambia, The	Banjul	Republic
Georgia	Tbilisi	In transition
Germany	Berlin	Federal republic
Ghana	Accra	Military
Greece	Athens	Presidential parl.

Capitals & Governments, Continued

Nation	Capital	Government
Grenada	St. George's	Parliamentary dem. [1]
Guatemala	Guatemala City	Republic
Guinea	Conakry	Republic
Guinea-Bissau	Bissau	Republic
Guyana	Georgetown	Republic
Haiti	Port-au-Prince	Military republic
Honduras	Tegucigalpa	Republic
Hungary	Budapest	Republic
Iceland	Reykjavik	Republic
India	New Delhi	Federal republic
Indonesia	Jakarta	Republic
Iran	Teheran	Theocratic rep.
Iraq	Baghdad	Republic
Ireland	Dublin	Republic
Israel	Jerusalem	Parliamentary dem.
Italy	Rome	Republic
Jamaica	Kingston	Parliamentary dem. [1]
Japan	Tokyo	Const. monarchy
Jordan	Amman	Const. monarchy
Kazakstan	Alma Alta	In transition
Kenya	Nairobi	Republic
Kiribati	Tarawa	Republic
Korea, North	Pyongyang	Communist
Korea, South	Seoul	Republic
Kuwait	Kuwait	Const. monarchy
Kyrgyzstan	Frunze	In transition
Laos	Vientiane	Communist
Latvia	Riga	Republic
Lebanon	Beirut	Republic
Lesotho	Maseru	Const. monarchy
Liberia	Monrovia	Republic
Libya	Tripoli	Military dictatorship
Liechtenstein	Vaduz	Const. monarchy
Lithuania	Vilnius	Republic

Capitals & Governments, Continued

Nation	Capital	Government
Luxembourg	Luxembourg	Const. monarchy
Macedonia	Skopje	Republic
Madagascar	Antananarivo	Republic
Malawi	Lilongwe	One-party state
Malaysia	Kuala Lumpur	Const. monarchy
Maldives	Male	Republic
Mali	Bamako	Republic
Malta	Valletta	Parliamentary dem.
Marshall Islands	Majuro	Republic
Mauritania	Nouakchott	Military republic
Mauritius	Port Louis	Parliamentary dem. [1]
Mexico	Mexico City	Federal republic
Micronesia	Palikir	Republic
Moldova	Kishinev	In transition
Monaco	Monaco	Const. monarchy
Mongolia	Ulaanbaatar	In transition
Morocco	Rabat	Const. monarchy
Mozambique	Maputo	Republic
Myanmar	Yangon	Military
Namibia	Windhoek	Republic
Nauru	Yaren	Republic
Nepal	Kathmandu	Const. monarchy
Netherlands	Amsterdam	Const. monarchy
New Zealand	Wellington	Parliamentary dem. [1]
Nicaragua	Managua	Republic
Niger	Niamey	Republic
Nigeria	Lagos	Military
Norway	Oslo	Const.monarchy
Oman	Muscat	Absolute monarchy
Pakistan	Islamabad	Federal republic
Palau	Koror	Republic
Panama	Panama	Centralized republic
Papua New Guinea	Port Moresby	Parliamentary dem. [1]
Paraguay	Asuncion	Republic

Capitals & Governments, Continued

Nation	Capital	Government
Peru	Lima	Republic
Philippines	Manila	Republic
Poland	Warsaw	Democratic state
Portugal	Lisbon	Republic
Qatar	Doha	Traditional monarchy
Romania	Bucharest	In transition
Russia	Moscow	In transition
Rwanda	Kigali	Republic
Saint Kitts & Nevis	Basseterre	Const. monarchy [1]
Saint Lucia	Castries	Parliamentary dem. [1]
Saint Vincent and the Grenadines	Kingstown	Const. monarchy [1]
San Marino	San Marino	Republic
São Tomé and Príncipe	São Tomé &Príncipe	Republic
Saudi Arabia	Riyadh	Monarchy
Senegal	Dakar	Republic
Seychelles	Victoria	Republic
Sierra Leone	Freetown	Republic
Singapore	Singapore	Republic
Slovakia	Bratislava	Parliamentary dem.
Slovenia	Ljubljana	Republic
Solomon Islands	Honiara	Parliamentary state [1]
Somalia	Mogadishu	Republic
South Africa	Pretoria	Republic
Spain	Madrid	Parliamentary mon.
Sri Lanka	Colombo	Republic
Sudan	Khartoum	Military
Suriname	Paramaribo	Military republic
Swaziland	Mbabane	Ind. monarchy [1]
Sweden	Stockholm	Const. monarchy
Switzerland	Bern	Federal republic
Syria	Damascus	Military republic
Taiwan	Taipei	Republic

Capitals & Governments, Continued

Nation	Capital	Government
Tajikistan	Dushanbe	In transition
Tanzania	Dar es Salaam	Republic
Thailand	Bangkok	Const. monarchy
Togo	Lome	Republic
Tonga	Nuku'alofa	Const. monarchy
Trinidad and Tobago	Port-of-Spain	Parliamentary dem.
Tunisia	Tunis	Republic
Turkey	Ankara	Rep. parl. dem.
Turkmenistan	Ashkhabad	In transition
Tuvalu	Funafuti	Democracy [1]
Uganda	Kampala	One-party republic
Ukraine	Kiev	In transition
United Arab Emirates	Abu Dhabi	Federation of seven emirates
United Kingdom	London	Const. monarchy
United States	Washington, D.C.	Federal republic
Uruguay	Montevideo	Republic
Uzbekistan	Tashkent	In transition
Vanuatu	Port-Vila	Republic
Venezuela	Caracas	Republic
Vietnam	Hanoi	Communist
Western Samoa	Apia	Const. monarchy
Yemen	Sanaa	Republic
Yugoslavia	Belgrade	Republic
Zaire	Kinshasa	Republic
Zambia	Lusaka	Multiparty state
Zimbabwe	Harare	Parliamentary dem.

[1] *Affiliated with the United Kingdom*

Most Populous Nations

CHINA

Population:	1,210,005,000
Land Area:	3,696,100 sq. mi.
Population Density:	327 per sq. mi.
Urban:	29%
Major Cities:	Shanghai, Beijing, Tianjin, Shenyang, Guangzhou
Official Language:	Mandarin
Religions:	Buddhism, Taoism
Government:	Communist-party led state
Active Troop Strength:	2.3 million
GDP (1994):	$2.61 trillion
Industries:	iron, steel, textiles, apparel, fishing, livestock
Crops:	grain, rice, cotton, potatoes, tea
Arable Land:	10%
Labor Force:	60% agricultural, forestry; 25% industrial, commercial
Imports (1994):	$115.7 billion
Exports (1994):	$121 billion
Monetary Unit:	Rinminbi
Private Motor Vehicles:	2.9 million
Literacy:	82%
Daily Newspaper Circ.:	23 per 1,000 population
Televisions:	1 per 5.3 persons
Radios:	1 per 5.4 persons
Telephones:	1 per 30 persons
Physicians:	1 per 630 persons
Birth Rate (per 1,000):	17
Death Rate (per 1,000):	7
Natural Increase:	1%
Life Expectancy:	68 male; 71 female

INDIA

Population:	952,108,000
Land Area:	1,222,243 sq. mi.
Population Density:	792 per sq. mi.
Urban:	27%
Major Cities:	Bombay, Calcutta, Delhi, Madras, Hyderabad, Bangalore
Official Language:	Hindi
Religions:	Hindu, Muslim, Christian
Government:	Federal Republic
Active Troop Strength:	1.145 million
GDP (1995):	$1.41 trillion
Industries:	textiles, steel, processed foods, cement, machinery, chemicals, mining, autos
Crops:	rice, grains, sugar, spices, tea, cashews, cotton, potatoes
Arable Land:	55%
Labor Force:	65% agricultural
Imports (1995):	$33.5 billion
Exports (1995):	$30 billion
Monetary Unit:	Rupee
Private Motor Vehicles:	3.5 million
Literacy:	52%
Daily Newspaper Circ.:	21 per 1,000 persons
Televisions:	1 per 25 persons
Radios:	1 per 12 persons
Telephones:	1 per 78 persons
Physicians:	1 per 2,173 persons
Birth Rate (per 1,000):	25
Death Rate (per 1,000):	9
Natural Increase:	1.6%
Life Expectancy:	59.5 males; 60.8 females

UNITED STATES

Population:	265,563,000
Land Area:	3,675,031 sq. mi.
Population Density:	72 per sq. mi.
Urban:	76%
Major Cities:	New York, Los Angeles, Chicago, Houston, Philadelphia
Official Language:	English
Government:	Federal Republic
Active Troop Strength:	1.484 million
GDP (1997):	$7.17 trillion
Industries:	electronics, industrial machinery, chemicals, food products, services
Crops:	corn, soybeans, wheat, hay, oats, cotton, sorghum, rice, potatoes, tobacco, peanuts
Arable Land:	20%
Labor Force:	35% service; 24% trade; 20% const., mfg., trans.
Imports (1995):	$749 billion
Exports (1995):	$685 billion
Monetary Unit:	Dollar
Private Motor Vehicles:	135 million
Literacy:	96%
Daily Newspaper Circ.:	228 per 1,000 population
Televisions:	1 per 1.2 persons
Radios:	1 per 1.5 persons
Telephones:	1 per 1.6 persons
Physicians:	1 per 381 persons
Birth Rate (per 1,000):	15
Death Rate (per 1,000):	9
Natural Increase:	0.6%
Life Expectancy:	72.8 males; 79.5 females

INDONESIA

Population:	206,612,000
Land Area:	741,052 sq. mi.
Population Density:	283 per sq. mi.
Urban:	36%
Major Cities:	Jakarta, Bandung, Surabaja
Official Language:	Bahasa Indonesian (Malay)
Religions:	Muslim, Protestant
Government:	Republic
Active Troop Strength:	299,200
GDP (1995):	$711 billion
Industries:	oil, gas, food processing, textiles, cement
Crops:	rice, cocoa, peanuts
Arable Land:	8%
Labor Force:	55% agriculture, 10% manuf.
Imports (1994):	$32 billion
Exports (1994):	$39.9 billion
Monetary Unit:	Rupiah
Private Motor Vehicles:	1.9 million
Literacy:	84%
Daily Newspaper Circ.:	20 per 1,000 population
Televisions:	1 per 16 persons
Radios:	1 per 6.8 persons
Telephones:	1 per 59 persons
Physicians:	1 per 7,402 persons
Birth Rate (per 1,000):	23
Death Rate (per 1,000):	8
Natural Increase:	1.5%
Life Expectancy:	59.9 males; 64.3 females

BRAZIL

Population:	162,661,000
Land Area:	3,300,171 sq. mi.
Population Density:	50 per sq. mi.
Urban:	79%
Major Cities:	Sao, Paulo, Rio de Janeiro, Belo Horizonte, Brasilia
Official Language:	Portuguese
Religions:	Roman Catholic
Government:	Federal Republic
Active Troop Strength:	295,000
GDP (1995):	$976.8 billion
Industries:	steel, autos, textiles, shoes, chemicals, machinery
Crops:	coffee, soy beans, sugar, cocoa, rice, corn, fruits, cotton
Arable Land:	7%
Labor Force:	42% service; 31% agricultural; 27% industrial
Imports (1995):	$49.7 billion
Exports (1995):	$46.5 billion
Monetary Unit:	Real
Private Motor Vehicles:	12 million
Literacy:	83%
Daily Newspaper Circ.:	45 per 1,000 population
Televisions:	1 per 4.8 persons
Radios:	1 per 2.5 persons
Telephones:	1 per 13 persons
Physicians:	1 per 681 persons
Birth Rate (per 1,000):	20
Death Rate (per 1,000):	9
Natural Increase:	1.1%
Life Expectancy:	56.8 males, 66.3 females

RUSSIA

Population:	148,178,000
Land Area:	6,592,800 sq. mi.
Population Density:	22 per sq. mi.
Urban:	76%
Major Cities:	Moscow, St. Petersburg, Novosibirsk
Official Language:	Russian
Religions:	Russian Orthodox, Muslim
Government:	Federation
Active Troop Strength:	1.27 million
GDP (1995):	$796 billion
Industries:	steel, machinery, vehicles, mining, footwear, textiles, appliances, paper
Crops:	grains, sugar beets, potatoes, vegetables, sunflowers
Arable Land:	8%
Labor Force:	84% production & service; 16% government
Imports (1995):	$33 billion
Exports (1995):	$66 billion
Monetary Unit:	Ruble
Private Motor Vehicles:	10.5 million
Literacy:	99%
Daily Newspaper Circ.:	267 per 1,000 population
Televisions:	1 per 2.7 persons
Radios:	1 per 2.9 persons
Telephones:	1 per 5.9 persons
Physicians:	1 per 253 persons
Birth Rate (per 1,000):	11
Death Rate (per 1,000):	16
Natural Increase:	-0.5%
Life Expectancy:	57.2 males; 70.7 females

PAKISTAN

Population:	129,276,000
Land Area:	307,374 sq. mi.
Population Density:	389 per sq. mi.
Urban:	35%
Major Cities:	Karachi, Lahore, Faisalabad
Official Language:	Urdu, English
Religions:	Sunni Muslim, Shi'a Muslim
Government:	Republic
Active Troop Strength:	587,000
GDP (1995):	$274 billion
Industries:	textiles, food processing, beverages
Crops:	rice, wheat, cotton
Arable Land:	23%
Labor Force:	46% agricultural; 18% mining & manufacturing; 17% service
Imports (1995):	$10.7 billion
Exports (1995):	$8.7 billion
Monetary Unit:	Rupee
Private Motor Vehicles:	770,000
Literacy:	38%
Daily Newspaper Circ.:	21 per 1,000 population
Televisions:	1 per 53 persons
Radios:	1 per 11 persons
Telephones:	1 per 61 persons
Physicians:	1 per 2,064 persons
Birth Rate (per 1,000):	35
Death Rate (per 1,000):	11
Natural Increase:	2.4%
Life Expectancy:	58 males; 59.6 females

JAPAN

Population:	125,450,000
Land Area:	145,850
Population Density:	861 per sq. mi.
Urban:	78%
Major Cities:	Tokyo, Osaka, Nagoya, Sapporo, Kyoto
Official Language:	Japanese
Religions:	Buddhism, Shintoism
Government:	Parliamentary Democracy
Active Troop Strength:	235,500
GDP (1995):	$2.68 trillion
Industries:	electronic equipment, vehicles, metallurgy, chemicals, fishing
Crops:	rice, potatoes, sugar, sugar beets, cabbage, fruits
Arable Land:	13%
Labor Force:	54% service & trade; 33% manuf., mining & const.
Imports (1995):	$336.1 billion
Exports (1995):	442.8 billion
Monetary Unit:	Yen
Private Motor Vehicles:	44.7 million
Literacy:	100%
Daily Newspaper Circ.:	576 per 1,000 population
Televisions:	1 per 1.5 persons
Radios:	1 per 1.1 persons
Telephones:	1 per 2.0 persons
Physicians:	1 per 546 persons
Birth Rate (per 1,000):	10
Death Rate (per 1,000):	8
Natural Increase:	0.2%
Life Expectancy:	76.7 males; 82.8 females

BANGLADESH

Population:	123,063,000
Land Area:	56,977 sq. mi.
Population Density:	2,200 per sq. mi.
Urban:	19%
Major Cities:	Dhaka, Chitagong, Khulna
Official Language:	Bangla
Religions:	Muslim, Hindu
Government:	Parliamentary Democracy
Active Troop Strength:	117,500
GDP (1995):	$144.5 billion
Industries:	food processing, jute, textiles, fertilizers, steel, fishing
Crops:	jute, rice, tea
Arable Land:	67%
Labor Force:	65% agricultural; 21% service; 14% ind., mining
Imports (1995):	$4.7 billion
Exports (1995):	$2.7 billion
Monetary Unit:	Taka
Private Motor Vehicles:	150,000
Literacy:	38%
Daily Newspaper Circ.:	6 per 1,000 population
Televisions:	1 per 172 persons
Radios:	1 per 21 persons
Telephones:	1 per 418 persons
Physicians:	1 per 5,264 persons
Birth Rate (per 1,000):	30
Death Rate (per 1,000):	11
Natural Increase:	1.9%
Life Expectancy:	56.4 males; 56.2 females

NIGERIA

Population:	103,912,000
Land Area:	356,669 sq. mi.
Population Density:	300 per sq. mi.
Urban:	40%
Major Cities:	Lagos, Ibadan
Official Language:	English
Religions:	Muslim, Christian
Government:	in transition
Active Troop Strength:	77,100
GDP (1995):	$136 billion
Industries:	crude oil, mining, food processing, textiles
Crops:	cocoa, palm products, corn, rice, yams, cassava
Arable Land:	31%
Labor Force:	54% agricultural; 19% ind.; 15% government
Imports (1993):	$7.5 billion
Exports (1993):	$9.9 billion
Monetary Unit:	Naira
Private Motor Vehicles:	590,000
Literacy:	57%
Daily Newspaper Circ.:	18 per 1,000 population
Televisions:	1 per 26 persons
Radios:	1 per 5.1 persons
Telephones:	1 per 275 persons
Physicians:	1 per 4,496 persons
Birth Rate (per 1,000):	43
Death Rate (per 1,000):	12
Natural Increase:	3%
Life Expectancy:	53.3 males; 56.0 females

2. These United States

See also 'Weather' and 'Travel.'

State Stats

State Name Origins

Comparative Stats

State Stats

ALABAMA

Abbreviation	AL
Capital	Montgomery
Total Area (sq. mi.)	52,423
Rank (area)	30
Nickname	Heart of Dixie
Bird	yellowhammer
Flower	camellia
Motto	We dare defend our rights
Song	Alabama

ALASKA

Abbreviation	AK
Capital	Juneau
Total Area (sq. mi.)	656,424
Rank (area)	1
Nickname	Last Frontier
Bird	willow ptarmigan
Flower	forget-me-not
Motto	North to the future
Song	Alaska's Flag

ARIZONA

Abbreviation	AZ
Capital	Phoenix
Total Area (sq. mi.)	114,006
Rank (area)	6
Nickname	Grand Canyon State
Bird	cactus wren
Flower	Saguaro cactus flower
Motto	God enriches
Song	Arizona

ARKANSAS

Abbreviation	AR
Capital	Little Rock
Total Area (sq. mi.)	53,182
Rank (area)	29
Nickname	Land of Opportunity
Bird	mockingbird
Flower	apple blossom
Motto	The people rule
Song	Arkansas

CALIFORNIA

Abbreviation	CA
Capital	Sacramento
Total Area (sq. mi.)	163,707
Rank (area)	3
Nickname	Golden State
Bird	Calif. valley quail
Flower	golden poppy
Motto	Eureka (I have found it)
Song	I Love You, California

COLORADO

Abbreviation	CO
Capital	Denver
Total Area (sq. mi.)	104,100
Rank (area)	8
Nickname	Centennial State
Bird	lark bunting
Flower	columbine
Motto	Nothing without providence
Song	Where the Columbines Grow

CONNECTICUT

Abbreviation	CT
Capital	Hartford
Total Area (sq. mi.)	5,544
Rank (area)	48
Nickname	Constitution or Nutmeg State
Bird	American robin
Flower	mountain laurel
Motto	He who transplanted still sustains
Song	Yankee Doodle

DELAWARE

Abbreviation	DE
Capital	Dover
Total Area (sq. mi.)	2,489
Rank (area)	49
Nickname	First, or Diamond State
Bird	blue hen chicken
Flower	peach blossom
Motto	Liberty and Independence
Song	Our Delaware

FLORIDA

Abbreviation	FL
Capital	Tallahassee
Total Area (sq. mi.)	65,756
Rank (area)	22
Nickname	Sunshine State
Bird	mockingbird
Flower	orange blossom
Motto	In God we trust
Song	Old Folks at Home

GEORGIA

Abbreviation	GA
Capital	Atlanta
Total Area (sq. mi.)	59,441
Rank (area)	24
Nickname	Empire or Peach State
Bird	brown thrasher
Flower	Cherokee rose
Motto	Wisdom, justice and moderation
Song	Georgia On My Mind

HAWAII

Abbreviation	HI
Capital	Honolulu
Total Area (sq. mi.)	10,932
Rank (area)	43
Nickname	Aloha State
Bird	Hawaiian goose
Flower	hibiscus
Motto	The life of the land is perpetuated in righteousness
Song	Hawaii Pono'i

IDAHO

Abbreviation	ID
Capital	Boise
Nickname	Gem State
Total Area (sq. mi.)	83,574
Rank (area)	14
Bird	mountain bluebird
Flower	lilac
Motto	It is perpetual
Song	Here We Have Idaho

ILLINOIS

Abbreviation	IL
Capital	Springfield
Total Area (sq. mi.)	57,918
Rank (area)	6
Nickname	Prairie State
Bird	cardinal
Flower	native violet
Motto	State sovereignty -- national union
Song	Illinois

INDIANA

Abbreviation	IN
Capital	Indianapolis
Total Area (sq. mi.)	36,420
Rank (area)	14
Nickname	Hoosier State
Bird	cardinal
Flower	peony
Motto	Crossroads of America
Song	On the Banks of the Wabash

IOWA

Abbreviation	IA
Capital	Des Moines
Total Area (sq. mi.)	56,276
Rank (area)	30
Nickname	Hawkeye State
Bird	eastern goldfinch
Flower	wild rose
Motto	Our liberties we prize and our rights we will maintain

KANSAS

Abbreviation	KS
Capital	Topeka
Total Area (sq. mi.)	82,282
Rank (area)	32
Nickname	Sunflower or Free State
Bird	western meadowlark
Flower	native sunflower
Motto	To the stars through difficulties
Song	Home On The Range

KENTUCKY

Abbreviation	KY
Capital	Frankfort
Total Area (sq. mi.)	40,411
Rank (area)	2
Nickname	Bluegrass State
Bird	cardinal
Flower	goldenrod
Motto	United we stand, divided we fall
Song	My Old Kentucky Home

LOUISIANA

Abbreviation	LA
Capital	Baton Rouge
Total Area (sq. mi.)	51,843
Rank (area)	31
Nickname	Pelican State
Bird	eastern brown pelican
Flower	magnolia
Motto	Union, justice, and confidence
Song	Give Me Louisiana

MAINE

Abbreviation	ME
Capital	Augusta
Total Area (sq. mi.)	35,387
Rank (area)	39
Nickname	Pine Tree State
Bird	chickadee
Flower	white pine cone and tassel
Motto	I direct
Song	State of Maine Song

MARYLAND

Abbreviation	MD
Capital	Annapolis
Total Area (sq. mi.)	12,407
Rank (area)	42
Nickname	Old Line or Free State
Bird	Baltimore oriole
Flower	black-eyed Susan
Motto	Manly deeds, womanly words
Song	Maryland, My Maryland

MASSACHUSETTS

Abbreviation	MA
Capital	Boston
Total Area (sq. mi.)	10,555
Rank (area)	44
Nickname	Bay State, Old Colony
Bird	chickadee
Flower	mayflower
Motto	By the sword we seek peace, but peace only under liberty
Song	All Hail to Massachusetts

MICHIGAN

Abbreviation	MI
Capital	Lansing
Total Area (sq. mi.)	96,705
Rank (area)	11
Nickname	Great Lakes State
Bird	robin
Flower	apple blossom
Motto	If you seek a pleasant peninsula, look about you
Song	Michigan, My Michigan

MINNESOTA

Abbreviation	MN
Capital	St. Paul
Total Area (sq. mi.)	86,943
Rank (area)	12
Nickname	North Star State
Bird	common loon
Flower	lady-slipper
Motto	The star of the north
Song	Hail! Minnesota

MISSISSIPPI

Abbreviation	MS
Capital	Jackson
Total Area (sq. mi.)	48,434
Rank (area)	32
Nickname	Magnolia State
Bird	mockingbird
Flower	magnolia
Motto	By valor and arms
Song	Go Mississippi

MISSOURI

Abbreviation	MO
Capital	Jefferson City
Total Area (sq. mi.)	69,709
Rank (area)	21
Nickname	Show-Me State
Bird	bluebird
Flower	white hawthorn
Motto	The welfare of the people shall be the supreme law
Song	Missouri Waltz

MONTANA

Abbreviation	MT
Capital	Helena
Total Area (sq. mi.)	147,046
Rank (area)	4
Nickname	Treasure State
Bird	western meadowlark
Flower	bitterroot
Motto	Gold and silver
Song	Montana

NEBRASKA

Abbreviation	NE
Capital	Lincoln
Total Area (sq. mi.)	77,358
Rank (area)	16
Nickname	Cornhusker State
Bird	western meadowlark
Flower	goldenrod
Motto	Equality before the law
Song	Nebraska

NEVADA

Abbreviation	NV
Capital	Carson City
Total Area (sq. mi.)	110,567
Rank (area)	7
Nickname	Sagebrush, or Silver State
Bird	mountain bluebird
Flower	sagebrush
Motto	All for our country
Song	Home Means Nevada

NEW HAMPSHIRE

Abbreviation	NH
Capital	Concord
Total Area (sq. mi.)	9,351
Rank (area)	46
Nickname	Granite State
Bird	purple finch
Flower	purple lilac
Motto	Live free or die
Song	Old New Hampshire

NEW JERSEY

Abbreviation	NJ
Capital	Trenton
Total Area (sq. mi.)	8,722
Rank (area)	47
Nickname	Garden state
Bird	eastern goldfinch
Flower	violet
Motto	Liberty and prosperity

NEW MEXICO

Abbreviation	NM
Capital	Santa Fe
Total Area (sq. mi.)	121,598
Rank (area)	5
Nickname	Land of Enchantment
Bird	pinon bird
Flower	yucca
Motto	It grows as it goes
Song	Oh Fair New Mexico
	Asi Es Nuevo Mexico

NEW YORK

Abbreviation	NY
Capital	Albany
Total Area (sq. mi.)	54,471
Rank (area)	27
Nickname	Empire State
Bird	bluebird
Flower	rose
Motto	Ever upward
Song	I Love New York

NORTH CAROLINA

Abbreviation	NC
Capital	Raleigh
Total Area (sq. mi.)	53,821
Rank (area)	28
Nickname	Tar Heel or Old North State
Bird	cardinal
Flower	dogwood
Motto	To be rather than to seem
Song	The Old North State

NORTH DAKOTA

Abbreviation	ND
Capital	Bismarck
Total Area (sq. mi.)	70,704
Rank (area)	19
Nickname	Peace Garden State
Bird	western meadowlark
Flower	wild rose
Motto	Liberty and union, now and forever, one and inseparable
Song	North Dakota Hymn

OHIO

Abbreviation	OH
Capital	Columbus
Total Area (sq. mi.)	44,828
Rank (area)	34
Nickname	Buckeye State
Bird	cardinal
Flower	scarlet carnation
Motto	With God, all things are possible
Song	Beautiful Ohio

OKLAHOMA

Abbreviation	OK
Capital	Oklahoma City
Total Area (sq. mi.)	69,903
Rank (area)	20
Nickname	Sooner State
Bird	scissor-tailed flycatcher
Flower	mistletoe
Motto	Labor conquers all things
Song	Oklahoma!

OREGON

Abbreviations	OR
Capital	Salem
Total Area (sq. mi.)	98,386
Rank (area)	9
Nickname	Beaver State
Bird	western meadowlark
Flower	Oregon grape
Motto	She flies with her own wings
Song	Oregon

PENNSYLVANIA

Abbreviations	PA
Capital	Harrisburg
Total Area (sq. mi.)	46,058
Rank (area)	33
Nickname	Keystone State
Bird	ruffed grouse
Flower	mountain laurel
Motto	Virtue, liberty and independence
Song	

RHODE ISLAND

Abbreviations	RI
Capital	Providence
Total Area (sq. mi.)	1,545
Rank (area)	50
Nickname	Little Rhody or Ocean State
Bird	Rhode Island red
Flower	violet
Motto	Hope
Song	Rhode Island

SOUTH CAROLINA

Abbreviations	SC
Capital	Columbia
Total Area (sq. mi.)	32,008
Rank (area)	40
Nickname	Palmetto State
Bird	Carolina wren
Flower	yellow Jessamine
Motto	While I breathe, I hope
Song	Carolina

SOUTH DAKOTA

Abbreviations	SD
Capital	Pierre
Total Area (sq. mi.)	77,121
Rank (area)	17
Nickname	Coyote or Mt. Rushmore State
Bird	ring-neck pheasant
Flower	pasque
Motto	Under God the people rule
Song	Hail! South Dakota

TENNESSEE

Abbreviations	TN
Capital	Nashville
Total Area (sq. mi.)	42,146
Rank (area)	36
Nickname	Volunteer State
Bird	mockingbird
Flower	iris
Motto	Agriculture and commerce
Song	The Tennessee Waltz

TEXAS

Abbreviations	TX
Capital	Austin
Total Area (sq. mi.)	268,601
Rank (area)	2
Nickname	Lone Star State
Bird	mockingbird
Flower	bluebonnet
Motto	Friendship
Song	Texas, Our Texas

UTAH

Abbreviations	UT
Capital	Salt Lake City
Nickname	Beehive State
Total Area (sq. mi.)	84,904
Rank (area)	13
Bird	California seagull
Flower	sego lily
Motto	Industry
Song	Utah, We Love Thee

VERMONT

Abbreviations	VT
Capital	Montpelier
Total Area (sq. mi.)	9,615
Rank (area)	45
Nickname	Green Mountain State
Bird	Hermit thrush
Flower	red clover
Motto	Freedom and unity
Song	Hail, Vermont

VIRGINIA

Abbreviations	VA
Capital	Richmond
Total Area (sq. mi.)	42,777
Rank (area)	35
Nickname	Old Dominion
Bird	cardinal
Flower	dogwood
Motto	Thus always to tyrants
Song	Carry me back to old Virginia

WASHINGTON

Abbreviations	WA
Capital	Olympia
Total Area (sq. mi.)	71,302
Rank (area)	18
Nickname	Evergreen State
Bird	willow goldfinch
Flower	Coast rhododendron
Motto	By and by
Song	Washington, My Home

WEST VIRGINIA

Abbreviations	WV
Capital	Charleston
Total Area (sq. mi.)	24,231
Rank (area)	41
Nickname	Mountain State
Bird	cardinal
Flower	big laurel
Motto	Mountaineers are always free
Song	The West Virginia Hills

WISCONSIN

Abbreviations	WI
Capital	Madison
Total Area (sq. mi.)	65,499
Rank (area)	23
Nickname	Badger State
Bird	robin
Flower	wood violet
Motto	Forward
Song	On Wisconsin!

WYOMING

Abbreviations	WY
Capital	Cheyenne
Total Area (sq. mi.)	97,818
Rank (area)	10
Nickname	Equality State
Bird	western meadowlark
Flower	Indian paintbrush
Motto	Equal rights
Song	Wyoming

OUTLYING AREAS

GUAM

Capital	Agana
Nickname	Where America's Day Begins
Song	Stand Ye Guamanians
State Bird	toto (fruit dove)
State Flower	bougainvillea
Total Area (sq. mi.)	210

COMMONWEALTH OF PUERTO RICO

Capital	San Juan
Motto	John is his name
Song	La Borinquena
State Bird	reinita
State Flower	maga
Total Area (sq. mi.)	3,492

VIRGIN ISLANDS

Capital	Charlotte Amalie, St. Thomas
Song	Virgin Islands March
State Bird	yellow breast
State Flower	yellow elder or yellow trumpet
Total Area (sq. mi.)	152

State Name Origins

What's in a Name?

State Name Origins

State	Name Origin
Alabama	Named for the Alabama Indians
Alaska	Aleutian word *alakshak* meaning "great lands"
Arizona	Prima indian word meaning "little spring place" or Aztec word *arizuma,* meaning "silver-bearing"
Arkansas	From French word for Quapaw Indians
California	Named for fictitious paradise in a 16th century Spanish novel
Colorado	A Spanish word meaning "red"
Connecticut	Algonquin word for "long river place"
Delaware	Named for Lord De La Warr, governor of Virginia
D.C.	Named for Christopher Columbus in 1791
Florida	Ponce de Leon named the region "flowery Easter" on Easter Sunday, 1513
Georgia	Named for King George II of England
Hawaii	English adaptation for native word *hawaiki,* meaning "homeland"
Idaho	Perhaps derived from Kiowa Apache word for the Comanche
Illinois	From Algonquin word *illini* meaning "soldiers"
Indiana	Settlers named the region "land of the Indians"
Iowa	Siouan word *Ouaouia,* meaning "puts to sleep"
Kansas	Siouan word *Kansa* or *Kaw,* meaning "people of the south wind"
Kentucky	Indian word meaning "dark and bloody ground"
Louisiana	Named for French king Louis XIV
Maine	Ancient French word for "province"
Maryland	Named for Queen Henrietta Maria
Massachusetts	Name of Indian tribe living near Milton, MA, meaning "large hill place"
Michigan	From the Chippewa word *micigama,* meaning "great water"
Minnesota	Sioux word for "sky-tinted water"

46

State	Name Origin
Mississippi	Probably from Chippewa words *mici* and *zibi*, meaning "great" and "river"
Missouri	Siouan word for "muddy water"
Montana	Latin word for "mountanous"
Nebraska	Omaha or Oto word meaning "flat water"
Nevada	Spanish word for "snow-clad"
N. Hampshire	Captain John Mason named the colony in 1629 for his home county in England
New Jersey	Named for the Isle of Jersey in England
New Mexico	Named by the Spanish
New York	Named for the Duke of York
North Carolina	Latin word *Carolus*, meaning "Charles," divided into North and South Carolina in 1710
North Dakota	Sioux word meaning "freind"
Ohio	Iroquois word meaning "great," or "good river"
Oklahoma	Choctaw Indian word meaning "red man"
Oregon	Perhaps from Algonquin word *wauregan*, meaning "beautiful water"
Pennsylvania	Named for William Penn, founder of the colony
Rhode Island	Perhaps named Roode (red) Eylandt by Dutch explorer Adrian Block, for its red clay soil
South Carolina	See North Carolina
South Dakota	Sioux word meaning "freind"
Tennessee	Named for Cherokee villages called *tanasi*
Texas	Variation of the Caddo Indian word for "friend"
Utah	From a name meaning "upper" used by the Navajo to refer to a Shoshone tribe
Vermont	From the French words *vert* and *mont* meaning "green" and "mountain"
Virginia	Named by Sir Walter Raleigh for the Virgin Queen of England, Elizabeth I
Washington	Named for George Washington
West Virginia	Named when the region refused to secede from the Union in 1863
Wisconsin	Chippewa word *Ouisconsin*
Wyoming	Algonquin word for "large prarie place"

Comparative Stats

Where the People Are
State Populations

State	1996 Population	Density (per sq. mi.)	Growth 1990-96
Alabama	4,273,084	83.8	+5.8%
Alaska	607,007	1.1	+10.4%
Arizona	4,428,068	37.1	+20.8%
Arkansas	2,509,793	47.7	+6.8%
California	31,878,234	202.5	+7.1%
Colorado	3,822,676	36.1	+16.0%
Connecticut	3,274,238	675.9	-0.4%
Delaware	724,842	366.9	+8.8%
Florida	14,399,985	262.3	+11.3%
Georgia	7,353,225	124.3	+13.5%
Hawaii	1,183,723	184.8	+6.8%
Idaho	1,189,251	14.1	+18.1%
Illinois	11,846,544	212.8	+3.6%
Indiana	5,840,528	161.8	+5.3%
Iowa	2,851,792	50.9	+2.7%
Kansas	2,572,150	31.4	+3.8
Kentucky	3,883,723	97.2	+5.3%
Louisiana	4,350,579	99.7	+3.1%
Maine	1,243,316	40.2	+1.3%
Maryland	5,071.604	515.9	+6.1%
Massachusetts	6,092,352	774.9	+1.3%
Michigan	9,594,350	168.1	+3.2%
Minnesota	4,657,758	57.9	+6.4%
Mississippi	2,716,115	57.5	+5.5%
Missouri	5,358,692	77.3	+4.7%
Montana	879,372	6.0	+10.1%
Nebraska	1,652,093	21.3	+4.7%
Nevada	1,603,163	13.9	+33.4%
Hew Hampshire	1,162,481	128.0	+4.8%
New Jersey	7,987,933	1,070.9	+3.3%
New Mexico	1,713,407	13.9	+13.1%

State	1996 Population	Density (per sq. mi.)	Growth 1990-96
New York	18,184,774	384.0	+1.1%
North Carolina	7,332,870	147.7	+10.4%
North Dakota	643,539	9.3	+0.7%
Ohio	11,172,782	272.3	+3.0%
Oklahoma	3,300,902	47.7	+4.9%
Oregon	3,203,735	32.7	+12.7%
Pennsylvania	12,056,112	269.3	+1.5%
Rhode Island	990,225	947.2	-1.3%
South Carolina	3,698,746	122.0	+6.1%
South Dakota	732,405	9.6	+5.2%
Tennessee	5,319,654	127.5	+9.1%
Texas	19,128,261	71.5	+12.6%
Utah	2,000,494	23.7	+16.1%
Vermont	588,654	63.2	+4.6%
Virginia	6,675,451	167.1	+7.9%
Washington	5,532,939	81.6	+13.7%
West Virginia	1,825,754	75.9	+1.8%
Wisconsin	5,159,795	94.3	+5.5%
Wyoming	481,400	4.9	+6.1%

The United States population density in 1996 was 75.0 people per square mile. That represents an increase of 11 people per square mile since 1980.

Fastest Growing States	**Most Densely Populated States**	**Most Sparsely Populated States**
1. Nevada	1. New Jersey	1. Alaska
2. Arizona	2. Rhode Island	2. Wyoming
3. Idaho	3. Massachusetts	3. Montana
4. Utah	4. Connecticut	4. North Dakota
5. Colorado	5. Maryland	5. South Dakota

State Birth & Death Rates

Birth & Death Rates by State, 1996

	Birth Rate	Death Rate		Birth Rate	Death Rate
U.S.	14.8	8.8	Missouri	13.6	10.0
Alabama	14.4	10.0	Montana	12.3	8.8
Alaska	16.8	4.2	Nebraska	14.1	9.4
Arizona	18.0	8.8	Nevada	14.6	8.0
Arkansas	14.3	10.2	New Hampshire	12.2	7.8
California	17.1	7.3	New Jersey	14.2	9.0
Colorado	12.5	6.8	New Mexico	15.9	7.2
Connecticut	13.4	8.9	New York	14.9	9.0
Delaware	14.0	8.9	North Carolina	14.5	9.1
Florida	13.2	10.7	North Dakota	13.0	8.9
Georgia	15.6	8.0	Ohio	13.6	9.4
Hawaii	15.5	6.6	Oklahoma	13.7	10.1
Idaho	15.9	7.3	Oregon	13.7	8.8
Illinois	15.6	9.0	Pennsylvania	14.2	9.0
Indiana	14.3	9.3	Rhode Island	12.7	9.7
Iowa	12.2	9.2	South Carolina	13.7	9.4
Kansas	15.6	9.3	South Dakota	13.8	8.6
Kentucky	13.5	9.7	Tennessee	13.8	9.4
Louisiana	15.2	9.3	Texas	16.5	7.1
Maine	11.0	8.9	Utah	20.6	5.5
Maryland	14.0	8.3	Vermont	11.5	8.3
Massachusetts	13.2	9.1	Virginia	13.4	7.9
Michigan	14.3	8.8	Washington	14.4	7.1
Minnesota	13.7	7.9	West Virginia	10.7	10.5
Mississippi	15.3	9.9	Wisconsin	12.9	8.7
			Wyoming	12.9	7.5

There are over 700 million acres of forested land in America. More than 500 million acres of it is timberland: land that is producing or could be producing industrial wood and is not withdrawn from use by law.

In the Woods
Number of Forested Acres, by State, 1996

State	Forested Acres	State	Forested Acres
Alabama	21,974,000	Montana	22,512,000
Alaska	129,131,000	Nebraska	722,000
Arizona	19,596,000	Nevada	8,938,000
Arkansas	17,864,000	New Hampshire	4,981,000
California	37,263,000	New Jersey	2,007,000
Colorado	21,338,000	New Mexico	15,296,000
Connecticut	1,819,000	New York	18,713,000
Delaware	398,000	North Carolina	19,278,000
Florida	16,549,000	North Dakota	462,000
Georgia	24,137,000	Ohio	7,863,000
Hawaii	1,748,000	Oklahoma	7,539,000
Idaho	21,621,000	Oregon	27,997,000
Illinois	4,266,000	Pennsylvania	16,969,000
Indiana	4,439,000	Rhode Island	401,000
Iowa	2,050,000	South Carolina	12,257,000
Kansas	1,359,000	South Dakota	1,690,000
Kentucky	12,714,000	Tennessee	13,612,000
Louisiana	13,864,000	Texas	19,193,000
Maine	17,533,000	Utah	16,234,000
Maryland	2,700,000	Vermont	4,538,000
Massachusetts	3,203,000	Virginia	15,858,000
Michigan	18,253,000	Washington	20,483,000
Minnesota	16,718,000	West Virginia	12,128,000
Mississippi	17,000,000	Wisconsin	15,513,000
Missouri	14,007,000	Wyoming	9,966,000

States with the Most Miles of Highways

1.	Texas	296,186
2.	California	170,389
3.	Illinois	137,413
4.	Kansas	133,323
5.	Minnesota	130,391
6.	Missouri	122,616
7.	Pennsylvania	118,648
8.	Michigan	117,611
9.	Ohio	114,956
10.	Florida	113,778

States with the Least Miles of Highways

1.	Hawaii	4,133
2.	Delaware	5,631
3.	Rhode Island	5,893
4.	Arkansas	13,486
5.	Vermont	14,184
6.	New Hampshire	15,086
7.	Maine	22,577
8.	Massachusetts	30,751
9.	West Virginia	35,110
10.	Wyoming	35,461

States with the Most Traffic Fatalities

1. California
2. Texas
3. Florida
4. New York
5. Illinois
6. Michigan
7. Georgia
8. Pennsylvania
9. North Carolina
10. Ohio

States with the Most Speeding-Related Traffic Fatalities

1. California
2. Texas
3. Florida
4. Arizona
5. Colorado
6. New Mexico
7. Nevada
8. South Carolina
9. North Carolina
10. Alabama

Source: U.S. Highway Traffic Safety Administration, 1995

Crime in the States

State Crime Rates, Incidents per 100,000 Population, 1996

State	Property Crime	Violent Crime
Alabama	4,217.5	632.4
Alaska	4,982.9	770.9
Arizona	7,500.1	713.5
Arkansas	4,137.7	553.2
California	4,865.1	966.0
Colorado	4,956.1	440.2
Connecticut	4,097.3	405.9
Delaware	4,433.8	725.0
Florida	6,630.6	1,071.0
Georgia	5,346.5	657.1
Hawaii	6,902.9	295.6
Idaho	4,079.4	322.0
Illinois	4,459.6	996.1
Indiana	4,106.8	524.7
Iowa	3,747.5	354.4
Kansas	4,466.2	420.7
Kentucky	2,987.0	364.7
Louisiana	5,668.6	1,007.4
Maine	3,153.3	131.4
Maryland	5,307.9	986.9
Massachusetts	3,654.4	687.2
Michigan	4,495.0	687.8
Minnesota	4,141.2	356.1
Mississippi	4,011.7	502.8
Missouri	4,456.8	663.8
Montana	5,134.4	170.6
Nebraska	4,162.5	382.0
Nevada	5,634.2	945.2
New Hampshire	2,540.9	114.5
New Jersey	4,103.9	599.8
New Mexico	5,608.8	819.2
New York	3,718.3	841.9
North Carolina	4,993.1	646.4

State	Property Crime	Violent Crime
North Dakota	2,779.6	86.7
Ohio	3,992.7	482.5
Oklahoma	4,932.7	664.1
Oregon	6,041.5	522.4
Pennsylvania	2,937.6	427.3
Rhode Island	3,876.6	368.0
South Carolina	5,081.8	981.9
South Dakota	2,853.1	207.5
Tennessee	4,591.2	771.5
Texas	5,020.5	663.9
Utah	5,762.0	328.8
Vermont	3,315.4	118.3
Virginia	3,627.7	361.5
Washington	5,785.5	484.3
West Virginia	2,248.0	210.2
Wisconsin	3,604.6	281.1
Wyoming	4,066.0	254.2

The 1996 national crime rate averaged 4,444.8 property crimes and 634.1 violent crimes per 100,000 people. In 1960, there were 1,726.3 property crimes and 160.9 violent crimes per 100,000 people.

States with Highest Violent Crime Rates	States with Lowest Violent Crime Rates
1. Florida	1. North Dakota
2. Louisiana	2. New Hampshire
3. Maryland	3. Vermont
4. South Carolina	4. Maine
5. California	5. Montana

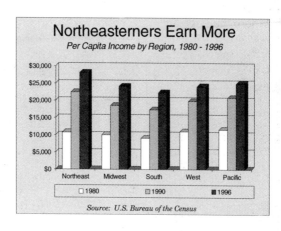

Northeasterners Earn More
Per Capita Income by Region, 1980 - 1996

Source: U.S. Bureau of the Census

States with the Highest Personal Income Per Capita	States with the Lowest Personal Income Per Capita
1. District of Columbia	1. Mississippi
2. Connecticut	2. West Virginia
3. New Jersey	3. New Mexico
4. Massachusetts	4. Arkansas
5. New York	5. Montana
6. Delaware	6. Utah
7. Maryland	7. Oklahoma
8. Illinois	8. Idaho
9. New Hampshire	9. Kentucky
10. Minnesota	10. South Carolina

Source: U.S. Bureau of Economic Analysis

Where the Poor Are

Americans Below the Poverty Level by State, in Percent

	1990	1996		1990	1996
U.S.	13.5	13.7	MO	13.4	9.5
AL.	19.2	17.1	MT	16.3	16.2
AK	11.4	7.7	NE	10.3	9.9
AZ	13.7	18.3	NV	9.8	9.6
AR	19.6	16.1	NH	6.3	5.9
CA	13.9	16.8	NJ	9.2	8.5
CO	13.7	9.7	NM	20.9	25.4
CT	6.0	10.7	NY	14.3	16.6
DE	6.9	9.5	NC	13.0	12.4
DC	21.1	23.2	ND	13.7	11.5
FL	14.4	15.2	OH	11.5	12.1
GA	15.8	13.5	OK	15.6	16.9
HI	11.0	11.2	OR	9.2	11.5
ID	14.9	13.2	PA	11.0	11.9
IL	13.7	12.3	RI	7.5	10.8
IN	13.0	8.6	SC	16.2	16.5
IA	10.4	10.9	SD	13.3	13.2
KS	10.3	11.0	TN	16.9	15.7
KY	17.3	15.9	TX	15.9	17.0
LA	23.6	20.1	UT	8.2	8.1
ME	13.1	11.2	VT	10.9	11.5
MD	9.9	10.2	VA	11.1	11.3
MA	10.7	10.6	WA	8.9	12.2
MI	14.3	11.7	WV	18.1	17.6
MN	12.0	9.5	WI	9.3	8.7
MS	25.7	22.1	WY	11.0	12.1

Source: U.S. Bureau of the Census

3. Government

Branches

U.S. Presidents

The Bill of Rights

The U.S. Flag

Income & Spending

Military Trends

Government Web Sites

Branches

United States Government

U.S. Constitution

Executive Branch	Legislative Branch	Judicial Branch
President	**Congress**	**U.S. Supreme Court**
Vice President	Senate - House	

- Exec. Office of the President
- White House Office
- Office of the Vice President
- Council of Economic Advisers
- Council on Environmental Quality
- National Security Council
- Office of Administration
- Office of Management and Budget
- Office of National Drug Control Policy
- Office of Policy Dev.
- Office of Science & Technology Policy
- Office of the U.S. Trade Representative

- Architect of the Capitol
- U.S. Botanic Garden
- General Accounting Office
- Government Printing Office
- Library of Congress
- Congressional Budget Office

- Courts of Appeals
- Disitrict Courts
- Territorial Courts
- Court of International Trade
- Court of Federal Claims
- Court of Appeals for the Armed Forces
- Tax Court
- Court of Veterans Appeals
- Admin. Office of the Courts
- Federal Judicial Center
- Sentencing Commission

There are 85,000 governments in America, and over half a million elected officials: about one for every 485 people. Only 542 of them serve in the federal government, and about 19,000 in state governments. The remainder are elected to local government offices.

Major Executive Departments

Department of State
Dept. of the Treasury
Dept. of Defense
Dept. of Justice
Dept. of the Interior
Dept. of Agriculture
Dept. of Commerce
Dept. of Labor
Dept. of Health & Human
  Services
Dept. of Housing and
  Urban Development
Dept. of Transportation
Dept. of Energy
Dept. of Education
Dept. of Veterans Affairs

The head of each major executive department -- its Secretary -- also serves as a member of the Cabinet. The Cabinet has no executive authority. It is an advisory panel to the President on policy matters and may also include other officials appointed by the President.

What Uncle Sam Pays
Annual Salaries of Selected Officials, 1997

Official	Salary
U.S. President	$200,000
U.S. Vice President	$171,500
U.S. Supreme Court Chief Justice	$171,500
U.S. Supreme Court Associate Justices	$164,100
U.S. Representatives	$133,600
Speaker of the House	$171,500
Majority and Minority Leader of the House	$148,400
U.S. Senators	$133,600
President Pro Tempore of the Senate	$148,400
Majority and Minority Leader of the Senate	$148,400

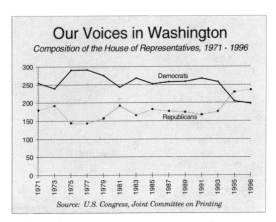

Source: U.S. Congress, Joint Committee on Printing

To serve in the House of Representatives, a person must be a resident of the state from which he or she is elected, at least 25 years of age, and an American citizen for at least 7 years.

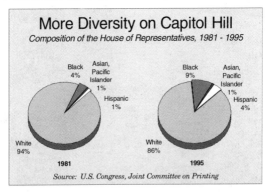

Source: U.S. Congress, Joint Committee on Printing

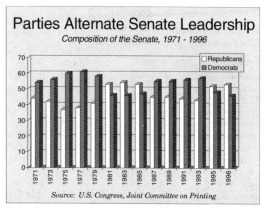

Parties Alternate Senate Leadership
Composition of the Senate, 1971 - 1996

□ Republicans
▥ Democrats

Source: U.S. Congress, Joint Committee on Printing

Ups and Downs of Politics
Composition of the House of Representatives and the Senate

		House		Senate	
Year	President/Party	R	D	R	D
1971	Nixon - R	180	254	44	54
1973	Nixon - R	192	239	42	56
1975	Ford - R	144	291	37	60
1977	Carter - D	143	292	38	61
1979	Carter - D	157	276	41	58
1981	Reagan - R	192	243	53	46
1983	Reagan - R	165	269	54	46
1985	Reagan - R	182	252	53	47
1987	Reagan - R	177	258	45	55
1989	Bush - R	174	259	45	55
1991	Bush - R	167	267	44	56
1993	Clinton - D	176	258	43	57
1995	Clinton - D	230	204	52	48
1996	Clinton - D	236	197	53	46

Source: U.S. Congress, Joint Committee on Printing

U.S. Presidents

Hail to the Chief
U.S. Presidents

President	Born	Party	Term
George Washington	Virginia	Federalist	1789 - 97
John Adams	Massachusetts	Federalist	1797 - 01
Thomas Jefferson	Virginia	Dem.-Rep.	1801 - 09
James Madison	Virginia	Dem.-Rep.	1809 - 17
James Monroe	Virginia	Dem.-Rep.	1817 - 25
John Quincy Adams	Massachusetts	Dem.-Rep.	1825 - 29
Andrew Jackson	North Carolina	Dem.-Rep.	1829 - 37
Martin Van Buren	New York	Dem.	1837 - 41
William H. Harrison	Virginia	Whig	1841
John Tyler	Virginia	Whig	1841 - 45
James Knox Polk	North Carolina	Dem.	1845 - 49
Zachary Taylor	Virginia	Whig	1849 - 50
Millard Fillmore	New York	Whig	1850 - 53
Franklin Pierce	New Hampshire	Dem.	1853 - 57
James Buchanan	Pennsylvania	Dem.	1857 - 61
Abraham Lincoln	Kentucky	Rep.	1861 - 65
Andrew Johnson	North Carolina	Dem.	1865 - 69
Ulysses S. Grant	Ohio	Rep.	1869 - 77
Rutherford B. Hayes	Ohio	Rep.	1877 - 81
James A. Garfield	Ohio	Rep.	1881
Chester Alan Arthur	Vermont	Rep.	1881 - 85
Grover Cleveland	New Jersey	Dem.	1885 - 97
Benjamin Harrison	Ohio	Rep.	1889 - 93
William McKinley	Ohio	Rep.	1897 - 01
Theodore Roosevelt	New York	Rep.	1901 - 09
William Howard Taft	Ohio	Rep.	1909 - 13
Woodrow Wilson	Virginia	Dem.	1913 - 21
Warren G. Harding	Ohio	Rep.	1921 - 23
Calvin Coolidge	Vermont	Rep.	1923 - 29
Herbert C. Hoover	Iowa	Rep.	1929 - 33

President	Born	Party	Term
Franklin D. Roosevelt	New York	Dem.	1933 - 45
Harry S. Truman	Missouri	Dem.	1945 - 53
Dwight D. Eisenhower	Texas	Rep.	1953 - 61
John F. Kennedy	Massachusetts	Dem.	1961 - 63
Lyndon B. Johnson	Texas	Dem.	1963 - 69
Richard M. Nixon	California	Rep.	1969 - 74
Gerald R. Ford	Nebraska	Rep.	1974 - 77
James E. Carter	Georgia	Dem.	1977 - 81
Ronald W. Reagan	Illinois	Rep.	1981 - 89
George H. W. Bush	Massachusetts	Rep.	1989 - 93
William J. Clinton	Arkansas	Dem.	1993 -

You can e-mail the at President this address:
president@whitehouse.gov.

To take a virtual tour of the White House, log on to this web site: **www.whitehouse.gov.**

Succession to the Presidency

Vice President
Speaker of the House of Representatives
President Pro Tempore of the Senate
Officer who is highest of the following:

Secretary of State
Sec. of the Treasury
Secretary of Defense
Attorney General
Secretary of Interior
Secretary of Agriculture
Secretary of Commerce
Secretary of Labor

Secretary of Health and
   Human Services
Sec. of Housing and
   Urban Development
Sec. of Transportation
Secretary of Energy
Secretary of Education
Sec. of Veterans Affairs

The Cheif Executive & His Right-hand Man
U.S. Presidents & Their Vice Presidents

President	Birth - Death	Vice President
George Washington	1732 - 1799	John Adams
John Adams	1735 - 1826	Thomas Jefferson
Thomas Jefferson	1743 - 1826	Aaron Burr,
		George Clinton
James Madison	1751 - 1836	George Clinton
		Elbridge Gerry
James Monroe	1758 - 1831	Daniel D. Tompkins
John Quincy Adams	1767 - 1848	John C. Calhoun
Andrew Jackson	1767 - 1845	John C. Calhoun,
		Martin Van Buren
Martin Van Buren	1782 - 1862	Richard M. Johnson
William H. Harrison	1773 - 1841	John Tyler
John Tyler	1790 - 1862	--
James Knox Polk	1795 - 1849	George M. Dallas
Zachary Taylor	1784 - 1850	Millard Fillmore
Millard Fillmore	1800 - 1874	--
Franklin Pierce	1804 - 1869	William R. King
James Buchanan	1791 - 1868	John C. Breckenridge
Abraham Lincoln	1809 - 1865	HannibalHamlin,
		Andrew Johnson
Andrew Johnson	1808 - 1875	--
Ulysses S. Grant	1822 - 1885	Schuyler Colfax,
		Henry Wilson
Rutherford B. Hayes	1822 - 1893	William A. Wheeler
James A. Garfield	1831 - 1881	Chester A. Arthur
Chester Alan Arthur	1829 - 1886	--
Grover Cleveland	1837 - 1908	Thomas A. Hendricks
Benjamin Harrison	1833 - 1901	Levi P. Morton
Grover Cleveland	1837 - 1908	Adlai E. Stevenson
William McKinley	1843 - 1901	Garret A. Hobart
		Theodore Roosevelt
Theodore Roosevelt	1858 - 1919	Charles W. Fairbanks
William Howard Taft	1857 - 1930	James S. Sherman
Woodrow Wilson	1856 - 1924	Thomas R. Marshall

President	Birth - Death	Vice President
Warren G. Harding	1865 - 1923	Calvin Coolidge
Calvin Coolidge	1872 - 1933	Charles G. Dawes
Herbert C. Hoover	1874 - 1964	Charles Curtis
Franklin D. Roosevelt	1882 - 1945	John N. Garner, Henry A. Wallace, Harry S. Truman
Harry S. Truman	1884 - 1972	Alben W. Barkley
Dwight D. Eisenhower	1890 - 1969	Richard M. Nixon
John F. Kennedy	1917 - 1963	Lyndon B. Johnson
Lyndon B. Johnson	1908 - 1973	Hubert Humphrey
Richard M. Nixon	1913 - 1994	Spiro T. Agnew, Gerald R. Ford
Gerald R. Ford	1913 -	Nelson A. Rockefeller
James E. Carter	1924 -	Walter F. Mondale
Ronald W. Reagan	1911 -	George Bush
George H. W. Bush	1924 -	J. Daforth Quayle
William J. Clinton	1946 -	Albert A. Gore, Jr.

More Presidential Facts

- The youngest president was Theodore Roosevelt, who began serving at age 42.
- The oldest president was Ronald Reagan, who was 77 when he left office after serving 2 terms.
- The only president to serve more than 2 terms was Franklin D. Roosevelt.
- William H. Harrison served the shortest term -- he died of pneumonia only 31 days after his inauguration.
- More presidents have been born in Virginia and Ohio than in any other states.
- The presidency is a high-risk position: eight presidents have died in office, and four of them were assasinated.

The First Family
U.S. Presidents and Their First Ladies

President	First Lady
G. Washington	Martha Dandridge Custis Washington
J. Adams	Abigail Smith Adams
T. Jefferson	Martha Wayles Skelton Jefferson
J. Madison	Dorothea "Dolly" Payne Todd Madison
J. Monroe	Elizabeth Kortight Monroe
J. Q. Adams	Louisa Catherine Johnson Adams
A. Jackson	Rachel Donelson Robards Jackson
M. Van Buren	Hannah Hoes Van Buren
W. H. Harrison	Anna Tuthill Symmes Harrison
J. Tyler	Letitia Christian Tyler
	Julia Gardiner Tyler
J. K. Polk	Sarah Childress Polk
Z. Taylor	Margaret Mackall Smith Taylor
M. Fillmore	Abigail Powers Fillmore
	Caroline C. Mackintosh Fillmore
F. Pierce	Jane Means Appleton Pierce
J. Buchanan	*never married*
A. Lincoln	Mary Todd Lincoln
A. Johnson	Eliza McCardle Johnson
U.S. Grant	Julia Boggs Dent Grant
R. B. Hayes	Lucy Ware Webb Hayes
J. A. Garfield	Lucretia Rudolph Garfield
C. A. Arthur	Ellen Lewis Herndon Arthur
G. Cleveland	Frances Folsom Cleveland
B. Harrison	Caroline Lavinia Scott Harrison
	Mary Scott Lord Dimmick Harrison
W. McKinley	Ida Saxton McKinley
T. Roosevelt	Alice Hathaway Lee Roosevelt
	Edith Kermit Carow Roosevelt
W. H. Taft	Helen Herron Taft
W. Wilson	Ellen Louise Axson Wilson
	Edith Bolling Galt Wilson
W. G. Harding	Florence Kling De Wolfe Harding

President	First Lady
C. Coolidge	Grace Anna Goodhue Coolidge
H. C. Hoover	Lou Henry Hoover
F. D. Roosevelt	Anna Eleanor Roosevelt
H. S. Truman	Elizabeth Virginia "Bess" Wallace Truman
D D. Eisenhower	Mamie Geneva Doud Eisenhower
J. F. Kennedy	Jacqueline Lee Bouvier Kennedy
L. B. Johnson	Claudia "Lady Bird" Alta Taylor Johnson
R. M. Nixon	Thelma Catherine Patricia Ryan Nixon
G. R. Ford	Elizabeth Bloomer Warren Ford
J. E. Carter	Rosalynn Smith Carter
R. W. Reagan	Anne Francis "Nancy" Robins Davis Reagan
G. H. W. Bush	Barbara Pierce Bush
W. J. Clinton	Hillary Rhodam Clinton

Proper forms of address when writing to the president are: Dear Sir or Madam; Mr. President or Madam President; Dear Mr. President or Dear Madam President. Send your letters to: The President, The White House, Washington DC 20500

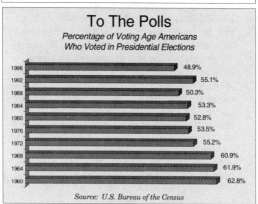

To The Polls
Percentage of Voting Age Americans Who Voted in Presidential Elections

Year	Percentage
1996	48.9%
1992	55.1%
1988	50.3%
1984	53.3%
1980	52.8%
1976	53.5%
1972	55.2%
1968	60.9%
1964	61.9%
1960	62.8%

Source: U.S. Bureau of the Census

The Bill of Rights

The Bill of Rights: The First Ten Amendments to the Constitution

I.   Congress shall make no law respecting an establishment of religion, or prohibiting the free exercise thereof; or abridging the freedom of speech, or of the press; or the right of the people peaceably to assemble, and to petition the Government for a redress of grievances.

II. A well regulated Militia, being necessary to the security of a free State, the right of the people to keep and bear Arms, shall not be infringed.

III. No Soldier shall, in time of peace be quartered in any house, without the consent of the Owner, nor in time of war, but in a manner to be prescribed by law.

IV. The right of the people to be secure in their persons, houses, papers, and effects, against unreasonable searches and seizures, shall not be violated, and no Warrants shall issue, but upon probable cause, supported by an Oath or affirmation, and particularly describing the place to be searched, and the persons or things to be seized.

V.   No person shall be held to answer for a capital, or otherwise infamous crime, unless on a presentment or indictment of a Grand Jury, except in cases arising in the land or naval forces, or in the Militia, when in actual service in time of War or public danger; nor shall any person be subject for the same offence to be twice put in jeopardy of life or limb; nor shall be compelled in any criminal case to be a witness against himself, nor be deprived of life, liberty, or property, without due process of law;

The Bill of Rights, Continued

nor shall private property be taken for public use, without just compensation.

VI. In all criminal prosecutions, the accused shall enjoy the right to a speedy and public trial, by an impartial jury of the State and district wherein the crime shall have been committed, which district shall have been previously ascertained by law, and to be informed of the nature and cause of the accusation; to be confronted with the witnesses against him; to have compulsory process for obtaining witnesses in his favor, and to have the Assistance of Counsel for his defence.

VII. In suits at common law, where the value in controversy shall exceed twenty dollars, the right of trial by jury shall be preserved, and no fact tried by a jury, shall be otherwise reexamined in any Court of the United States, than according to the rules of the common law.

VIII. Excessive bail shall not be required, nor excessive fines imposed, nor cruel and unusual punishments inflicted.

IX. The enumeration in the Constitution, of certain rights, shall not be construed to deny or disparage others retained by the people.

X. The powers not delegated to the United States by the Constitution, nor prohibited by it to the States, are reserved to the States respectively, or to the people.

The U.S. Flag

Taking Care of Old Glory
Proper Display and Care of the United States Flag

Handling	Instruction
Flying at full staff (from sunrise to sunset)	Only in good weather
	On all holidays
	On official buildings, such as schools when in session, post offices, courthouses, etc.
Raising	Quickly
Lowering	Slowly, to the tempo of "Taps"
Hanging from a building	Hang with the field of stars facing away from the building
Displaying over a street	Hang with the Union side facing north or east
Displaying on a platform	Above the speaker with the field of stars to the audience's left
Flying at night	Fly only if lit
Fly at half staff	To commemorate the death of an official
	Until noon on Memorial Day
Folding	Never let it touch the ground
Flying with another flag	Place to its right (left, viewed from the front) and with its staff in front of the other flag if against a wall
Flying with a group of flags	Display prominently, above other flags and in the center
In a church	Stand on its staff to the right of the speaker, with other flags to the speaker's left
At the White House	Only when the President is in residence, from sunrise to sunset
Flag passes in a parade, or is raised or lowered	Civilians should salute the flag by placing their right hands over their hearts; men should remove hats and hold them over left shoulder with right hand

Adding New Stars

Number of Stars on the U.S. Flag, as States Joined the Union

Date	Stars	States
1777	13	Delaware, Pennsylvania, New Jersey, Georgia, Connecticut, Massachusetts, Maryland, South Carolina, New Hampshire, Virginia, New York, North Carolina, Rhode Island
1795	15	Vermont, Kentucky
1818	20	Tennessee, Ohio, Louisiana, Indiana, Mississippi
1819	21	Illinios
1820	23	Alabama, Maine
1822	24	Missouri
1836	25	Arkansas
1837	26	Michigan
1845	27	Florida
1846	28	Texas
1847	29	Iowa
1848	30	Wisconsin
1851	31	California
1858	32	Minnesota
1859	33	Oregon
1861	34	Kansas
1863	35	West Virginia
1865	36	Nevada
1867	37	Nebraska
1877	38	Colorado
1890	43	North Dakota, South Dakota, Montana, Washington, Idaho
1891	44	Wyoming
1896	45	Utah
1908	46	Oklahoma
1912	48	New Mexico, Arizona
1959	49	Alaska
1960	50	Hawaii

The Pledge of Allegiance

I pledge allegiance to the flag of the United States of America, and to the Republic for which it stands, one nation under God, indivisible, with liberty and justice for all.

Income & Spending

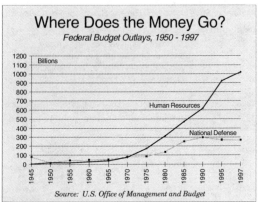

Where Does the Money Go?
Federal Budget Outlays, 1950 - 1997

Billions

Human Resources

National Defense

Source: U.S. Office of Management and Budget

Federal Spending Outpaces Receipts
Federal Budget Summary, in Millions of Dollars

Year	Receipts	Outlays	Surplus or Deficit (-)	Federal Debt
1945	45,159	92,712	-47,553	260,123
1950	39,443	42,562	-3,119	256,853
1960	92,492	92,191	301	290,525
1970	192,807	195,649	-2,842	380,921
1980	517,112	590,847	-73,835	909,050
1985	734,165	946,499	-212,334	1,817,521
1990	1,031,969	1,253,163	-221,194	3,206,564
1991	1,055,041	1,324,400	-269,359	3,598,4998
1992	1,091,279	1,381,681	-290,402	4,002,136
1993	1,154,401	1,409,414	-255,013	4,351,416
1994	1,258,627	1,461,731	-203,104	4,643,705
1995	1,351,830	1,515,729	-163,899	4,921,018
1996	1,426,775	1,572,411	-145,636	5,207,298
1997	1,505,425	1,631,016	-125,591	5,453,677

Source: U.S. Office of Management and Budget

Military Trends

In Uniform
Department of Defense Manpower, 1950 - 1995

Source: *U.S. Department of Defense*

Serving Their Country
Number of Armed Services Personnel, in Thousands

Year	Army	Navy	Marine Corps	Air Force
1950	593	381	74	411
1955	1,109	661	205	960
1960	873	617	171	815
1965	969	670	190	825
1970	1,323	691	260	791
1975	784	535	196	613
1980	777	527	188	558
1985	781	571	198	602
1990	732	579	197	535
1995	509	435	175	400

There are more than 20 million war veterans living in America.

When expansion of military programs for women began in 1973, they accounted for only 2.5% of active duty troops. By 1997, women represented 13.6%.

Government Web Sites

Our Government, On Line
Selected Government Web Sites

Agency, Bureau or Department	Address
House of Representatives	www.house.gov
Senate	www.senate.gov
Supreme Court	www.supct.law.cornell.edu/supct
Dept. of Agriculture	www.usda.gov
Dept. of Commerce	www.doc.gov
Dept. of Defense	www.dtic.dla.mil/defenselink
Dept. of Education	www.ed.gov
Dept. of Energy	www.doe.gov
Dept. of Health & Human Services	www.os.dhhs.gov
Dept. of Housing & Urban Development	www.hud.gov
Dept. of the Interior	www.doi.gov
Dept. of Justice	www.usdoj.gov
Dept. of Labor	www.dol.gov
Dept. of Transportation	www.dot.gov
Dept. of Treasury	www.ustreas.gov
Dept. of Veterans Affairs	www.va.gov
Census Bureau	www.census.gov
Central Intelligence Agency	www.odci.gov/cia
Env. Protection Agency	www.epa.gov
Federal Bueau of Investigation	www.fbi.gov
Fed.l Emerg. Mgmnt Agency	www.fema.gov
Federal Trade Commission	www.ftc.gov
Library of Congress	www.loc.gov
NASA	www.nasa.gov
National Institutes of Health	www.nih.gov
National Weather Service	www.noaa.gov
Postal Service	www.usps.gov
Social Security Administration	www.ssa.gov
Bureau of Economic Analysis	www.bea.gov
Bureau of Labor Statistics	www.bls.gov

4. We the People

See also 'These United States.'

U.S. Population

Who Are Americans?

Families & Households

Life & Death Statistics

U.S. Population

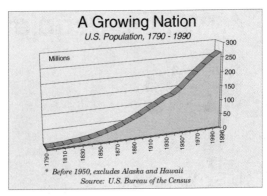

A Growing Nation
U.S. Population, 1790 - 1990

Millions

* Before 1950, excludes Alaska and Hawaii
Source: U.S. Bureau of the Census

We the People
U.S. Resident Population, 1790 - 2050

Year	Population	Year	Population
1790	3,929,214	1930	122,775,046
1800	5,308,483	1940	131,669,275
1810	7,239,881	1950[1]	151,325,798
1820	9,638,453	1960	179,323,175
1830	12,866,020	1970	203,302,031
1840	17,069,453	1980	226,542,199
1850	23,191,876	1990	248,718,301
1860	31,443,321	2000[2]	274,634,000
1870	39,818,449	2010[2]	297,716,000
1880	50,155,783	2020[2]	322,742,000
1890	62,947,718	2030[2]	346,899,000
1900	75,994,575	2040[2]	369,980,000
1910	91,972,266	2050[2]	393,931,000
1920	105,710,620		

1 Before 1950, excludes Alaska and Hawaii

2 Projections

76

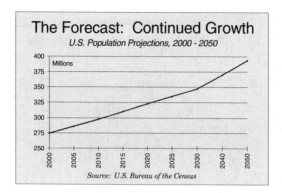

The Forecast: Continued Growth
U.S. Population Projections, 2000 - 2050

Source: U.S. Bureau of the Census

America Reborn Each Year
Population Changes, in Rate per 1,000 Population

Year	Net Growth Rate	Birth Rate	Death Rate	Net Migration
1980	11.1	16.0	8.6	4.2
1985	9.1	15.8	8.8	2.7
1990	10.2	16.6	8.6	2.2
1995	9.4	14.8	8.8	3.4
2000	8.4	14.2	8.8	3.0
2005	8.0	14.0	8.9	2.9
2010	8.1	14.3	8.9	2.8
2020	7.8	14.2	9.0	25
2030	6.7	13.9	9.5	2.4
2040	6.4	14.2	10.1	2.2
2050	6.4	14.4	10.1	2.1

Source: U.S. Bureau of the Census

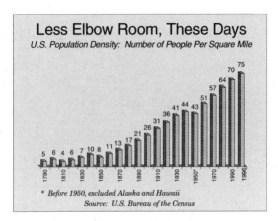

Less Elbow Room, These Days

U.S. Population Density: Number of People Per Square Mile

5 6 4 6 7 10 8 11 13 17 21 26 31 36 41 44 43 51 57 64 70 75

1790 1810 1830 1850 1870 1890 1910 1930 1950* 1970 1990 1996

* Before 1950, excluded Alaska and Hawaii
Source: U.S. Bureau of the Census

Rubbing Elbows

The Most Crowded of America's Largest Cities

City	Number of People per Square Mile
New York	23,739
San Francisco	15,738
Chicago	12,025
Philadelphia	11,280
Washington, DC	9,235
Baltimore	8,700
Los Angeles	7,349
Detroit	7,152
Milwaukee	6,420
Seattle	6,222

In 1960, 30% of Americans lived in rural areas. By 1994, only 25% refused to call cities and towns their home.

Urban population is defined by the U.S. Census Bureau as the people living in cities, villages, boroughs, and towns of at least 2,500.

Where the People Live
Urban Population, by Size of Place of Residence

Population Size	Number of Cities & Towns	Population (millions)	Percent of Total Urban
Total	19,314	160.7	100.0
1,000,000 +	8	20.0	12.4
500,000 - 999,999	16	10.8	6.7
250,000 - 499,999	41	14.8	9.2
100,000 - 249,999	144	21.1	13.1
50 000 - 99,999	343	23.4	14.6
25,000 - 49,999	588	20.6	12.8
10,000 - 24,999	1,372	21.5	13.4
Under 10,000	16,802	28.6	17.8

Source: U.S. Bureau of the Census

*New York is America's largest city. It is the
fourth largest in the world, after Tokyo, Mexico
City, and Sao Paolo.*

Calling the City Home
Population of America's Largest Cities, in Thousands

Rank	City	1980	1990	1994
1.	New York, NY	7,072	7,323	7,333
2.	Los Angeles, CA	2,969	3,486	3,449
3.	Chicago, IL	3,005	3,784	2,732
4.	Houston, TX	1,595	1,631	1,702
5.	Philadelphia, PA	1,688	1,586	1,524
6.	San Diego, CA	876	1,111	1,152
7.	Phoenix, AZ	1,688	1,586	1,524
8.	Dallas, TX	905	1,008	1,023
9.	San Antonio, TX	786	935	999
10.	Detroit, MI	1,203	1,028	992
11.	San Jose, CA	629	782	817
12.	Indianapolis, IN	701	731	752
13.	San Francisco, CA	679	724	735
14.	Baltimore, MD	787	736	703
15.	Jacksonville, FL	541	635	665
16.	Columbus, OH	565	633	636
17.	Milwaukee, WI	636	628	617
18.	Memphis, TN	646	619	614
19.	El Paso, TX	425	515	579
20.	Washington, DC	638	607	567
21.	Boston, MA	563	574	548
22.	Seattle, WA	494	516	521
23.	Austin, TX	346	466	514
24.	Nashville, TN	456	488	505
25.	Denver, CO	493	468	494

Source: U.S. Bureau of the Census

The Urban Sprawl

Population of America's Largest Metropolitan Areas, in Thousands

Rank	Metropolitan Area	1990	1994
1.	New York-Northern NJ-Long Island	19,550	19,796
2.	Los Angeles-Riverside-Orange Co.	14,532	15,302
3.	Chicago-Gary-Kenosha	8,240	8,527
4.	Washington-Baltimore	6,726	7,051
5.	San Francisco-Oakland-San Jose	6,250	6,513
6.	Philadelphia-Wilmington-Atlantic City	5,893	5,959
7.	Boston-Worcester-Lawrence	5,455	5,497
8.	Detroit-Ann Arbor-Flint	5,187	5,256
9.	Dallas-Ft. Worth	4,037	4,362
10.	Houston-Galveston-Brazoria	3,731	4,099
11.	Miami-Ft. Lauderdale	3,193	3,408
12.	Atlanta	2,960	3,331
13.	Seattle-Tacoma-Bremerton	2,970	3,226
14.	Cleveland-Akron	2,860	2,899
15.	Minneapolis-St. Paul	2,539	2,688
16.	San Diego	2,498	2,632
17.	St. Louis	2,492	2,536
18.	Phoenix-Mesa	2,238	2,473
19.	Pittsburgh	2,395	2,402
20.	Tampa-St. Petersburg-Clearwater	2,068	2,157
21.	Denver-Boulder-Greeley	1,980	2,190
22.	Portland-Salem	1,793	1,982
23	Cincinnati-Hamilton	1,818	1,894
24.	Kansas City	1,583	1,347
25.	Milwaukee-Racine	1,607	1,637
26.	Sacramento-Yolo	1,481	1,588
27.	Norfolk-Virginia Beach-Newport News	1,445	1,529
28.	Indianapolis	1,380	1,462
29.	Columbus, OH	1,345	1,423
30.	Orlando	1,225	1,361

Source: U.S. Bureau of the Census

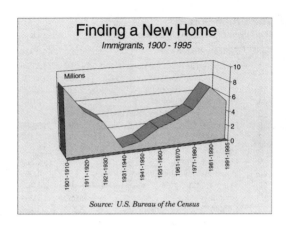

Finding a New Home
Immigrants, 1900 - 1995

Millions

Source: U.S. Bureau of the Census

Where Do They Come From?

Number of U.S. Immigrants, by Continent, in Thousands

Continent	1981-90	1991-93	1994	1995
Asia	2,817.4	1,073.5	292.6	267.9
N. America	3,125.0	1,896.4	272.2	231.5
Europe	705.6	438.9	160.9	128.2
S. America	455.9	189.2	47.4	45.7
Africa	192.3	91.0	26.7	42.5

Leading Countries of Birth of American Immigrants

1. Mexico
2. Former Soviet Union
3. Philippines
4. Vietnam
5. Dominican Republic
6. China
7. India
8. Jamaica
9. Korea
10. Colombia

Who Are Americans?

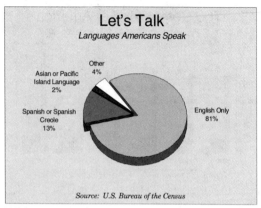

Let's Talk
Languages Americans Speak

Other 4%

Asian or Pacific Island Language 2%

Spanish or Spanish Creole 13%

English Only 81%

Source: U.S. Bureau of the Census

Not Just English

Number of Americans by Language Spoken, in Thousands

Language	People	Language	People
English Only	198,601	Hindi (Urdu)	331
Spanish	17,339	Russian	242
French	1,702	Yiddish	213
German	1,547	Thai (Laotian)	206
Italian	1,309	Persian	202
Chinese	1,249	French Creole	188
Tagalog	843	Armenian	150
Polish	723	Navaho	149
Korean	626	Hungarian	148
Vietnamese	507	Hebrew	144
Portuguese	430	Dutch	143
Japanese	428	Cambodian	127
Greek	388	Gujarathi	102
Arabic	355		

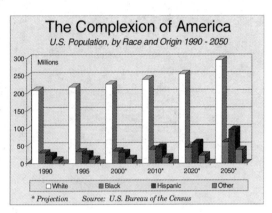

The Complexion of America
U.S. Population, by Race and Origin 1990 - 2050

□ White   ■ Black   ■ Hispanic   ▨ Other

* Projection   Source: U.S. Bureau of the Census

*About 86% of Americans were white in 1980.
By 2025, though, whites will account for only
75%. The fastest growing groups are Hispanics
and Asian / Pacific Islanders.*

A Diverse People

U.S. Resident Population by Race and Origin, in Thousands

Year	White	Black	Am. Ind. Eskimo, Aleut	Asian, Pacific Islander	Hispanic
1980	194,713	26,683	1,420	3,729	14,609
1990	208,710	30,486	2,065	7,458	22,354
1996	219,749	33,503	2,288	9,743	28,269
2000[1]	225,532	35,454	2,402	11,245	31,366
2010[1]	239,588	40,109	2,754	15,265	41,139
2020[1]	254,887	45,075	3,129	19,651	52,652
2025[1]	262,227	47,539	3,319	21,965	58,930
2050[1]	294,615	60,592	4,371	34,352	96,508

[1] *Projection*

City populations generally have more diversity than the population in general.

The Melting Pot
Diversity of America's Largest Cities, in Percent

City	Black	Am. Ind. Eskimo, Aleut	Asian, Pacific Islander	Hispanic
New York, NY	28.7	0.4	7.0	24.4
Los Angeles, CA	14.0	0.5	9.8	39.9
Chicago, IL	39.1	0.3	3.7	19.6
Houston, TX	28.1	0.3	4.1	27.6
Philadelphia, PA	39.9	0.2	2.7	5.6
San Diego, CA	9.4	0.6	11.8	20.7
Phoenix, AZ	5.2	1.9	1.7	20.0
Dallas, TX	29.5	0.5	2.2	20.9
San Antonio, TX	7.0	0.4	1.1	55.6
Detroit, MI	75.7	1.4	0.8	2.8
San Jose, CA	4.7	0.7	19.5	26.6
Indianapolis, IN	22.6	0.2	0.9	1.1
San Francisco, CA	10.9	0.5	29.1	13.9
Baltimore, MD	59.2	0.3	1.1	1.0
Jacksonville, FL	25.2	0.3	1.9	2.6
Columbus, OH	22.6	0.2	2.4	1.1
Milwaukee, WI	30.5	0.9	1.9	6.3
Memphis, TN	54.8	0.2	0.8	0.7
El Paso, TX	3.4	0.4	1.2	69.0
Washington, DC	65.8	0.2	1.8	5.4
Boston, MA	25.6	0.3	5.3	10.8
Seattle, WA	10.1	1.4	11.8	3.6
Austin, TX	12.4	0.4	3.0	23.0
Nashville, TN	24.3	0.2	1.4	0.9
Denver, CO	12.8	1.2	2.4	23.0

Source: U.S. Bureau of the Census

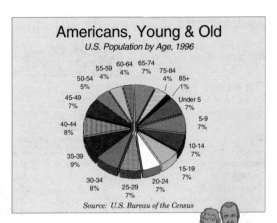

Americans, Young & Old

U.S. Population by Age, 1996

- 55-59 4%
- 60-64 4%
- 65-74 7%
- 75-84 4%
- 85+ 1%
- 50-54 5%
- 45-49 7%
- 40-44 8%
- 35-39 9%
- 30-34 8%
- 25-29 7%
- 20-24 7%
- 15-19 7%
- 10-14 7%
- 5-9 7%
- Under 5 7%

Source: U.S. Bureau of the Census

By the year 2030, 20% of the U.S. population will be age 65 or older.

The Graying of America

Population Distribution by Age, in Percent

Age	1995	2000	2010	2020	2030	2040
Under 5	7.4	6.9	6.7	6.8	6.6	6.8
5 - 13	13.0	13.1	12.0	12.0	12.0	11.9
14 - 17	5.6	5.7	5.7	5.3	5.4	5.4
18 - 24	9.6	9.6	10.1	9.3	9.2	9.3
25 - 34	15.5	13.6	12.9	13.3	12.3	12.4
35 - 44	16.2	16.3	12.9	12.3	12.8	11.9
45 - 64	19.9	22.2	26.5	24.6	21.7	22.0
65 +	12.8	12.6	13.2	16.5	20.0	20.3
85 +	1.4	1.6	1.9	2.0	2.4	3.7
100 +	0.0	0.0	0.0	0.1	0.1	0.1

Source: U.S. Bureau of the Census

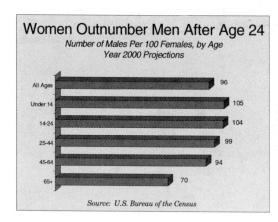

Women Outnumber Men After Age 24
Number of Males Per 100 Females, by Age
Year 2000 Projections

Age	Males per 100 Females
All Ages	96
Under 14	105
14-24	104
25-44	99
45-64	94
65+	70

Source: U.S. Bureau of the Census

More Women Than Men in America
U.S. Resident Population, by Sex, in Thousands

Year	Total	Males	Females
1996	265,284	129,810	135,474
1997	267,645	130,712	136,933
1998	270,002	131,883	138,119
1999	272,330	133,039	139,291
2000	274,634	134,181	140,453
2005	285,981	139,785	146,196
2010	297,716	145,584	146,196
2015	310,134	151,750	158,383
2020	322,742	158,021	164,721
2025	335,050	164,119	170,931
2030	346,899	169,950	176,949
2040	369,980	181,261	188,719
2050	393,931	193,234	200,696

Source: U.S. Bureau of the Census

Families & Households

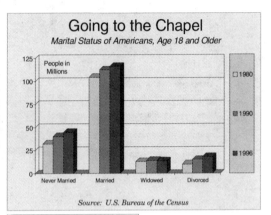

Going to the Chapel
Marital Status of Americans, Age 18 and Older

People in Millions

- □ 1980
- ▨ 1990
- ▨ 1996

Never Married · Married · Widowed · Divorced

Source: U.S. Bureau of the Census

Favorite U.S. Honeymoon Spots

1. Florida
2. Hawaii
3. California
4. Pennsylvania
5. Nevada

Favorite Foreign Honeymoon Spots

1. Mexico
2. Jamaica
3. Virgin Islands
4. The Bahamas
5. Europe

Source: Modern Bride

The marriage rate (number of marriages per 1,000 unmarried women) fell from 77 in 1970 to 51 in 1995. The divorce rate (the number of divorces per 1,000 married women) climbed from 15 to 20 during the same period.

Source: National Cntr. for Health Statistics

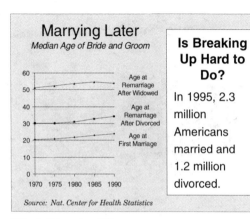

Marrying Later
Median Age of Bride and Groom

Age at Remarriage After Widowed

Age at Remarriage After Divorced

Age at First Marriage

1970 1975 1980 1985 1990

Source: Nat. Center for Health Statistics

Is Breaking Up Hard to Do?

In 1995, 2.3 million Americans married and 1.2 million divorced.

Who's Marrying Whom
Marriages of the Same or Mixed Race, in Thousands

Race or Origin	1980	1990	1996
White/White	44,910	47,202	48,056
Black/Black	3,354	3,687	3,560
Hispanic/Hispanic	1,906	3,085	3,888
Black/White	167	211	337
White/Other	450	720	884
Black/Other	34	33	39

States with the Highest Marriage Rates	States with the Highest Divorce Rates
1. Nevada	1. Nevada
2. Hawaii	2. New Mexico
3. Tennessee	3. Oklahoma
4. Idaho	4. Wyoming
5. South Carolina	5. Arizona

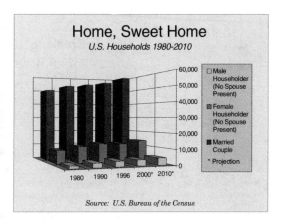

Home, Sweet Home
U.S. Households 1980-2010

Legend:
- ☐ Male Householder (No Spouse Present)
- ▨ Female Householder (No Spouse Present)
- ■ Married Couple
- * Projection

Years: 1980, 1990, 1996, 2000*, 2010*

Source: U.S. Bureau of the Census

Of women divorced in America, 20% marry again within one year. By the end of five years, 50% are remarried.
Source: *National Center for Health Statistics*

The Lady of the House
Female Householders with No Spouse Present

	Never Married	Married Spouse Absent	Widowed	Divorced
White	19%	17%	21%	43%
Black	42%	19%	14%	25%
Hispanic	31%	26%	14%	29%

64% of Americans own their homes.

Each year, 17% of us move to a different home.

Most Expensive Places to Live
Metropolitan Areas by Cost of Living Index, 1996

Metropolitan Area	% of U.S. Average
U.S. Average	100.0
New York, NY	234.5
Salinas, CA	143.6
Philadelphia, PA	125.5
Washington, DC	125.4
Anchorage, AK	124.8
San Diego, CA	121.9
Los Angeles-Long Beach, CA	119.7
Seattle-Bellvue-Everett, WA	115.0
Detroit, MI	113.4
Santa Barbara-Santa Maria, CA	113.2
Reno, NV	112.4
Elmira, NY	112.3
Madison, WI	112.2
Flagstaff, AZ	111.4
Bremerton, WA	111.1
Wilmington-Newark, DE, MD	110.1
Boulder-Longmont, CO	109.5
Pittsburgh, PA	109.5
Portland-Vancouver, OR, WA	109.1
Riverside-San Bernardino, CA	108.7
Visalia-Toulare-Porterville, CA	108.6
Eugene-Springfield, OR	108.3
Miami, FL	107.7
West Palm Beach-Boca Raton, FL	107.7
South Bend, IN	107.7
Dubuque, IA	107.6

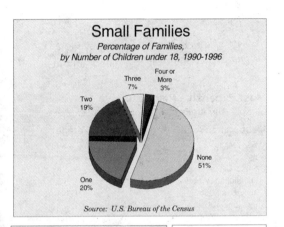

Small Families
*Percentage of Families,
by Number of Children under 18, 1990-1996*

Three 7%

Four or More 3%

Two 19%

None 51%

One 20%

Source: U.S. Bureau of the Census

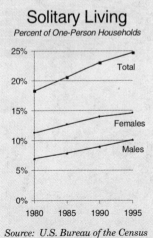

Solitary Living
Percent of One-Person Households

25%

20%

15%

10%

5%

0%

Total

Females

Males

1980   1985   1990   1995

Source: U.S. Bureau of the Census

Of the 70 million families in America, about 43% are comprised of two people, 23% of three people, and 21% of four people. Large families -- with seven or more people -- account for only 2%. The average family size is 3 people.

The birth rate (number of births per 1,000 women ages 15 - 44) was 70.9 in 1990, and fell to 65.6 in 1996.

Working Moms

38% of the women who had babies in 1980 were employed outside the home. By 1995, that number had risen to 55%.

Most Common Names for Boys

1. Michael
2. Christopher
3. Matthew
4. Joshua
5. Andrew
6. James
7. John
8. Nicholas
9. Justin
10. David

Most Common Names for Girls

1. Brittany
2. Ashley
3. Jessica
4. Amanda
5. Sarah
6. Megan
7. Caitlin
8. Samantha
9. Stephanie
10. Katherine

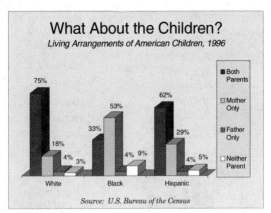

What About the Children?

Living Arrangements of American Children, 1996

Legend:
- ■ Both Parents
- □ Mother Only
- ■ Father Only
- □ Neither Parent

White: 75%, 18%, 4%, 3%
Black: 33%, 53%, 4%, 9%
Hispanic: 62%, 29%, 4%, 5%

Source: U.S. Bureau of the Census

In 1980, 77% of America's children under age 18 lived with both parents. By 1996, only 68% had both parents at home.

More than half of all divorces effect children. Every year, over one million children have parents who separate or divorce. The divorce rate in 1996 was 4.3 per 1,000 population -- the lowest for over two decades. Still, it was almost double the 1960 rate of 2.2 per 1,000, and more than six times the rate of 0.7 per 1,000 in 1900.

Life & Death Statistics

Higher Expectations
Life Expectancy in Years, by Year of Birth, Race, and Sex

Birth Year	All Races M	All Races F	White M	White F	Black & Other M	Black & Other F
1920	53.6	54.6	54.4	55.6	45.5	45.2
1940	60.8	65.2	62.1	66.6	51.5	54.9
1960	66.6	73.1	67.4	74.1	61.1	66.3
1980	70.0	77.5	70.7	78.1	65.3	73.6
1985	71.2	78.2	71.9	78.7	64.8	69.3
1990	71.8	78.8	72.9	79.4	67.0	75.2
1991	72.0	78.9	72.9	79.2	67.4	75.5
1992	72.1	78.9	73.0	79.5	67.5	75.8
1993	72.1	78.9	73.0	79.5	67.4	75.5
1994	72.4	79.0	73.3	79.6	67.5	75.8
1995	72.5	78.9	73.4	79.6	67.9	75.7
1996	73.0	79.0	73.8	79.6	68.8	76.2

Source: National Center for Health Statistics

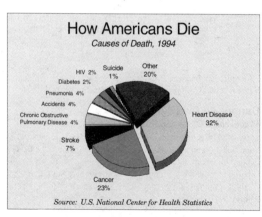

How Americans Die
Causes of Death, 1994

- HIV 2%
- Suicide 1%
- Other 20%
- Diabetes 2%
- Pneumonia 4%
- Accidents 4%
- Chronic Obstructive Pulmonary Disease 4%
- Stroke 7%
- Cancer 23%
- Heart Disease 32%

Source: U.S. National Center for Health Statistics

Accidents Claim Young Lives
Leading Causes of Death by Age, 1994

Age Group	Leading Causes of Death	Age Group	Leading Causes of Death	Age Group	Leading Causes of Death
1-4	Accidents	15-24	Accidents	45-64	Cancer
	Congenital		Homicide		Heart Dis.
	Cancer		Suicide		Pneumonia
	Homicide		Cancer		HIV Inf.
	Heart Dis.		Stroke		Stroke
	Pneumonia		COPD [1]		Accidents
	HIV Inf.		Congenital		COPD [1]
5-14	Accidents		Heart Dis.		Liver Dis.
	Cancer		Pneumonia		Diabetes
	Congenital		HIV Inf.		Suicide
	Suicide	25-44	Accidents	65+	Heart Dis.
	Homicide		Cancer		Cancer
	Heart Dis.		Stroke		Stroke
	Pneumonia		HIV Inf.		COPD [1]
	HIV Inf.		Heart Dis.		Pneumonia
			Pneumonia		Diabetes
			Diabetes		Accidents
			Homicide		
			Suicide		

[1] *Chronic Obstructive Pulmonary Disease*
Source: U.S. National Center for Health Statistics

Danger on the Highway
Motor Vehicle Occupants Killed and Injured in Crashes

Year	Total	Cars	Light Trucks	Motorcycles	Buses
Killed					
1990	37,134	24,092	8,601	3,244	32
1995	35,274	22,358	9,539	2,221	32
Injured, in Thousands					
1990	3,044	2,376	505	84	33
1995	3,232	2,416	709	55	18

Source: U.S. National Highway Traffic Safety Admin.

5. Food, Fitness & Health

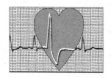

Nutrition & Weight

Exercise & Fitness

Home Safety

Immunizations

Nutrition & Weight

Cooking Up Dinner
Roasting Times for Beef, at 325° F

Cut	Donness	Size	Min. per Pound	Internal Temp.
Standing rib	rare	4 -8 lbs.	20 - 25	140°
	medium	4 -8 lbs.	25 - 30	160°
	well-done	4 -8 lbs.	30 - 35	170°
Rolled rib	rare	5 - 7 lbs.	30 - 35	140°
	medium	5 - 7 lbs.	35 - 40	160°
	well	5 - 7 lbs.	40 - 45	170°
Rib eye	rare	4 - 6 lbs.	20	140°
	medium	4 - 6 lbs.	22	160°
	well-done	4 - 6 lbs.	24	170°
Sirloin tip		3 ½ - 4 lbs.	35 - 40	160°

Broiling Times for Steak, 2 Inches from Broiler

Cut	Donness	Size	Time
Porterhouse,	rare	1 inch thick	5 min. each side
or T-bone	medium	1 inch thick	7 min. each side
	well-done	1 inch thick	10 min. each side
Porterhouse,	rare	1½ inch thick	6 min. each side
or T-bone	medium	1½ inch thick	8 min. each side
	well-done	1½ inch thick	12 min. each side

Roasting Times for Pork, at 350° F

Cut	Size	Min. per Pound	Internal Temp.
Loin, center	3 - 5 lbs.	40	185°
Loin, half	5 - 7 lbs.	45	185°
Loin, rolled	3 - 5 lbs.	50	185°
Sirloin	3 - 4 lbs.	50	185°

Roasting Times for Turkey, at 325° F

	Oven Temp.	Size	Time	Internal Temp.
Turkey, whole (unstuffed)	325°	4 - 8 lbs.	3 - 4 hrs.	185°
	325°	8 - 12 lbs.	3½ - 4½ hrs.	185°
	325°	12 - 16 lbs.	4 - 5 hrs.	185°
	325°	16 - 20 lbs.	4½ - 5½ hrs.	185°
Breast	325°	4 - 6 lbs.	1½ - 2¼ hrs.	185°
	325°	6 - 8 lbs.	2¼ - 3¼ hrs.	185°

Cooking Times for Chicken Breasts

Cooking Method	Minutes
Baking, at 375°	45 - 60
Boneless, at 325°	25 - 35
Broiling	25 - 35
Boneless	12 - 15
Kabobs	8 - 10
Grilling	15 - 25, each side
Boneless	8 - 10, each side
Kabobs	4 - 5, each side
Pan-frying	30 - 40
Deep-frying	20 - 25
Stewing	40

Cooking Times for Fish

Cooking Method	Minutes
Baking, at 500°	10
Broiling	15
Deep-frying, at 370°	2
Pan-frying	10
Poaching	10 per lb.

Is This Still Good?
Maximum Recommended Refrigerated Storage Time

Beef	3 - 5 days	Hot Dogs	1 week
Butter	2 weeks	Ground	
Cheese	1 - 3 weeks	meat	1 - 2 days
Eggs	1 - 2 weeks	Milk	1 week
Fish	1 day	Poultry	1 - 2 days

The Vegetable Steamer
Cooking Times for Vegetables

Vegetable	Method	Minutes
Artichoke	Steam/boil	30 - 40
Asparagus	Steam/boil	10 - 15
Beans (green)	Steam/boil	5 - 10
Beans (lima)	Steam/boil	20 - 25
Beets (whole)	Steam/boil	35 - 45
Broccoli	Steam/boil	10 - 15
Brussels sprouts	Steam/boil	5 - 10
Cabbage	Steam/boil	5
Carrots	Steam/boil	10 - 15
Cauliflower	Steam/boil	10 - 15
Corn	Steam/boil	5 - 10
Eggplant	Broil/saute	5 - 10
Mushrooms	Saute	5
Peas	Steam/boil	5 - 10
Peppers (green)	Saute	3 - 5
Potatoes	Steam/boil	20 - 25
Potatoes	Bake	60 - 90
Potatoes (new)	Steam/boil	20 - 25
Potatoes (sweet)	Steam/boil	30 - 35
Spinach	Steam/boil	5
Squash	Boil/saute	5 - 10
Tomatoes	Steam/boil	5 - 10
Turnips	Steam/boil	25 - 30

Steaming and boiling are both fat-free ways to cook vegetables.

Weighing In
Acceptable Weight Ranges for Adults

	Height	Small Frame	Medium Frame	Large Frame
Men	5' 1"	123-129	126-136	133-145
	5' 2"	125-131	128-138	135-148
	5' 3"	127-133	130-140	137-151
	5' 4"	129-135	132-143	139-155
	5' 5"	131-137	134-146	141-159
	5' 6"	133-140	137-149	144-163
	5' 7"	135-143	140-152	147-167
	5' 8"	137-146	143-155	150-171
	5' 9"	139-149	146-158	153-175
	5' 10"	141-152	149-161	156-179
	5' 11"	144-155	152-165	159-183
	6' 0"	147-159	155-169	163-187
	6' 1"	150-163	159-173	167-192
	6' 2"	153-167	162-177	171-197
	6' 3"	157-171	166-182	176-202
Women	4' 9"	99-108	106-118	115-128
	4' 10"	100-110	108-120	117-131
	4' 11"	101-112	110-123	119-134
	5' 0"	103-115	112-126	122-137
	5' 1"	105-118	115-129	125-140
	5' 2"	108-121	118-132	128-144
	5' 3"	111-124	121-135	131-148
	5' 4"	114-127	124-138	134-152
	5' 5"	117-130	127-141	137-156
	5' 6"	120-133	130-144	140-160
	5' 7"	123-136	133-147	143-164
	5' 8"	126-139	136-150	146-167
	5' 9"	129-142	139-153	149-170
	5' 10"	132-145	142-156	152-173
	5' 11"	135-148	145-159	155-176

Source: American Medical Assoc. <u>Family Medical Guide</u>

How Much Is Too Much?

Using weight tables is a good place to start in determining if your weight is appropriate. Another, perhaps more accurate way to check your weight is to calculate your body mass index. This method minimizes the effect of height and provides useful guidelines.

Body Mass Index Calculation:

- Convert your weight to kilograms (divide the pounds by 2.2).
- Convert your height to meters (divide the inches by 39.4). Then square it (multiply it by itself).
- Divide your weight in kilograms by your height in meters, squared.

Example: 5' 3" 125 pound woman

- 125 lbs. / 2.2 = 56.8 kg
- 63" / 39.4 = 1.6 meters
- 1.6 x 1.6 = 2.56
- 56.8 / 2.56 = 22.1

Interpreting Your Score:

- For men, a desirable body mass index is 22 to 24. Above about 28.5 is overweight. Above 33 is seriously overweight.
- For women, a desirable body mass index is 21 to 23. Above about 27.5 is overweight. Above 31.5 is seriously overweight.

Source: The Wellness Encyclopedia, UCLA Berkeley

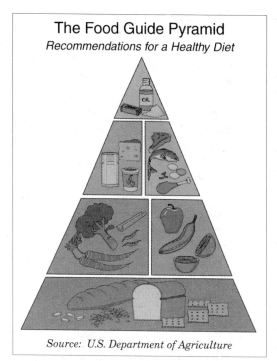

Source: U.S. Department of Agriculture

Serving recommendations are presented in ranges because calorie needs vary based on age, size, and activity level. Smaller, older, and less active people need less food than larger, younger, and more active people. See next page for information on serving sizes.

Recommended Serving Sizes

Grain Products

- 1 slice bread
- 1 ounce ready-to-eat cereal
- 1/2 cup cooked cereal, rice, or pasta

Vegetables

- 1 cup raw leafy vegetables
- 1/2 cup other vegetables, cooked or chopped raw
- 3/4 cup juice

Fruit

- 1 medium apple, banana, or orange
- 1/2 cup chopped, cooked, or canned fruit
- 3/4 cup juice

Milk Products

- 1 cup milk or yogurt
- 1-1/2 ounces natural cheese
- 2 ounces processed cheese

Meat and Beans

- 2-3 ounces cooked lean meat, poultry, or fish
- 1/2 cup cooked dry beans or 1 egg counts as one ounce of meat

Source: U.S. Department of Agriculture, U.S. Department of Health and Human Services, Nutrition and Your Health: Dietary Guidelines for Americans, Fourth Edition, 1995

What's for Dinner?

Nutritive Value of Foods

Food	Calories	Protein	Carbo-hydrates	Fat
Grains & Breads				
Bagel, plain	200	7g	38g	2g
Bread, white, 1 slice	65	2g	12g	1g
Bread, wheat, 1 slice	70	3g	13g	1g
Bread, pita, 1	165	6g	12g	1g
Oatmeal, 1 cup	145	6g	25g	2g
Muffin, bran, 1	140	3g	24g	4g
Muffin, corn, 1	145	3g	21g	5g
Angel Food Cake, 1/12	125	3g	29g	T
Graham Crackers, 2	60	1g	11g	1g
Noodles, 1 cup, cooked	200	7g	37g	2g
Pretzels, 10	10	T	2g	T
Fruits & Vegetables				
Apple, raw, small	80	T	21g	T
Banana, raw	50	1g	11g	1g
Lemonade, unsw., 6 oz.	55	1g	16g	1g
Orange Juice, 1 cup	110	2g	27g	T
Peach, small	35	1g	10g	T
Raisins, 1 cup	435	5g	115g	1g
Strawberries, 1 cup	45	1g	10g	T
Asparagus, 4 spears	15	2g	3g	T
Green Beans, 1 cup cooked	35	2g	8g	T
Broccoli, 1 spear	50	5g	10g	1g
Carrot, 1 raw	30	1g	7g	T
Cauliflower, 1 cup, cooked	20	2g	6g	T
Green Peas, 1 cup	125	8g	23g	T
Potato, 1, baked	145	3g	34g	T
Potato Chips, 10	105	1g	10g	7g
Meats, Fish & Poultry				
Roast Beef, 2.6 oz.	135	22g	0g	5g
Ground Beef, 3 oz.	245	20g	0g	18g

Proteins and carbohydrates supply about 4 calories per gram. Fats provide about 9 calories per gram.

Food	Calories	Protein	Carbo-hydrates	Fat
Ham, 3 oz.	205	18g	0g	14g
Bacon, crisp, 3 slices	110	6g	T	9g
Pork chop, 3 oz.	275	24g	0g	19g
Pork sausage, 1 link	50	3g	T	4g
Trout, broiled, 3 oz.	175	21g	T	9g
Shrimp, fried, 3 oz.	200	16g	11g	10g
Chicken breast, no skin	140	27g	0g	3g
Chicken drumstick, fried	195	16g	6g	11g
Dairy Products				
Cheese, cheddar, 1 oz.	115	7g	T	9g
Cheese, Swiss, 1 oz.	95	7g	1g	7g
Sour Cream, 1 Tbsp.	25	T	1g	3g
Milk, whole, 1 cup	150	8g	11g	8g
Milk, skim, 1 cup	85	8g	12g	T
Milkshake, 10 oz.	355	9g	60g	8g
Ice Cream, hard, 1 cup	270	5g	32g	14g
Yogurt, 8 oz.	23	10g	43g	2g
Egg, fried in margarine	90	6g	1g	7g
Fats & Sweets				
Butter, 1 Tbsp.	100	T	T	11g
Margarine, 1 Tbsp.	100	T	T	11g
Mayonnaise	100	T	T	11g
Apple Pie, 1/6	405	3g	60g	18g
Pecan Pie, 1/6	575	7g	71g	32g
Choc. Chip Cookies, 4	185	2g	26g	11g
Sheetcake, frosted, 1/9	445	4g	77g	14g
Pound Cake, 1/17	110	2g	15g	5g
Cheesecake, 1/12	280	5g	26g	18g
Brownies with nuts, 1	100	1g	16g	4g
Cake Doughnut, 1	210	3g	24g	12g

Source: U.S. Department of Agriculture

Vitamin Packed Foods
Best Sources of Vitamins

Vitamin	Good Sources
Vitamin A	animal fats, fish liver oil, liver, vegetables (especially green leafy ones like kale, and escarole, and yellow ones like carrots)
Vitamin B_1 (Thiamine)	yeast, whole grain cereals, peas, beans, peanuts, oranges, liver, many vegetables
Vitamin B_2 (Riboflavin)	eggs, green vegetables, liver, kidney, lean meat, milk, wheat germ, dried yeast
Vitamin B_6 (Pyridoxine)	Blackstrap molasses, meat, whole grain cereals, wheat germ
Vitamin B_{12}	liver, kidney, dairy products
Niacin	yeast, lean meat, fish, legumes, whole grain cereals, and peanuts
Vitamin C	fresh fruits and vegetables, escpeially citrus fruits and juices, and tomatoes
Vitamin D	butter, egg yolks, fish liver oils, liver, oysters, yeast, fatty fish such as salmon, tuna, herring
Vitamin E	lettuce, other green leafy vegetables, wheat germ oil, rice
Folacin	glandular meats, yeast, green leafy vegetables

Vitamins are necessary for good health. Vitamin A, for example, promotes resistance to infection. Vitamin B_1 is essential for metabolism, digestion, and appetite. Vitamin B_2 is important for normal growth, while vitamin B_{12} is required for the development of red blood cells. Niacin is important in fat synthesis. Vitamin C helps maintain skin, cartilage, and bones and aids in the healing of wounds.

Recent studies have shown that a group of vitamins known as antioxidants (A,C, and E) may have profound protective effects against cancer, heart disease, and even the aging process. They work by neutralizing free radicals, or oxidants. Oxidants are a by-product of breathing and other ordinary metabolic processes, but are also supplied by radiation, air pollutants, toxic industrial chemicals, pesticides, cigarette smoke and some drugs. To get the best antioxidant rich foods, choose vegetables with rich color, like dark green leafy vegetables, red grapes, and deep orange carrots and sweet potatoes.

The Vitamins You Need
Recommended Daily Allowances of Vitamins

Vitamin	Males	Females	During Pregnancy	Children
A	1,000 mg	800 mg	1,000 mg	400-700 mg
B_1	1.2 - 1.5 mg	1.0 - 1.1 mg	1.4 - 1.6 mg	0.7 - 1.2 mg
B_2	1.4 - 1.7 mg	1.2 - 1.3 mg	1.6 mg	
B_6	1.8 - 2.2 mg	1.8 - 2.2 mg	2.6 mg	0.9 - 1.6 mg
B_{12}	3 mcg	4 mcg	5 mcg	2 - 5 mcg
Niacin	16 -19 mg	13 - 15 mg	17 mg	9 - 16 mg
C	50 - 60 mg	50 - 60 mg	80 mg	45 mg
D	200-400 IU[1,2]	200-400 IU[1,2]	400-600 IU[1,2]	400 IU[1]
E	8 - 10 mg	8 mg	10 mg	10 - 15 IU[1]
Folacin	0.4 mg	0.4 mg	800 mg	100 - 300 mg

[1] *International units*

[2] *After age 22, none except during pregnancy*

Exercise Recommendations

Current recommendations for cardiovascular health include engaging in moderate exercise on most, or preferably all, days, for 30 minutes or more. Those already exercising can get even greater health benefits by increasing the amount (duration, frequency, or intensity) of physical activity.

Examples of moderate exercise:

- Walking
- Golf
- Gardening
- Mowing lawn
- Cycling

Source: U.S. Department of Health and Human Services

Great Sports for Building Muscles

Weight Training
Stair Climbing
Rowing/Canoeing
Martial Arts
Bicycling
Swimming Laps
Alpine Skiing

Great Sports for Improving Heart and Lung Health

Jogging/Running
Jumping Rope
Bicycling
Cross-country Skiing
Rowing/Canoeing
Swimming Laps
Aerobic Dance
Basketball
Hiking/Climbing
Hockey
Martial Arts
Racquetball/Squash
Soccer
Speed Walking

Go for the Burn
Calories Burned During Various Activities, Per Minute

	Body Weight		
	110 lbs	**150 lbs**	**190 lbs**
Boxing	11.1	15.1	19.2
Squash	10.6	14.5	18.3
Running, 9 minute mile	9.6	13.1	16.6
Swimming, fast	8.1	11.0	14.0
Basketball	6.9	9.4	11.9
Horsebackriding, galloping	6.8	9.3	11.7
Aerobic Dance, intense	6.7	9.1	11.6
Swimming, slow	6.4	8.7	11.1
Skiing, cross country, moderate	5.9	8.0	10.2
Lawn Mowing	5.6	7.6	9.7
Tennis	5.4	7.4	9.3
Aerobic Dance, medium	5.1	7.0	8.8
Cycling, 9.5 m.p.h.	5.0	6.8	8.6
Weight Training, circuit	4.6	6.3	7.9
Golf	4.2	5.7	7.3
Walking, brisk pace	4.1	5.6	7.1
Weeding	3.6	4.9	6.2
Cycling, 5.5 m.p.h.	3.2	4.4	5.5
Fishing	3.1	4.2	5.4
Mopping Floors	3.1	4.2	5.4
Raking	2.7	3.7	4.7
Volleyball	2.5	3.4	4.3
Canoeing	2.2	3.0	3.8
Billiards	2.1	2.9	3.6
Driving Tractor	1.8	2.5	3.1
Typing	1.3	1.8	2.2
Card Playing	1.2	1.6	2.1
Sitting Still	1.0	1.4	1.7

Source: Wellness Encyclopedia, UCLA Berkeley

To avoid soreness or injury, start slowly and gradually build up. People with chronic health problems such as heart disease, diabetes, or obesity, or who are at high risk for these problems should consult a physician before beginning new exercise programs. Also men over 40 and women over 50 who plan to begin new vigorous exercise should consult a physician.

To improve your heart's health, the American Heart Association recommends exercising within your 'target zone' -- which is 50% - 70% of your maximum heart rate. See table below.

Get in the Zone
Target Heart Rate

Age	Target beats/min.	Maximum beats/min.
20	100-150	200
25	98-146	195
30	95-142	190
35	93-138	185
40	90-135	180
45	88-131	175
50	85-127	170
55	83-123	165
60	80-120	160
65	78-116	155
70	75-113	150

Most Common Sports Injuries

1. Bruise
2. Sprained Ankle
3. Sprained Knee
4. Low Back Strain
5. Hamstring Tear
6. Jumper's Knee
7. Achilles Tendonitis
8. Shin Splints
9. Tennis Elbow
10. Shoulder Strain

Health Benefits of Exercise for Older Adults

1. Reduces risk of falling and fracturing bones
2. Improves ability to live independently
3. Helps control joint swelling and pain of arthritis
4. Helps reduce symptoms of anxiety and depression
5. Helps reduce the risk of dying from heart disease
6. Helps people with chronic, disabling conditions improve stamina

Source: Centers for Disease Control and Prevention

Previously sedentary older adults who begin to exercise should start with short intervals of moderate activity (5 - 10 minutes) and gradually build up to the desired amount. Older adults should consult a physician before starting an exercise program.

Among adults aged 65 and older, walking and gardening are by far the most popular physical activities.

Home Safety

Home Safety Checklist

1. Install a smoke detector on each floor and outside each bedroom three feet from vents and windows. Test monthly.
2. Buy a portable fire extinguisher. In case of fire, remain to use it only if fire is small and you have a clear path to an exit.
3. Keep a screen around your fireplace.
4. Do not allow candles to burn unattended.
5. Never smoke in bed.
6. Make two fire escape plans. Practice with the entire family, using a stopwatch.
7. Do not overload outlets. Cover with protective plates if there are small children in your home.
8. Anchor carpet on stairs and in hallways.
9. Keep stairs well-lit (bright enough to read).
10. Make it a rule that nothing is left on the stairs.
11. If something is spilled, clean it up immediately.
12. Keep non-skid mats inside and outside tubs and showers.
13. Find places to put toys and miscellaneous items when not in use.
14. Keep cleaning supplies in a locked or firmly latched cabinet. Take only one out at a time and keep it in your hand, if there are small children in your home.
15. Keep all medicines in a locked or securely latched cabinet. Close lids tightly each time you use them.
16. Lower the temperature on your water heater to 120°F to avoid scalding.
17. Do not leave small children alone in kitchen or bathroom.

Source: National Safety Council

Immunizations

This Won't Hurt a Bit.
Recommended Immunization Schedule

Age	Vaccine
Birth	Hepatitis [1]
1 month	Hepatitis
2 months	DTP [2], Influenza, Poliomyelitis
4 months	DTP, Influenza, Poliomyelitis
6 months	DTP, Influenza, Hepatitis
12-15 months	H.ib, MMR[3]
12-18 months	Poliomyelitis, Chicken pox
4-6 years	DTP, Poliomyelitis, MMR
11-16 years	DT, Chicken pox

[1] *If infant's mother is Hepatitis B-positive, the infant should receive vaccine within 12 hours of birth*
[2] *DTP = Diphtheria, Tetanus, Pertussus*
[3] *MMR = Measles, Mumps, Rubella (German measles)*
Source: Advisory Committee on Immunization Practices, American Academy of Pediatrics, American Academy of Family Physicians, 1997

If you are planning to travel abroad, you may need immunizations against diseases no longer common in the United States. For example, some countries require a yellow fever or cholera vaccination. Prophylactic medications for malaria are advisable for travel to some countries. To get information regarding required immunizations, call the U.S. Centers for Disease Control and Prevention at (404) 639-2572, and ask for the brochure *Health Information for International Travel*.

6. Education Trends

*See also 'Jobs &
Careers' and
'Earning & Spending.'*

Primary & Secondary

Colleges & Universities

Primary & Secondary

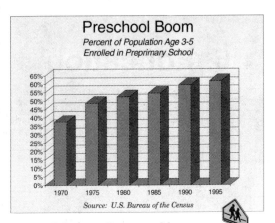

Preschool Boom
Percent of Population Age 3-5 Enrolled in Preprimary School

65%
60%
55%
50%
45%
40%
35%
30%
25%
20%
15%
10%
5%
0%

1970 1975 1980 1985 1990 1995

Source: U.S. Bureau of the Census

62% of three to five-year olds attended school in 1995, compared to 38% in 1970.

The First Day of School
Three- to Five-Year-Olds Enrolled in School, in Thousands

	1970	1980	1990	1995
Population Age 3-5	10,949	9,284	11,207	12,518
Number Enrolled	4,104	4,878	6,659	7,739
Percent Enrolled	37.5%	52.5%	59.4%	61.8%
Nursery School	1,094	1,981	3,378	4,331
Public	332	628	1,202	1,950
Private	762	1,353	2,177	2,381
Kindergarten	3,010	2,897	3,281	3,408
Public	2,498	2,438	2,767	2,799
Private	511	459	513	608

Five-year-olds attending elementary school are excluded.
Source: U.S. Bureau of the Census

116

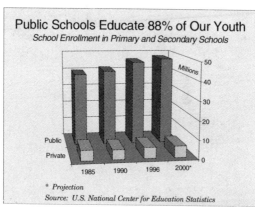

Public Schools Educate 88% of Our Youth
School Enrollment in Primary and Secondary Schools

* Projection
Source: U.S. National Center for Education Statistics

America benefits from the service of more than three million teachers. That's more than the doctors, lawyers, and engineers combined.

Off to School
School Enrollment, in Thousands

	K - 8th		9 - 12th	
	Public	Private	Public	Private
1980	27,647	3,992	13,231	1,339
1990	29,878	4,095	11,338	1,137
1995	32,085	4,431	12,576	1,269
2000*	33,852	4,632	13,804	1,380
2005*	33,680	4,609	14,818	1,481

* Projections Source: U.S. Nat. Cntr. for Education Statistics

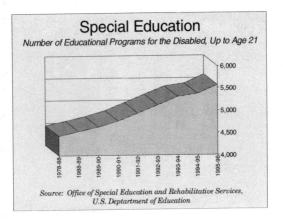

Special Education
Number of Educational Programs for the Disabled, Up to Age 21

Source: *Office of Special Education and Rehabilitative Services,*
U.S. Deptartment of Education

Teaching Children with Special Needs
Children Served in Special Education Programs, in Thousands

	1987-88	1990-91	1995-96
Learning disabilities	1,928	2,130	2,579
Speech impairments	953	987	1,022
Mental retardation	582	536	570
Serious emotional disturbance	373	391	438
Hearing impairments	56	58	67
Orthopedic impairments	47	49	63
Other health impairments	45	55	133
Multiple disabilities	77	96	93
Visual impairments	22	23	25
Deafness/blindness	12	1	1
Autism	-	-	39
Preschool disabilities	361	441	544

Source: U.S. Department of Education

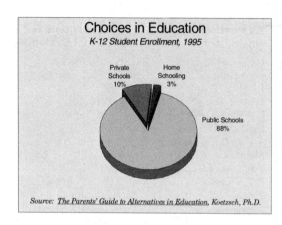

Choices in Education
K-12 Student Enrollment, 1995

Private Schools 10%

Home Schooling 3%

Public Schools 88%

Source: *The Parents' Guide to Alternatives in Education,* Koetzsch, Ph.D.

The American public school system developed in the late 19th century. Over time, a good number of religious and private schools closed, as almost all Protestants, Jews, and a majority of Catholics sent their children to public schools. But in recent decades, religious schools have begun to grow again. And other alternatives have emerged both inside and outside the public school system.

Of the 5 million children being educated outside the public school system, about 40% (2 million) are in Catholic schools.

Alternatives to Mainstream Education Exist Inside and Outside Public School System

Carden Schools	Christian Schools
Comer Schools	Core Knowledge Schools
Essential Schools	Foxfire Schools
Free Schools	Friends Schools
Holistic Schools	Home Schooling
Int. Baccalaureate	Islamic Schools
Jewish Day Schools	Mennonite/Amish Schools
Montessori Schools	Multiple Intelligence Ed.
Progressive Schools	Protestant Schools
Reggio Emilia Approach	Roman Catholic Schools
Teenage Liberation	Waldorf Education

Source: The Parents' Guide to Alternatives in Education

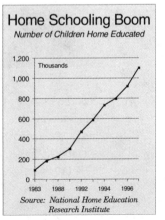

Home Schooling Boom
Number of Children Home Educated

Thousands

1,200
1,000
800
600
400
200
0

1983　1988　1992　1994　1996

Source: National Home Education Research Institute

Christian schools, which offer nonde-nominational religion-based education, are the fastest growing among private schools.

U.S. public schools face a tough job: educate anyone who walks through their doors. They do it with 86,000 schools and 2.6 million teachers in 15,000 school districts, and at a yearly cost of $3,000 to $12,000 per student.

In high school, enrollment in daily physical education classes dropped from 42% in 1991 to 25% in 1995.

Top Disciplinary Problems, in the Opinion of Public School Teachers

1940
1. Talking out of turn
2. Chewing gum
3. Making noise
4. Running in the halls
5. Cutting in line
6. Dress code violations
7. Littering

1990
1. Drug abuse
2. Alcohol abuse
3. Pregnancy
4. Suicide
5. Rape
6. Robbery
7. Assault

Source: Congressional Quarterly

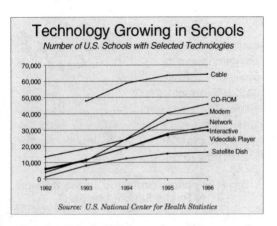

Between 7th and 12th grade, most teenagers listen to 10,500 hours of rock music -- about the same amount of time spent in school.

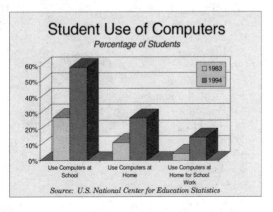

Computers Break into Education

During the 1984/85 school year, there were 62.7 students per computer in U.S. elementary and secondary schools. By 1996/97, there were 7.4 students per computer.

Source: Market Data Retrieval, Shelton, CT

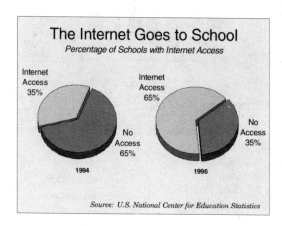

The Internet Goes to School
Percentage of Schools with Internet Access

Internet Access 35%

No Access 65%

1994

Internet Access 65%

No Access 35%

1996

Source: U.S. National Center for Education Statistics

Of the schools without internet access in 1996, 87% plan to have it by the year 2000.

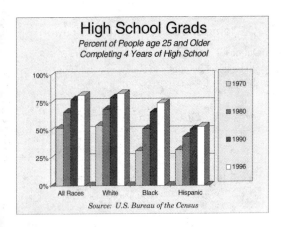

High School Grads
*Percent of People age 25 and Older
Completing 4 Years of High School*

Source: U.S. Bureau of the Census

States with Highest Percentage High School Graduation

1. Alaska
2. Utah
3. Colorado
4. Washington
5. Wyoming
6. Minnesota
7. New Hampshire
8. Nebraska
9. Oregon
10. Kansas

Source: U.S. Bureau of the Census

An estimated 20% of adult Americans are functionally illiterate.
Source: Literacy League

Nearly half a million General Educational Development (GED) credentials are issued each year. About 1/3 of them are earned by people under 19 years of age and 1/4 to people between 20 and 24.

School's Out!

High School Graduates and Dropouts by State, in Percent

	Grad-uates	Drop-outs		Grad-uates	Drop-outs
U.S.	75.2	14.4	MO	73.8	14.5
AL	66.8	19.4	MT	81.0	10.9
AK	86.5	8.2	NE	81.9	10.2
AZ	78.6	12.2	NV	78.8	15.2
AR	66.4	18.4	NH	82.1	11.2
CA	76.2	12.6	NJ	76.6	13.9
CO	84.4	10.0	NM	75.0	13.5
CT	79.2	12.4	NY	74.8	15.0
DE	77.5	15.3	NC	70.0	17.3
DC	73.2	17.3	ND	76.5	8.3
FL	74.4	16.1	OH	75.6	16.4
GA	70.9	17.1	OK	74.6	15.6
HI	80.0	9.8	OR	81.4	12.3
ID	79.8	12.9	PA	74.6	15.9
IL	79.3	13.5	RI	72.1	16.9
IN	75.7	15.8	SC	68.2	18.1
IA	80.1	10.7	SD	77.1	9.5
KS	81.2	11.0	TN	67.0	17.0
KY	64.7	16.4	TX	72.3	14.4
LA	68.3	17.0	UT	85.1	11.5
ME	78.9	12.4	VT	80.8	10.6
MD	79.4	13.7	VA	75.1	13.7
MA	79.9	12.0	WA	83.7	10.7
MI	76.7	15.5	WV	65.9	17.3
MN	82.5	9.0	WI	78.6	11.9
MS	64.4	20.1	WY	83.1	11.2

Source: National Center for Education Statistics, U.S. Dept. of Education, 1996

This Is Only a Test
Scholastic Aptitude Test (SAT) Scores
Mean Scores by State Based on Recentered Scale

	1987		1997	
	Verbal	**Math**	**Verbal**	**Math**
National Average	507	501	505	511
Alabama	553	535	561	555
Alaska	521	504	520	517
Arizona	539	526	523	522
Arkansas	556	540	567	558
California	500	507	496	514
Colorado	542	535	536	539
Connecticut	515	499	509	507
Delaware	517	496	505	498
Dist. of Columbia	482	462	490	475
Florida	501	497	499	499
Georgia	478	470	486	481
Hawaii	481	502	483	512
Idaho	548	524	544	539
Illinois	539	540	562	578
Indiana	492	487	494	497
Iowa	588	586	589	601
Kansas	572	562	578	575
Kentucky	554	538	548	546
Louisiana	548	530	560	553
Maine	510	493	507	504
Maryland	513	502	507	507
Massachusetts	511	500	508	508
Michigan	534	533	557	566
Minnesota	548	549	582	592
Mississippi	561	540	567	551
Missouri	549	538	567	568
Montana	555	548	545	548
Nebraska	563	562	562	564
Nevada	516	508	508	509
New Hampshire	527	512	521	518

	1987		1997	
	Verbal	**Math**	**Verbal**	**Math**
New Jersey	502	493	497	508
New Mexico	559	544	554	545
New York	501	495	495	502
North Carolina	477	468	490	488
North Dakota	583	573	588	595
Ohio	532	521	535	536
Oklahoma	560	539	568	560
Oregon	521	509	525	524
Pennsylvania	505	491	498	495
Rhode Island	509	492	499	493
Carolina	474	466	479	474
South Dakota	587	577	574	570
Tennessee	563	543	564	556
Texas	493	486	494	501
Utah	577	557	576	570
Vermont	518	500	508	502
Virginia	511	499	506	497
Washington	532	519	523	523
West Virginia	534	519	524	508
Wisconsin	550	551	576	590
Wyoming	557	551	543	543

Source: The College Board

The SAT scoring was adjusted, or 'recentered' in 1995 for the first time since 1941. The difficulty of the test was not altered, but earlier scores are not comparable to current ones. For a free score converter, write to SAT Score Converter, 45 Columbus Ave., New York, NY 10023.

Colleges & Universities

Average SAT Scores of College-Bound Seniors

	1990	1996
Verbal	500	505
Male Students	505	507
Female Students	496	503
Math	501	508
Male Students	521	527
Female Students	483	492

Source: The College Entrance Examination Board

Profile of College Freshmen

Average Grade in High School
- A 32% • B 54% • C 14%

Political Orientation
- Liberal 22% • Middle 53% • Conservative 21%

Attitudes -- Agree or Strongly Agree
- Activities of married women are best confined to home and family — 24%
- Capital punishment should be abolished — 22%
- Legalize marijuana — 33%
- There is too much concern for the rights of criminals — 72%
- Abortion should be legalized — 56%
- Aspires to advanced degree — 67%

Source: The Higher Education Research Institute, University of California, Los Angeles, CA, 1996

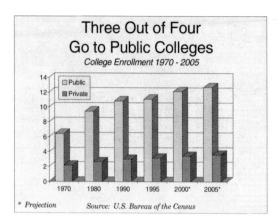

Three Out of Four Go to Public Colleges
College Enrollment 1970 - 2005

* Projection   Source: U.S. Bureau of the Census

In 1995, 62% of recent high school graduates were enrolled in college. That's up from 49% in 1980.

Better Start Saving
Average Annual Cost of American Colleges, in Dollars

	Tuition	Dormitory	Board
Public			
1990	1,356	1,513	1,635
1992	1,624	1,731	1,780
1994	1,942	1,873	1,880
1996	2,176	2,057	2,019
Private			
1990	8,174	1,923	1,948
1992	9,434	2,221	2,252
1994	10,572	2,490	2,434
1996	11,858	2,739	2,610

Source: National Center for Education Statistics

College Student Demographics

45% Male
54% Female
58% Age 18 - 24
23% Age 25 - 34
18% Age 35 +
81% White
11% Black
8% Hispanic

40% of the American adult population (age 17 and older) is enrolled in some form of adult education. Of those taking classes, 44% do so for personal or social reasons, 54% to advance on the job, 11% to train for a new job, and 10% to complete a degree.

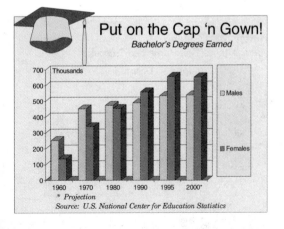

Put on the Cap 'n Gown!
Bachelor's Degrees Earned

* Projection
Source: U.S. National Center for Education Statistics

Top 10 National Universities

1. Yale University (CT)
2. Princeton University (NJ)
3. Harvard University (MA)
4. Duke University (NC)
5. Massachusetts Inst. of Technology (MA)
6. Stanford University (CA)
7. Dartmouth College (NH)
8. Brown University (RI)
9. California Institute of Technology
10. Northwestern University (IL)

Source: U.S. News & World Report, 1996-97 Survey

Top 10 Liberal Arts Colleges

1. Swarthmore College (PA)
2. Amherst College (MA)
3. Williams College (MA)
4. Wellesley College (MA)
5. Pomona College (CA)
6. Haverford College (PA)
7. Middlebury College (VT)
8. Bowdoin College (ME)
9. Carleton College (MN)
10. Bryn Mawr College (PA)

Source: U.S. News & World Report, 1996-97 Survey

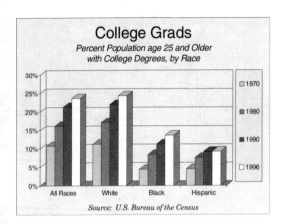

College Grads

*Percent Population age 25 and Older
with College Degrees, by Race*

Source: U.S. Bureau of the Census

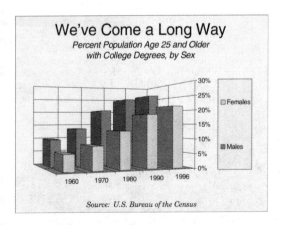

We've Come a Long Way

*Percent Population Age 25 and Older
with College Degrees, by Sex*

Source: U.S. Bureau of the Census

7. Jobs & Careers

See also 'Money & Business,' and 'Earning & Spending.'

Working in America

Payday

Job Troubles

Career Trends

Working in America

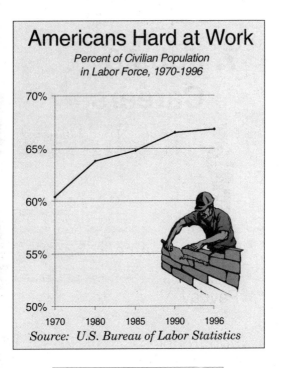

Americans Hard at Work

*Percent of Civilian Population
in Labor Force, 1970-1996*

Source: U.S. Bureau of Labor Statistics

6% of employed Americans have
more than one job.

26% of the American labor force
work only part-time.

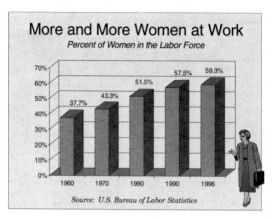

More and More Women at Work
Percent of Women in the Labor Force

70% — 37.7% (1960), 43.3% (1970), 51.5% (1980), 57.5% (1990), 59.3% (1996)

Source: U.S. Bureau of Labor Statistics

Married or Not, Women Work
Labor Force Participation Rates for Women, in Percent

	1960	1970	1980	1990	1996
Total	37.7	43.3	51.5	57.5	59.3
Single	58.6	56.8	64.4	66.7	67.1
Married	31.9	40.5	49.9	58.4	61.2
Other [1]	41.6	40.3	43.6	47.2	48.1

[1] *Divorced, Widowed, or Separated*
Source: U.S. Bureau of Labor Statistics

Mommy Goes to the Office

In 1975, 36.7% of married women with husbands at home and children under age 6 worked outside the home. By 1996, this number had risen to 62.7%.

People's Choice
The 50 Best Companies to Work for in America

Rank	Company	Emp-loyees	% Min-orities	% Women
1.	Southwest Airlines	24,757	24	55
2.	Kingston Tech.	552	70	48
3.	SAS Institute	3,154	13	53
4.	Fel-Pro	2,577	50	36
5.	TDIndustries	976	26	10
6.	MBNA	18,050	22	58
7.	W.L. Gore	4,118	13	43
8.	Microsoft	14,936	19	29
9.	Merck	31,767	24	52
10.	Hewlett-Packard	66,300	21	37
11.	Synovus Financial	8,037	18	65
12.	Goldman Sachs	6,546	NA	40
13.	Moog	2,346	10	19
14.	Deloitte & Touche	19,875	19	45
15.	Corning	8,127	11	38
16.	Wegmans Food Mkts.	23,292	10	54
17.	Harley Davidson	5,288	9	22
18.	Federal Express	106,300	40	32
19.	Procter & Gamble	37,164	17	40
20.	Peoplesoft	3,010	19	44
21.	First Tenn. Bank	6,094	26	70
22.	J.M. Smucker	1,785	24	48
23.	Granite Rock	558	26	17
24.	Patagonia	615	12	52
25.	Cisco Systems	11,005	35	25
26.	Erie Insurance	3,338	6	61
27.	Marriott International	94,891	59	47
28.	Four Seasons Hotels	10,246	60	39
29.	Rosenbluth International	3,771	26	83
30.	American Mgmt. Sys.	5,984	20	43
31.	S.C. Johnson Wax	3,561	11	34

Rank	Company	Emp-loyees	% Min-orities	%Women
32.	Intel	37,580	29	30
33.	Unum	3,785	9	71
34.	Whole Foods Market	10,628	32	44
35.	Minn. Mining & Manuf.	38,395	12	34
36.	L.L. Bean	3,917	2	62
37.	REI	4,907	11	41
38.	ACXIOM	2,598	13	47
39.	USAA	15,696	36	63
40.	CMP Media	1,589	16	61
41.	Eddie Bauer	4,865	18	65
42.	Life Technologies	1,085	21	48
43.	Lands' End	3,595	1	79
44.	J.P. Morgan	8,989	26	49
45.	Publix Super Markets	104,396	30	50
46.	Gillette	11,319	22	43
47.	Medtronic	9,436	26	49
48.	Worthington Ind.	5,005	9	28
49.	BE&K	7,991	9	20
50.	Baldor Electric	3,501	20	28

Source: Fortune Magazine, January 1998

Who's Hiring?

10 Fastest Growing Among the 50 Best Companies

Company	New Jobs(2 Years)	PercentGrowth
Intel	11,000	43%
Cisco Systems	7,200	189%
Federal Express	6,000	11%
Hewlett Packard	6,000	10%
Mariott International	5,936	8%
Publix Super Markets	5,665	16%
Merck	5,740	24%
Southwest Airlines	4,917	29%
MBNA	4,234	48%
Whole Foods Markets	4,203	94%

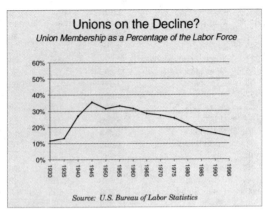

Unions on the Decline?
Union Membership as a Percentage of the Labor Force

Source: *U.S. Bureau of Labor Statistics*

Not Just Auto Workers
U.S. Membership in AFL-CIO Affiliated Unions, in Thousands

Union	1975	1985	1995
Total	11,119	13,287	13,014
Actors & Artists	76	100	80
Automobile, Aerospace & Agriculture	x	974	751
Bakery, Confectionery & Tobacco	x	115	96
Bricklayers	143	95	84
Carpenters	700	609	378
Clothing and Textile Workers	x	228	129
Communication Workers	476	524	478
Electrical Workers	856	791	679
Electronic, Electrical & Salaried	x	x	135
Operating Engineers	300	330	298
Fire Fighters	123	142	151
Food & Commercial Workers	x	989	983
Garment Workers	363	210	123
Glass, Molders, Pottery & Plastics	x	72	69
Government, American Federation	255	199	153
Graphic Communications	x	141	194

Union	1975	1985	1995
Hotel & Restaurant Employees	421	327	241
Iron Workers	160	140	82
Laborers	475	383	352
Letter Carriers	151	186	210
Longshoreman's Association	60	65	61
Machinists & Aerospace	780	520	448
Mine Workers	x	x	75
Office & Professional Employees	74	90	86
Oil, Chemical, Atomic Workers	145	108	83
Painters	160	133	95
Paperworkers International	275	232	233
Plumbing & Pipefitting	228	226	220
Postal Workers	249	232	261
Retail, Wholesale, Dept. Stores	118	106	76
Rubber, Cork, Linoleum, Plastic	173	106	79
Seafarers	80	80	80
Service Employees	480	688	1,027
Sheet Metal Workers	120	108	106
Stage & Moving Picture	50	50	51
State, County, Municipal	647	997	1,183
Steelworkers	1,062	572	403
Teachers	396	470	613
Teamsters	x	x	1,285
Transit Union	90	94	95
Transport Workers	95	85	75
Transportation-Communications	x	x	58
Transportation Union, United	134	188	58

Source: American Federation of Labor and Congress of Industrial Organizations

In 1945, more than one in three (35.5%) American workers were union members. By 1996, union membership had declined to 14.5%, or about one in seven workers.

Payday

The average pay for production and nonsupervisory employees increased from $2 per hour in 1960 to $12 per hour in 1996.

Comparing Paychecks
Average Hourly Earnings of Production Workers and Nonsupervisory Employees, by Industry

Mining
Construction
Transportation
Manufacturing
Wholesale
Fiance
Services
Retail

Source: U.S. Bureau of Labor Statistics

What's Your Pay Worth?

Federal Minimum Wage Compared to Its Value in 1995 Dollars

Source: U.S. Bureau of Labor Statistics

Metropolitan Areas with the Highest Average Annual Pay

1. San Jose, CA
2. New York, NY
3. San Francisco, CA
4. Middlesex-Somerset-Hunterdon, NJ
5. New Haven-Bridgeport-Stamford-Danbury-Waterbury, CT
6. Newark, NJ
7. Trenton, NJ
8. Bergen-Passaic, NJ
9. Washington, DC-MD-VA-WV
10. Detroit, MI

Source: U.S. Bureau of Labor Statistics, 1997

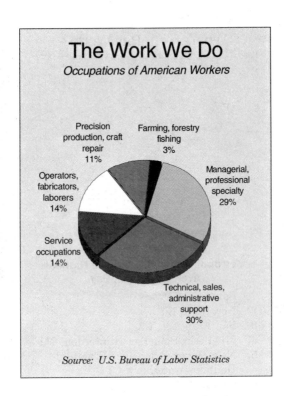

The Work We Do
Occupations of American Workers

Precision production, craft repair
11%

Farming, forestry fishing
3%

Operators, fabricators, laborers
14%

Managerial, professional specialty
29%

Service occupations
14%

Technical, sales, administrative support
30%

Source: U.S. Bureau of Labor Statistics

Full-time workers are working more than full time, averaging 43.3 hours per week.

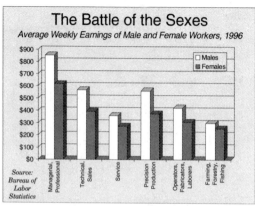

The Battle of the Sexes
Average Weekly Earnings of Male and Female Workers, 1996

Source: Bureau of Labor Statistics

How Much Does It Pay, for Men & Women?

Average Weekly Earnings of Full-Time Workers, in Dollars

Occupation	1985	1990	1996
Managerial, Professional			
Men	583	729	852
Women	399	510	616
Technical, Sales, Administrative Support			
Men	420	493	567
Women	269	331	394
Service			
Men	272	317	357
Women	185	230	273
Precision Production			
Men	408	486	560
Women	268	316	373
Operators, Fabricators, Laborers			
Men	325	375	422
Women	216	261	307
Farming, Forestry, Fishing			
Men	216	261	300
Women	176	185	255

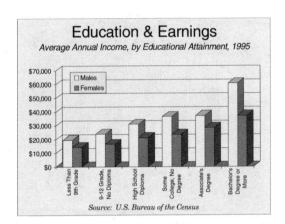

Education & Earnings
Average Annual Income, by Educational Attainment, 1995

Source: U.S. Bureau of the Census

Race & Earnings
Average Weekly Earnings for Full-Time Workers, by Race and Sex

Source: U.S. Bureau of Labor Statistics

Education Pays Off
Earnings by Highest Degree Earned, 1996, in Dollars

	All	White	Black	Hispanic
Not a H.S. Grad	14,013	14,234	12,956	13,068
Male	16,748	17,032	14,877	14,774
Female	9,790	9,582	9,809	
H.S. Only	21,431	22,154	17,072	18,333
Male	26,333	27,467	19,514	20,882
Female	15,970	16,196	14,473	14,989
Some College	22,392	22,898	20,275	18,903
Male	28,458	29,206	24,894	21,705
Female	16,152	16,125	16,627	15,699
Associate's	27,780	28,137	26,818	23,406
Male	33,881	34,286	33,674	24,021
Female	22,429	22,547	22,113	22,883
Bachelor's	36,980	37,711	29,666	30,602
Male	46,111	47,016	36,026	35,109
Female	26,841	26,916	25,557	25,338
Master's	47,609	48,029	38,284	36,633
Male	58,302	58,817	41,777	38,539
Female	34,911	35,125	35,222	33,390
Professional	85,322	85,229	B	B
Male	101,730	100,856	B	B
Female	47,959	48,562	B	B
Doctorate	64,550	64,608	B	B
Male	71,016	72,542	B	B
Female	47,733	45,202	B	B

B: Base figure too small for statistical accuracy
Source: U.S. Bureau of the Census

Job Troubles

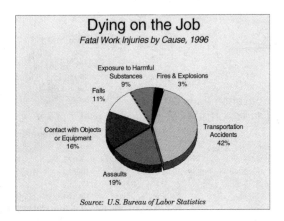

Dying on the Job
Fatal Work Injuries by Cause, 1996

Exposure to Harmful Substances 9%

Fires & Explosions 3%

Falls 11%

Contact with Objects or Equipment 16%

Transportation Accidents 42%

Assaults 19%

Source: U.S. Bureau of Labor Statistics

Most Common Types of Injuries on the Job

1. Sprains, Strains
2. Bruises, Contusions
3. Cuts, Lacerations
4. Fractures
5. Carpal Tunnel Syndrome
6. Heat Burns
7. Tendonitis
8. Chemical Burns
9. Amputations
10. Multiple Injuries

Most Common Sources of Injuries on the Job

1. Floor, Ground
2. Worker Motion
3. Containers
4. Parts, Materials
5. Vehicles
6. Machinery
7. Tools
8. Worker
9. Furniture, Fixtures
10. Chemicals

Source: U.S. Bureau of Labor Statistics

Most Stressful Jobs

1. U.S. President
2. Firefighter
3. Senior Corp. Exec.
4. Racecar Driver
5. Taxi Driver
6. Surgeon
7. Astronaut
8. Police Officer
9. NFL Player
10. Air Traffic Cont.
11. Highway Patrol Officer
12. Public Relations Executive
13. Mayor
14. Jockey
15. College Basketball Coach
16. Advertising Account Executive
17. Real Estate Agent
18. Photo Journalist
19. Member of Congress

Source: National Employment Weekly

Least Stressful Jobs

1. Medical Records Technician
2. Janitor
3. Forklift Operator
4. Musical Instrument Repairer
5. Florist
6. Actuary
7. Appliance Repairer
8. Medical Secretary
9. Librarian
10. Bookkeeper
11. File Clerk
12. Piano Tuner
13. Photographic Process Worker
14. Dietitian
15. Paralegal Assistant
16. Vending Machine Repairer
17. Bookbinder
18. Barber
19. Electrical Tech.
20. Typist, Word Processor

Source: National Employment Weekly

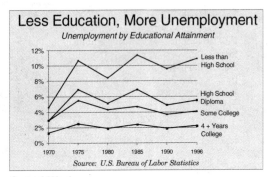

Less Education, More Unemployment

Unemployment by Educational Attainment

Source: U.S. Bureau of Labor Statistics

Out of Work

Unemployment by Education, Race and Sex, in Percent

	1980	1990	1996
Males	4.9	4.8	5.3
Less than High School	8.2	9.6	11.0
High School	5.3	5.3	6.4
Some College	4.4	3.9	4.5
4+ Years College	1.7	2.1	2.3
Females	5.0	4.2	4.1
Less than High School	8.9	9.5	10.7
High School	5.0	4.6	4.4
Some College	4.1	3.5	3.8
4+ Years College	2.2	1.7	2.1
White	4.4	4.0	4.2
Less than High School	7.8	8.3	10.2
High School	4.6	4.4	4.6
Some College	3.9	3.3	3.7
4+ Years College	1.8	1.8	2.1
Black	9.6	8.6	8.9
Less than High School	11.7	15.9	15.3
High School	9.5	8.6	10.8
Some College	9.0	6.5	6.9
4+ Years College	4.0	1.9	3.3

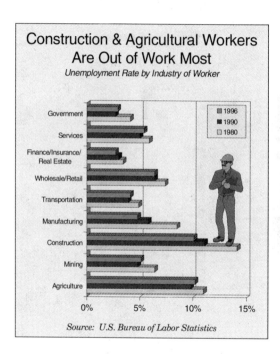

Construction & Agricultural Workers Are Out of Work Most

Unemployment Rate by Industry of Worker

Legend: 1996, 1990, 1980

Government
Services
Finance/Insurance/Real Estate
Wholesale/Retail
Transportation
Manufacturing
Construction
Mining
Agriculture

0%   5%   10%   15%

Source: U.S. Bureau of Labor Statistics

Occupations with Highest Unemployment

1. Construction Laborer
2. Handlers, Helpers, Laborers
3. Private Household Service Occupations
4. Construction Trades
5. Machine Operators, Assemblers, Inspectors

Source: U.S. Bureau of Labor Statistics

Career Trends

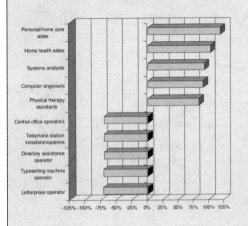

The Best & Worst Job Prospects

Fastest Growing and Declining Occupations
Percent Change, 1994 - 2005

- Personal/home care aides
- Home health aides
- Systems analysts
- Computer engineers
- Physical therapy assistants
- Central office operators
- Telephone station installers/repairers
- Directory assistance operator
- Typesetting machine operator
- Letterpress operator

-125% -100% -75% -50% -25% 0% 25% 50% 75% 100% 125%

Source: U.S. Bureau of Labor Statistics

What's Hot & What's Not

Civilian Employment in the Fastest Growing & Fastest Declining Occupations 1994 - 2005, in Thousands

Fastest Growing	1994	2005	% Change
Personal/Home Care Aides	179	391	118.7
Home Health Aides	420	848	102.0
Systems Analysts	483	928	84.9
Computer Engineers	195	372	81.8
Physical Therapy Assistants	78	142	82.3
Electronic Pagination Systems	18	33	82.8
Occupational Therapy Aides	16	29	82.1
Physical Therapists	102	183	80.0
Residential Counselors	165	290	76.5
Human Services Workers	168	293	74.5
Occupational Therapists	54	93	72.2
Manicurists	38	64	69.5
Medical Assistants	206	327	59.0
Paralegals	110	175	85.3
Medical records Technicians	81	126	55.8
Teachers, Special Education	388	593	53.0
Amusement Attendants	267	406	52.0
Corrections Officers	310	468	50.9
Fastest Declining	**1994**	**2005**	**% Change**
Letterpress operators	14	4	-71.3
Typesetting Operators	20	6	-71.1
Directory Assistance Operators	33	10	-70.4
Telephone Station Installers	37	11	-70.4
Central Office Operators	48	14	-70.3
Billing, posting operators	96	32	-66.7
Data Entry Keyers, Composing	19	6	-66.6
Shoe Sewing Machine Op.	14	5	-6..6
Roustabouts	28	13	-55.0
Peripheral EDP operators	30	13	-54.8

Industries with the Most Self-Employed People

1. Services
2. Agriculture
3. Trade
4. Construction
5. Finance, Insurance & Real Estate

Top Occupations of Self-Employed People

1. Managerial/ Professional Specialty
2. Technical, Sales, Administrative Support
3. Precision Production, Craft, Repair
4. Farming, Forestry, Fishing
5. Service Occupations

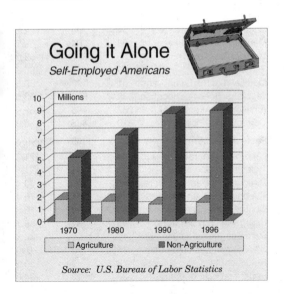

Going it Alone
Self-Employed Americans

Millions

1970 1980 1990 1996

☐ Agriculture ■ Non-Agriculture

Source: U.S. Bureau of Labor Statistics

8. Money & Business

See also 'Jobs & Careers.'

Productivity

Prices

Exchange Rates

Stock Market

Trends in Business

Productivity

America's Producing More
Gross Domestic Product, in Chained 1992 Dollars

Source: U.S. Bureau of Economic Analysis, U.S. Bureau of Commerce

Production on the Rise
Gross Domestic Product, in Billions of Chained 1992 Dollars

Year	GDP	% Change	Exports	Imports
1982	4,620.3	2.3	311.4	325.5
1983	4,803.7	4.0	3.3.3	987.3
1984	5,140.1	7.0	328.4	455.7
1985	5,323.5	3.6	337.3	485.2
1986	5,487.7	3.1	362.2	526.1
1987	5,649.5	2.9	402.0	558.2
1988	5,865.2	3.8	465.8	580.2
1989	6,062.0	3.4	520.2	603.0
1990	6,136.3	1.2	564.4	626.3
1991	6,079.4	-0.9	599.9	622.2
1992	6,244.4	2.7	639.4	669.0
1993	6,389.6	2.3	658.2	728.4
1994	6,610.7	3.5	712.4	817.0
1995	6,742.1	2.0	791.2	890.1
1996	6,928.4	2.8	857.0	971.5
1997	7,189.6	3.8	963.6	1,110.1

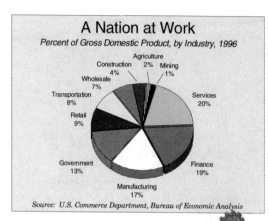

A Nation at Work
Percent of Gross Domestic Product, by Industry, 1996

- Agriculture 2%
- Mining 1%
- Construction 4%
- Wholesale 7%
- Transportation 8%
- Retail 9%
- Government 13%
- Manufacturing 17%
- Finance 19%
- Services 20%

Source: U.S. Commerce Department, Bureau of Economic Analysis

The 1997 gross domestic product in current dollars is $8,081 billion.

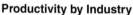

Productivity by Industry
Gross Domestic Product, in Billions of Current Dollars

Industry	1992	1993	1994	1995	1996
Total GDP	6,244.4	6,558.1	6,947.0	7,265.4	7,636.0
Agriculture	112.4	106.1	119.2	111.0	129.8
Mining	92.2	94.6	94.9	99.8	113.6
Construction	229.7	242.4	268.7	286.4	306.1
Manufacturing	1,063.6	1,116.5	1,216.1	1,286.3	1,332.1
Transportation	528.7	561.7	598.7	622.4	645.3
Wholesale	406.4	423.3	468.0	484.4	516.8
Retail	544.3	573.2	615.3	637.6	667.9
Finance	1,147.9	1,218.1	1,267.6	1,361.3	1,448.5
Services	1,200.8	1,267.0	1,350.4	1,440.3	1,539.5
Government	873.6	902.7	933.5	964.1	996.3

Prices

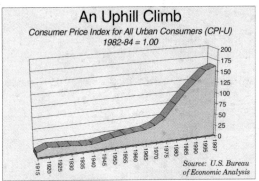

An Uphill Climb
Consumer Price Index for All Urban Consumers (CPI-U)
1982-84 = 1.00

Source: U.S. Bureau
of Economic Analysis

*To calculate inflation using the consumer price
index (next page), subtract the index for the
earlier year from that for the recent year, then
divide by the index for the earlier year. For
example, to figure inflation from 1990 to 1997:
160.5 - 130.7 = 29.8 ÷ 130.7 = .228, or 22.8%.*

Prices Rising
Consumer Price Index, Percent Change of Annual Averages

Source: Bureau of
Labor Statistics

156

Inflation's Climb

Consumer Price Index for All Urban Consumers, 1982-84 = 1.00

Year	CPI Avg	% Change Avg - Avg	Year	CPI Avg	% Change Avg - Avg
1914	10.0	1.0	1956	27.2	1.5
1915	10.1	1.0	1957	28.1	3.3
1916	10.9	7.9	1958	28.9	2.8
1917	12.8	17.4	1959	29.1	0.7
1918	15.1	18.0	1960	29.6	1.7
1919	17.3	14.6	1961	29.9	1.0
1920	20.0	15.6	1962	30.2	1.0
1921	17.9	-10.5	1963	30.6	1.3
1922	16.8	-6.1	1964	31.0	1.3
1923	17.1	1.8	1965	31.5	1.6
1924	17.1	0.0	1966	32.4	2.9
1925	17.5	2.3	1967	33.4	3.1
1926	17.7	1.1	1968	34.8	4.2
1927	17.4	-1.7	1969	36.7	5.5
1928	17.1	-1.7	1970	38.8	5.7
1929	17.1	0.0	1971	40.5	4.4
1930	16.7	-2.3	1972	41.8	3.2
1931	15.2	-9.0	1973	44.4	6.2
1932	13.7	-9.9	1974	49.3	11.0
1933	13.0	-5.1	1975	53.8	9.1
1934	13.4	3.1	1976	56.9	5.8
1935	13.7	2.2	1977	60.6	6.5
1936	13.9	1.5	1978	65.2	7.6
1937	14.4	3.6	1979	72.6	11.3
1938	14.1	-2.1	1980	82.4	13.5
1939	13.9	-1.4	1981	90.9	10.3
1940	14.0	0.7	1982	96.5	6.2
1941	14.7	5.0	1983	99.6	3.2
1942	16.3	10.9	1984	103.9	4.3
1943	17.3	6.1	1985	107.6	3.6
1944	17.6	1.7	1986	109.6	1.9
1945	18.0	2.3	1987	113.6	3.6
1946	19.5	8.3	1988	118.3	4.1
1947	22.3	14.4	1989	124.0	4.8
1948	24.1	8.1	1990	130.7	5.4
1949	23.8	-1.2	1991	136.2	4.2
1950	24.1	1.3	1992	140.3	3.0
1951	26.0	7.9	1993	144.5	3.0
1952	26.5	1.9	1994	148.2	2.6
1953	26.7	0.8	1995	152.4	3.0
1954	26.9	0.7	1996	156.9	3.0
1955	26.8	-0.4	1997	160.5	2.3

Exchange Rates

Foreign Currency Exchange Rates
National Currency Units per Dollar, Except as Indicated

Country	Currency	1980	1990	1996	7/7/1998
Australia [1]	dollar	1.14	0.7813	0.7829	0.6159
Austria	schilling	12.945	11.37	10.587	12.763
Belgium	franc	29.237	33.418	30.962	37.4475
Canada	dollar	1.1693	1.1668	1.3635	1.4728
Denmark	kroner	5.634	6.189	5.799	6.9191
France	franc	4.225	5.4453	5.1155	6.0814
Germany	mark	1.8175	1.6157	1.5048	1.8138
Greece	drachma	42.62	158.51	240.71	303.09
India	rupee	7.887	17.504	35.433	42.46
Ireland [1]	pound	2.0577	1.6585	1.6006	1.3881
Italy	lira	856	1,198	1,543	1,787
Japan	yen	226.63	144.79	108.78	139.75
Malaysia	ringgit	2.1767	2.7049	2.5159	—
Mexico	new peso	—	2.8126	7.6009	
Netherlands	guilder	1.9875	1.8209	1.6859	2.0449
Norway	kroner	4.9381	6.2597	6.4498	7.702
Portugal	escudo	50.08	142.55	154.24	185.607
Singapore	dollar	2.1412	1.8125	1.4100	1.7035
S. Korea	won	607.43	707.76	804.45	—
Spain	peseta	71.76	101.93	126.66	153.94
Sweden	krona	4.2309	5.9188	6.7060	8.0825
Switzerland	franc	1.6772	1.3892	1.2360	1.5228
Thailand	baht	20.476	25.585	25.343	—
UK	pound	2.3243	1.7847	1.5617	1.6356

[1] *Value of one unit of foreign currency in U.S. dollars*

Source: International Monetary Fund

www.imf.org

Stock Market

Ups and Downs
Dow Jones Ind. Average

Year	High	Low
1970	842.00	631.16
1971	950.82	797.97
1972	1036.27	889.15
1973	1051.70	788.31
1974	891.66	577.60
1975	881.81	632.04
1976	1014.79	858.71
1977	999.75	800.85
1978	907.74	742.12
1979	897.61	796.67
1980	1000.17	759.13
1981	1024.05	824.01
1982	1070.55	776.92
1983	1287.20	1027.04
1984	1286.64	1086.57
1985	1553.10	1184.96
1986	1955.57	1502.29
1987	2722.42	1738.74
1988	2183.50	1879.14
1989	2791.41	2144.64
1990	2999.75	2365.10
1991	3168.83	2470.30
1992	3413.21	3136.58
1993	3794.33	3241.95
1994	3978.36	3593.35
1995	5216.47	3832.08
1996	6010.00	5032.94
1997	8254.90	6391.69
1998 [1]	9184.90	7580.40

[1] *Through April, 1998*

www.dowjones.com

A 30% rise in the Dow Jones Industrial Average after 50 days or a 13% rise after 155 days is called a Bull Market. A Bear Market is a 30% drop after 50 days or a 13% drop after 145 days.

Dow Jones Firsts	
100	1906
500	1956
1,000	1972
1,500	1985
2,000	1987
2,500	1987
3,000	1991
3,500	1993
4,000	1995
4,500	1995
5,000	1995
5,500	1996
6,000	1996
6,500	1996
7,000	1997
7,500	1997
8,000	1997
9,000	1998

Trends in Business

Largest U.S. Corporations, by Revenue

1. General Motors
2. Ford Motor Co.
3. Exxon
4. Wal-Mart Stores
5. General Electric
6. IBM
7. Chrysler
8. Mobil
9. Philip Morris
10. AT&T
11. Boeing
12. Texaco
13. State Farm Group
14. Hewlett-Packard
15. E. I. Du Pont de Nemours
16. Sears Roebuck
17. Travelers Group
18. Prudential Ins. Co. of America
19. Chevron
20. Procter & Gable
21. Citicorp
22. Amoco
23. Kmart
24. Merrill Lynch
25. J.C. Penney

Source: Fortune Magazine, 1998

Fastest Growing U.S. Companies

1. Global Marine
2. Harnischfeger Ind.
3. CompUSA
4. EVI
5. Rent Way
6. Just for Feet
7. Employee Solutions
8. YorkResearch
9. U. S. Cellular
10. Semtech

Source: Fortune Magazine, 1998

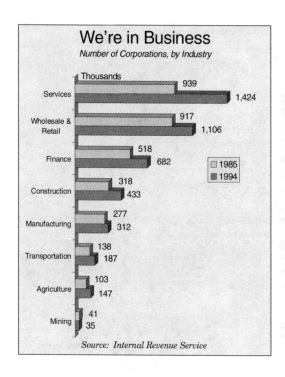

We're in Business
Number of Corporations, by Industry

Thousands

Industry	1985	1994
Services	939	1,424
Wholesale & Retail	917	1,106
Finance	518	682
Construction	318	433
Manufacturing	277	312
Transportation	138	187
Agriculture	103	147
Mining	41	35

Source: Internal Revenue Service

About one third of all businesses in the nation are owned by women. 4% are owned by blacks, and 5% are owned by Americans of Hispanic origin.

Top U.S. Franchises

1. McDonald's
2. Burger King Corp.
3. Yogen Fruz/ Bressler's Ice Cream/ICBIY
4. Subway
5. 7-Eleven Convenience Stores
6. Baskin-Robbins
7. GNC Franchising
8. Dairy Queen
9. Mail Boxes Etc.
10. Taco Bell
11. KFC
12. Jani-King
13. Arby's
14. Radio Shack
15. Midas Int'l. Corp.
16. Choice Hotels
17. Blimpie Int'l., Inc.
18. Coverall Cleaning Concepts
19. Snap-On Tools
20. Carlson Wagonlit Travel

Source: Entrepreneur Magazine
www.entrepreneurmag.com

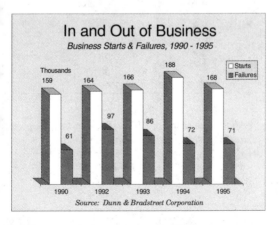

In and Out of Business
Business Starts & Failures, 1990 - 1995

Thousands

	1990	1992	1993	1994	1995
Starts	159	164	166	188	168
Failures	61	97	86	72	71

Source: Dunn & Bradstreet Corporation

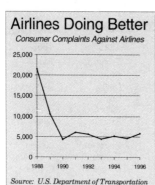

Airlines Doing Better
Consumer Complaints Against Airlines

Most Common Complaints Against Airlines

1. Cancellations and Delays
2. Customer Service
3. Ticketing
4. Baggage
5. Refunds
6. Oversales

Source: U.S. Department of Transportation

Airline Fatality Rate Down
Worldwide Airline Fatalities

Year	Fatal Accidents	Deaths	Death Rate*
1970	29	700	0.29
1975	20	467	0.13
1980	22	814	0.14
1985	22	1,066	0.15
1990	25	495	0.04
1995	26	710	0.04
1996	23	1,135	0.08

* Deaths per 100 million passenger miles flown
Source: Federal Aviation Administration

Leading U.S. Airlines

1. AMR
2. UAL
3. Delta Air Lines
4. Northwest Airlines
5. USAir Group
6. Continental Airlines
7. Southwest Airlines
8. Trans World Airlines
9. America West
10. Alaska Air Group

Source: Fortune Magazine, 1998

That's My Car

Top-Selling Automobile Models, by Year

1993	1994	1995	1996
Taurus	Taurus	Taurus	Taurus
Accord	Accord	Accord	Accord
Camry	Escort	Camry	Camry
Cavalier	Camry	Civic	Civic
Escort	Saturn	Saturn	Escort
Civic	Civic	Escort	Saturn
Saturn	Grand Am	Neon	Cavalier
Lumina	Corsica	Grand Am	Lumina
Tempo	Corolla	Lumina	Grand Am
Grand Am	Cavalier	Corolla	Corolla

Americans on the Road

Number of Registered Cars, 1900 - 1995

Source: *U.S. Department of Transportation*

Leading U.S. Motor Vehicle & Parts Companies

1. General Motors
2. Ford Motor
3. Chrysler
4. Johnson Controls
5. TRW
6. ITT Industries
7. Dana
8. Lear
9. Tenneco
10. Paccar

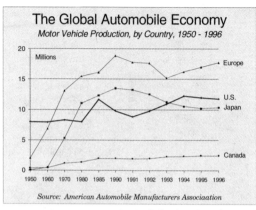

The Global Automobile Economy
Motor Vehicle Production, by Country, 1950 - 1996

Source: *American Automobile Manufacturers Associaation*

71% of the imported cars sold in the U.S. during the 1990's came from Japan. Another 12% were imported from Germany.

Most Americans Buy American Cars
Car Sales in the U.S.

Year	Total	Domestic	Imported	Percent Imported
1980	8,979,194	6,581,307	2,397,887	26.7%
1982	7,982,143	5,758,586	2,223,557	27.9%
1984	10,390,365	7,951,523	2,438,842	23.5%
1986	11,459,518	8,214,897	3,244,621	28.3%
1988	10,529,730	7,526,038	3,003,692	28.5%
1990	9,300,211	6,896,888	2,403,323	25.8%
1992	8,213,112	6,276,557	1,936,555	23.6%
1994	8,990,517	7,255,303	1,735,214	19.3%
1996	8,526,753	7,253,582	1,273,171	14.9%

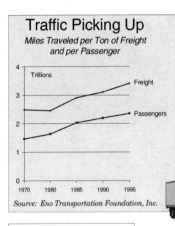

Traffic Picking Up

Miles Traveled per Ton of Freight and per Passenger

Trillions

Freight

Passengers

1970 1980 1985 1990 1995

Source: Eno Transportation Foundation, Inc.

About 37% of our freight travels by train. Another 26% travels by truck, 16% by water, and 20% moves across the country via oil pipelines.

Leading U.S. Trucking Companies

1. CNF Transportation
2. Yellow
3. Roadway Express
4. Consol. Freightways
5. Arkansas Best

The Federal Highway Administration reports that 38% of roads are in good condition, 15% are mediocre, 38% are fair, and 9% are poor.

Leading U.S. Transportation Equipment Companies

1. Brunswick
2. Trinity Industries
3. Harley Davidson
4. Polaris Industries

Leading U.S. Package & Freight Delivery Companies

1. UPS
2. FDX
3. Pittston
4. Airborne Freight
5. NEI

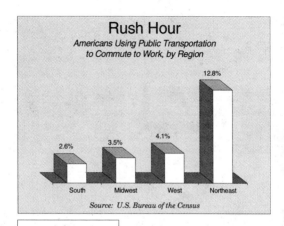

Rush Hour

*Americans Using Public Transportation
to Commute to Work, by Region*

			12.8%
2.6%	3.5%	4.1%	
South	Midwest	West	Northeast

Source: U.S. Bureau of the Census

Americans travel an average of 17 million miles per day in urban areas. That's 13,000 miles per lane-mile of freeway. We spend 226,000 hours held up in traffic every day, or about 80 hours per 1,000 people.

On average, only 5.3% of Americans use public transportation to commute to work, but in certain areas it is very common. In the District of Columbia, for example, 36% use public transport.

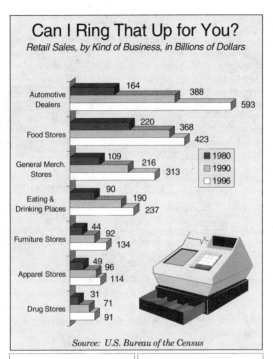

Can I Ring That Up for You?

Retail Sales, by Kind of Business, in Billions of Dollars

- Automotive Dealers: 164, 388, 593
- Food Stores: 220, 368, 423
- General Merch. Stores: 109, 216, 313
- Eating & Drinking Places: 90, 190, 237
- Furniture Stores: 44, 92, 134
- Apparel Stores: 49, 96, 114
- Drug Stores: 31, 71, 91

■ 1980 ▨ 1990 □ 1996

Source: U.S. Bureau of the Census

Leading U.S. Toys, Sporting Goods Companies	Leading U.S. Apparel Companies
1. Mattel	1. Nike
2. Hasbro	2. VF
3. Coleman Holdings	3. Reebok Int.
	4. Liz Claiborne
	5. Fruit of the Loom

Leading U.S. Food Companies

1. Conagra
2. Sara Lee
3. RJR Nabisco
4. Archer Daniels Midland
5. IBP
6. Bestfoods
7. H.J. Heinz
8. Farmland
9. Campbells Soup
10. Kellog

Leading U.S. Food and Drug Stores

1. Kroger
2. Safeway
3. American Stores
4. Albertson's
5. Walgreen
6. Winn-Dixie Stores
7. CVS
8. Publix Super Mkts.
9. Rite Aid
10. Food 4 Less

Leading U.S. General Merchandisers

1. Wal-Mart Stores
2. Sears Roebuck
3. Kmart
4. J. C. Penney
5. Dayton Hudson

Leading U.S. Specialty Retailers

1. Home Depot
2. Costco
3. Toys "R" Us
4. Republic Industries
5. Lowes

Leading U.S. Beverage Companies

1. Pepsico
2. Coca-Cola
3. Coca-Cola Ent.
4. Anheuser-Busch
5. Whitman
6. Adolph Coors

Leading U.S. Tobacco Companies

1. Philip Morris
2. Universal
3. Dimon
4. UST
5. Standard Commercial

Source: Fortune Magazine, 1998

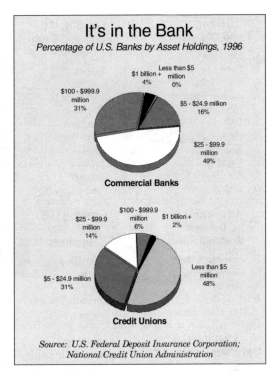

It's in the Bank
Percentage of U.S. Banks by Asset Holdings, 1996

Commercial Banks

- Less than $5 million 0%
- $1 billion + 4%
- $100 - $999.9 million 31%
- $5 - $24.9 million 16%
- $25 - $99.9 million 49%

Credit Unions

- $25 - $99.9 million 14%
- $100 - $999.9 million 6%
- $1 billion + 2%
- $5 - $24.9 million 31%
- Less than $5 million 48%

Source: U.S. Federal Deposit Insurance Corporation; National Credit Union Administration

There were 85,000 banking offices in America in 1985. By 1996, the total had declined to 82,000. The number of credit unions dropped from 27,000 to 15,000 during the decade, while the number of commercial banks grew from 58,000 to 67,000.

Leading U.S. Brokerage Companies

1. Merrill Lynch
2. Lehman Brothers
3. Salomon
4. Paine Webber
5. Bear Stearns
6. Charles Schwab

Leading U.S. Diversified Financial Companies

1. Travelers Group
2. Fannie Mae
3. American Express
4. Fed. Home Loan
5. Marsh & McLennan
6. AON
7. Household Int.
8. SLM Holdings
9. Beneficial
10. Franklin Resources

Leading U.S. Commercial Banks

1. Citicorp
2. Chase Manhattan
3. Bankamerica Corp.
4. Nationsbank Corp.
5. J.P. Morgan & Co.
6. First Union Corp.
7. Banc One Corp.
8. Bankers Trust N.Y.
9. First Chicago NBD
10. Norwest Corp.

Leading U.S. Life & Health Ins. Companies

1. Prudential
2. Metropolitan Life
3. Cigna
4. Aetna Life & Casualty
5. American General

Leading U.S. Property & Casualty Ins. Companies

1. American Intl.
2. Allstate
3. Loews
4. Hartfield
5. National Ins.

Source: Fortune Magazine, 1998

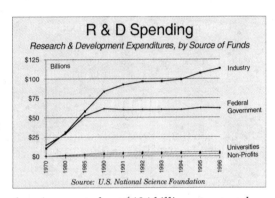

R & D Spending
Research & Development Expenditures, by Source of Funds

Source: U.S. National Science Foundation

America spent about $184 billion on research and development during 1996 -- nearly ten times its 1965 spending. The Federal government financed only about 1/3 of this research.

Leading U.S. Scientific, Photographic & Control Companies	Leading U.S. Aerospace Companies
1. Minn. Mining & Mfg.	1. Boeing
2. Eastman Kodak	2. Lockheed Martin
3. Honeywell	3. United Technologies
4. Baxter Int.	4. AlliedSignal
5. Thermo Electron	5. Textron
6. Becton Dickinson	6. Northrop Grumman
7. Medtronic	7. General Dynamics
8. Polaroid	9. Gulfstream
9. Tecktronic	10. Sundstrand
10. Bausch & Lomb	

Leading U.S. Pharmaceuticals Companies

1. Merck
2. Johnson & Johnson
3. Bristol-Myers Squibb
4. American Home
5. Pfizer

Source: Fortune Magazine, 1998

Leading U.S. Telecommunications Companies

1. AT&T
2. Bell Atlantic
3. SBC Communications
4. GTE
5. BellSouth
6. MCI Communications
7. Ameritech
8. US West
9. Sprint
10. Tele-Communications

Leading U.S. Computer & Data Services Companies

1. Electronic Data Systems
2. Unisys
3. Computer Sciences
4. First Data
5. Automatic Data Proc.

Leading U.S. Electronics, Electrical Equipment Companies

1. General Electric
2. Motorola
3. Lucent Technologies
4. Raytheon
5. Emerson Electric
6. Rockwell Int.
7. Whirlpool
8. Eaton
9. Sci Systems
10. AMP

Leading U.S. Computer & Office Equipment Companies

1. IBM
2. Hewlett-Packard
3. Compaq Computer
4. Xerox
5. Digital Equipment
6. Dell Computer
7. Sun Microsystems
8. Apple Computer
9. NCR
10. Gateway 2000

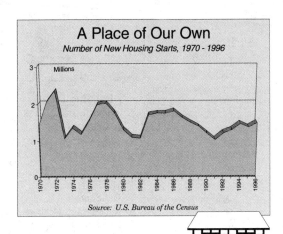

A Place of Our Own
Number of New Housing Starts, 1970 - 1996

Source: U.S. Bureau of the Census

Homes More Affordable
Average Mortgage Expense, 1987 - 1997

Year	Median Priced Home	Average Mortgage Rate	Monthly Payment	% of Median Income
1987	$85,600	9.28	$565	21.9
1988	90,600	9.31	591	22.0
1989	93,100	10.11	660	23.1
1990	97,500	10.04	673	22.7
1991	99,700	9.51	671	22.3
1992	103,700	8.11	615	20.0
1993	106,800	7.16	578	18.8
1994	109,800	7.47	612	19.3
1995	112,900	7.85	653	19.8
1996	122,700	7.93	715	21.3
1997	123,200	7.91	717	19.9

Source: National Association of Realtors

Buying a Home

Monthly Mortgage Payments, at 11% Interest

Amount Financed	10 Years	20 Years	30 Years
50,000	688.75	516.09	476.16
60,000	826.50	619.31	571.39
70,000	964.25	722.53	666.63
80,000	1102.00	825.75	761.86
90,000	1239.75	928.97	857.09
100,000	1377.50	1032.19	952.32
120,000	1653.00	1238.62	1142.78
140,000	1928.50	1445.06	1333.26
160,000	2204.00	1651.50	1523.72
180,000	2479.50	1857.94	1714.18
200,000	2755.00	2064.38	1904.64

Monthly Mortgage Payments, at 8% Interest

Amount Financed	10 Years	20 Years	30 Years
50,000	606.64	418.22	366.88
60,000	727.97	501.86	440.26
70,000	849.29	585.51	513.64
80,000	970.62	669.15	587.01
90,000	1091.95	752.80	660.39
100,000	1213.28	836.44	733.76
120,000	1455.94	1003.72	880.52
140,000	1698.58	1171.02	1027.28
160,000	1941.24	1338.30	1174.02
180,000	2183.90	1505.60	1320.78
200,000	2426.56	1672.88	1467.52

Source: Federal Trade Commission

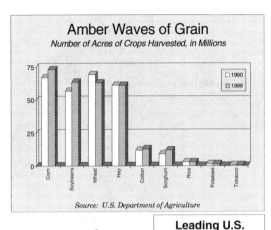

Amber Waves of Grain
Number of Acres of Crops Harvested, in Millions

Legend: □ 1990 ▨ 1996

Categories: Corn, Soybeans, Wheat, Hay, Cotton, Sorghum, Rice, Potatoes, Tobacco

Source: U.S. Department of Agriculture

Leading U.S. Farm Equipment Companies

1. Caterpillar
2. John Deere
3. Dresser Ind.
4. Ingersoll-Rand
5. CASE

Working the Land
U.S. Farm Land, in Millions

Year	Land Used for Crops	Cropland Harvested	Crop Failure	Summer Fallow
1980	382	342	10	30
1985	372	334	7	31
1990	341	310	6	25
1992	337	305	8	24
1994	339	310	7	22
1996	346	314	10	22

Source: U.S. Department of Agriculture

9. Travel

See also 'The Environment' and 'Nations of the World.'

U.S. Travel

International Travel

U.S. Travel

SITES TO SEE IN ALABAMA

First White House of the Confederacy, Montgomery
Alabama Space and Rocket Center, Huntsville
Russell Cave National Monument, Bridgeport
U.S.S. Alabama Memorial Park, Mobile
Civil Rights Memorial, Montgomery
Shakespeare Festival, Montgomery

SITES TO SEE IN ALASKA

Portage Glacier
Ketchikan Totems
Mendenhall Glacier
Iditerod Dog Sled Race
Mt. Roberts Tramway, Juneau
Denali National Park, Mt. McKinley
Katmai National Park and Preserve
Glacier Bay National Park and Preserve

SITES TO SEE IN ARIZONA

Meteor Crater
The Grand Canyon
The Painted Desert
The Petrified Forest National Park
Navajo National Monument, Sedona

SITES TO SEE IN ARKANSAS

Hot Springs National Park
Ozark Folk Center, Mountain View
Blanchard Caverns, Mountain View
Toltek Mounds Archeological State Park, Little Rock

SITES TO SEE IN CALIFORNIA

Sequoia-Kings Canyon National Park
Los Angeles County Art Museum
Universal Studios, Hollywood
Mojave and Colorado Deserts
Chanel Islands National Park
Death Valley National Park
Yosemite National Park
Rose Bowl, Pasadena
Disneyland, Anaheim
Golden Gate Bridge
Lake Tahoe

SITES TO SEE IN COLORADO

Mesa Verde National Park
Grand Mesa National Forest
Dinosaur National Monument
Colorado National Monument
Rocky Mountain National Park
Great Sand Dunes National Monument
Black Canyon of the Gunnison National Monument

SITES TO SEE IN CONNECTICUT

Yale University Art Gallery, New Haven
P.T. Barnum Museum, Bridgeport
U.S.S. Nautilus Memorial, Groton
Peabody Museum, New Haven
Mystic Marine Life Aquarium
Mark Twain House, Hartford

SITES TO SEE IN DELAWARE

New Castle Historic District
Hagley Museum, Wilmington
Dover Downs International Speedway
Fort Christina Monument, Holy Trinity Church, Wilmington

SITES TO SEE IN THE DISTRICT OF COLUMBIA

White House
Lincoln Memorial
National Archives
Jefferson Memorial
Library of Congress
United States Capitol
Korean War Memorial
Smithsonian Institution
Washington Monument
John F. Kennedy Center
Vietnam Veterans Memorial
Federal Bueau of Investigation
Franklin Delano Roosevelt Memorial

SITES TO SEE IN FLORIDA

Walt Disney World's Magic Kingdom, Epcot Center, Orlando
Castillo de San Marcos, St. Augustine
Cypress Gardens, Winter Haven
Universal Studios, Orlando
Everglades National Park
Busch Gardens, Tampa
Kennedy Space Center
Sea World, Orlando

SITES TO SEE IN GEORGIA

Franklin D. Roosevelt's Little White House, Warm Springs
Martin Luther King Jr. National Historic Site, Atlanta
Kennesaw Mt. National Battlefield Park, Atlanta
Jimmy Carter Library and Museum, Atlanta
Savannah's Historic Riverfront District
Andersonville National Historic Site
Okefenokee Swamp, Waycross
Chattahoochee National Forest
Callaway Gardens, Pine Mt.
Stone Mountain State Park
Underground Atlanta

SITES TO SEE IN HAWAII

Hawaii Volcanoes, Haleakala National Parks
Wailoa and Wailuku River State Parks
Waikiki Beach, Diamond Head, Honolulu
U.S.S. Arizona Memorial, Pearl Harbor
Polynesian Cultural Center, Laie
Waimea Canyon

SITES TO SEE IN IDAHO

Shoshone Falls
Hells Canyon
Lava Hot Springs
World Center for Birds of Prey
Sawtooth National Rereation Area
River of No Return Wilderness Area

SITES TO SEE IN ILLINOIS

Starved Rock State Park
Shawnee National Forest
Cahokia Mounds, Collinsville
Chicago Museums and Parks
Crab Orchard Wildlife Refuge
Illinois State Museum, Springfield

SITES TO SEE IN INDIANA

National College Football Hall of Fame, South Bend
Lincoln Log Cabin Historic Site, Charleston
Indianapolis 500 Raceway and Museum
Benjamin Harrison Home, Indianapolis
Tippecanoe Battlefield Memorial Park
Indiana State Museum, Indianapolis
Indianapolis Children's Museum
Eiteljorg Museum, Indianapolis
Hoosier National Forest
Wyandott Cave

SITES TO SEE IN IOWA

Herbert Hoover Birthplace and Library, West Branch
Effigy Mounds National Monument, Marquette
Davenport Municipal Art Gallery
Council Bluffs Greyhound Park
Prairie Meadows Horse Racing
Dubuque Greyhound Park
Adventureland, Altoona

SITES TO SEE IN KANSAS

Agriculture Hall of Fame and National Center, Bonner Springs
Kansas Cosmosphere and Space Center, Hutchinson
Dodge City-Boot Hill and Frontier Town
Woodlands Race Track, Kansas City
U.S. Calvary Museum, Fort Riley
Old Cow Town Museum, Wichita
Eisenhower Center, Abilene

SITES TO SEE IN KENTUCKY

Cumberland Gap National Historical Park, Middleboro
Land Between the Lakes National Recreation Area
My Old Kentucky Home State Park, Bardstown
Lincoln's Birthplace, Hodgenville
Shaker Village, Pleasant Hill
Mamoth Cave National Park
Kentucky Derby, Louisville

SITES TO SEE IN LOUISIANA

Longfellow-Evangeline Memorial Park, St. Martinville
Audobon Zoo and Gardens, New Orleans
Aquarium of the Americas, New Orleans
Mardi Gras, French Quarter, New Orleans
U.S.S. Kidd Memorial, Baton Rouge
Hodges Gardens, Natchitoches
Kent House Museum, Alexandria

ouisiana

SITES TO SEE IN MAINE

Bar Harbor
Kennebunkport
Baxter State Park
Old Orchard Beach
Portland's Old Port
Acadia National Park
Common Ground Country Fair

SITES TO SEE IN MARYLAND

Ocean City
Fort McHenry
Camden Yards, Baltimore
National Aquarium, Baltimore
U.S. Naval Academy, Annapolis
Antietam Battlefield, Hagarstown
Maryland State House, Annapolis
Edgar Allen Poe House, Baltimore
The Preakness at Pimlico Track, Baltimore

SITES TO SEE IN MASSACHUSETTS

Cape Cod
Walden Pond
Boston Museums
JFK Library, Boston
Boston Pops, Boston
Boston Ballet, Boston
Mayflower II, Plymouth
Plymouth Rock, Plymouth
Plymouth Plantation, Plymouth
Boston Symphony Orchestra, Boston
Hancock Shaker Village, the Berkshires
Naismith Memorial Basketball Hall of Fame, Springfield

SITES TO SEE IN MICHIGAN

St. Mary's Falls Ship Canal, Sault Ste. Marie
Kalamazoo Aviation History Museum
Henry Ford Museum, Deerborn
Michigan Space Center, Jackson
Greenfield Village, Deerborn
DeZwaan Windmill and
  Tulip Festival, Holland
Mackinac Island
Hiawatha Falls

SITES TO SEE IN MINNESOTA

Mall of the Americas, Minneapolis
Minneapolis Sculpture Garden
Minneapolis Institute of Arts
Ordway Theater, St. Paul
St. Paul Winter Carnival
Voyagers National Park
Mayo Clinic, Rochester
Walker Arts Center

SITES TO SEE IN MISSISSIPPI

Natchez Trace
Mynelle Gardens, Jackson
Gulf Islands National Seashore
Smith Robertson Museum, Jackson
Mardi Gras and Shrimp Festival, Biloxi
Vicksburg National Military Park and Cemetery

SITES TO SEE IN MISSOURI

Pony Express Museum, St. Joseph
State Capitol, Jefferson City
Mark Twain Area, Hannibal
Churchill Memorial, Fulton
Silver Dollar City, Branson
Gateway Arch, St. Louis
Harry S. Truman Library
Lake of the Ozarks

SITES TO SEE IN MONTANA

Museum of the Plains Indian, Blackfeet Res., Browning
Lewis and Clark Caverns State Park, Whitehall
Little Bighorn Battlefield National Monument
Museum of the Rockies, Bozeman
Custer National Cemetery
Yellowstone National Park
Glacier National Park
Flathead Lake

SITES TO SEE IN NEBRASKA

Buffalo Bill Ranch State Historic Park, North Platte
Stuhr Museum of the Prairie Pioneer, Grand Island
Strategic Air Command Museum, Bellevue
Arbor Lodge State Park, Nebraska City
Museum of the Fur Trade, Chadron
Scotts Bluff National Monument
Joslyn Art Museum, Omaha
Henry Doorly Zoo, Omaha
Pioneer Village, Minden
State Capitol, Lincoln
Boys Town, Omaha

SITES TO SEE IN NEVADA

Lake Mead
Hoover Dam
Laughlin, Elko County
Valley of Fire State Park
Great Basin National Park
Liberace Museum, Las Vegas
Guinness World Records Museum, Las Vegas
Red Rock Canyon National Conservation Area
Legalized Gambling at Las Vegas, Lake Tahoe, Reno

SITES TO SEE IN NEW HAMPSHIRE

Mount Washington
Lake Winnipesaukee
Shaker Village, Canterbury
Strawbery Banke, Portsmouth
White Mountain National Forest
The Aerial Tramway, Cannon Mountain
Saint-Gaudens National Historic Site, Cornish

SITES TO SEE IN NEW JERSEY

Edison National Historic Site, West Orange
Six Flags Great Adventure, Jackson
Miss America Pagent, Atlantic City
Liberty State Park, Jersey City
Pine Barrens Wilerness Area
Grover Cleveland Birthplace
State Aquarium, Camden
Cape May Historic District

SITES TO SEE IN NEW MEXICO

Pueblo Bonito Ruins, Chaco Canyon
White Sands National Monument
Carlsbad Caverns National Park
Taos Historic District
Ute Lake State Park
Acoma Pueblo

SITES TO SEE IN NEW YORK

Franklin D. Roosevelt National Historic Site, Hyde Park
Corning Glass Center and Steuben Factory, Corning
National Baseball Hall of Fame, Cooperstown
Statue of Liberty, Ellis Island, New York City
Theodore Roosevelt Estate, Sagamore Hill
Empire State Building, New York City
Adirondack Mountains
Saratoga Springs
Niagara Falls

SITES TO SEE IN NORTH CAROLINA

Wright Brothers National Memorial, Kitty Hawk
The Biltmore Home and Gardens, Asheville
Cape Hatteras National Sea Shore
North Carolina Symphony, Raleigh
Cape Lookout National Seashore
American Revolution Battle Sites
North Carolina Zoo, Asheboro
Great Smokey Mountains
Blue Ridge Parkway

NORTH CAROLINA

SITES TO SEE IN NORTH DAKOTA

Fort Abraham Lincoln State Park and Museum
Fort Union Trading Post National Historic Site
Theodore Roosevelt National Park, Badlands
North Dakota Heritage Center, Bismark
Dakota Dinosaur Museum, Dickinson
MandanLake Sakakawea
Bonanzaville, Fargo

NORTH
DAKOTA

SITES TO SEE IN OHIO

Birthplaces of Presidents W.H. Harrison, Grant, Garfield,
   Hayes, McKinley, Harding, Taft, and Benjamin Harrison
Neil Armstrong Air and Space Museum, Wapakoneta
Rock and Roll Hall of Fame, Cleveland
Pro Football Hall of Fame, Canton
Air Force Museum, Dayton
German Village, Columbus
Sea World, Aurora

SITES TO SEE IN OKLAHOMA

Tulsa's Art Deco District
Ouachita National Forest
Will Rogers Memorial, Claremore
White Water Frontier Park, Oklahoma
Cherokee Heritage Center, Tahlequah
Wichita Mountains Wildlife Refuge, Lawton
National Cowboy Hall of Fame, Oklahoma City
Woolaroc Museum and Wildlife Preserve, Bartlesville

SITES TO SEE IN OREGON

Multnomah Falls
Columbia River Gorge
Crater Lake National Park
High Desert Museum, Bend
Shakespearean Festival, Ashland
Oregon Dunes National Recreation Area

SITES TO SEE IN PENNSYLVANIA

Independence National Historic Park, Philadelphia
Franklin Institute Science Museum, Philadelphia
Valley Forge National Historic Park
Gettysburg National Military Park
Carnegie Institute, Pittsburgh
Pennsylvania Dutch Country
Pocono Mountains

SITES TO SEE IN RHODE ISLAND

Yachting Races
Newport Mansions
Touro Synagogue, Newport
First Baptist Church, Providence
Skater Mill Historic Site, Pawtucket
Gilbert Stuart Birthplace, Saunderstown

SITES TO SEE IN SOUTH CAROLINA

Hilton Head Island
Historic Charleston
Riverbanks Zoo, Columbia
Middleton Place, Charleston
Cypress Gardens, Charleston
Andrew Jackson State Park and Museum

SITES TO SEE IN SOUTH DAKOTA

Black Hills
Deadwood
Harney Peak
Mount Rushmore
Custer State Park
Crazy Horse Memorial
Badlands National Park
Wind Cave National Park
Jewel Cave National Monument
Great Plains Zoo and Museum, Sioux Falls

SITES TO SEE IN TENNESSEE

Casey Jones Home and Museum, Jackson
Great Smoky Mountains National Park
Dollywood Themepark, Pigeon Forge
Grand Old Opryland, USA, Nashville
Andrew Jackson's Home, Nashville
Tennessee Aquarium, Chattanooga
Lookout Mountain, Chattanooga
Cumberland Gap National Park
Alex Haley Museum, Henning
Graceland, Memphis

SITES TO SEE IN TEXAS

The Alamo
Cowgirl Hall of Fame, Fort Worth
Padre Island National Seashore
Lyndon B. Johnson National Park
San Antonio Missions National Park
George Bush Library, College Station
Texas State Aquarium, Corpus Christi
Sea World and Fiesta Texas, San Antonio

SITES TO SEE IN UTAH

Great Salt Lake
Capitol Reef National Park
Bryce Canyon National Park
Dinosaur National Monument
Rainbow Bridge National Monument
Flaming Gorge National Recreation Area
Temple Square Mormon Church, Salt Lake City

SITES TO SEE IN VERMONT

Maple Grove Maple Museum, St. Johnsbury
Calvin Coolidge Homestead, Plymouth
Rock of Ages Quarry, Graniteville
Ben & Jerry's Factory, Waterbury
Vermont Marble Exhibit, Proctor

SITES TO SEE IN VIRGINIA

Monticello, Home of Thomas Jefferson, Charlottesville
Mount Vernon, Home of George Washington
Arlington National Cemetery
Colonial Williamsburg
Blue Ridge Parkway

SITES TO SEE IN WASHINGTON

Puget Sound
Olympic National Park
Museum of Flight, Seattle
Seattle Waterfront, Seattle
Mount Ranier National Park
North Cascades National Park
Seattle Center and Space Needle
Columbia R. Gorge National Scenic Area

SITES TO SEE IN WEST VIRGINIA

Science and Cultural Center, Charleston
Harpers Valley National Historic Park
Showshoe Ski Resort, Slaty Fork
Sternwheel Regatta, Charleston
Mountain State Forest Festival
New River Gorge, Fayetteville
Whites Sulphur Springs
Berkeley Springs

SITES TO SEE IN WISCONSIN

Old Wade House and Carriage Museum, Greenbush
Circus World Museum, Baraboo
Chequamegon National Forest
Old World Wisconsin, Eagle
Villa Louis, Prarie du Chien
Monona Terrace, Madison
Door County Peninsula
Lake Winnebago

SITES TO SEE IN WYOMING

Devils Tower
Fort Laramie
National Elk Refuge
Yellowstone National Park
Grand Teton National Park
Buffalo Bill Museum, Cody
Cheyenne Frontier Days Celebration

Tell Me More!

United States Tourist Information, by State

State	Phone	Web Site
Alabama	1-800-ALABAMA	http://alaweb.asc.edu
Alaska	1-907-465-2010	http://www.state.ak.us
Arizona	1-602-254-6500	http://www.state.az.us
Arkansas	1-800-NATURAL	http://www.state.ar.us
California	1-800-862-2543	http://ww.ca.gov/s/
Colorado	1-800-265-6723	http://www.state.co.us
Connecticut	1-800-CTBOUND	http://www.state.ct.us
Delaware	1-800-441-8846	http://www.state.de.us
D.C.	1-202-789-7000	http://ci.washington.dc.us
Florida	1-904-487-1462	http://www.state.fl.us
Georgia	1-404-880-9000	http://www.state.ga.us
Hawaii	1-800-464-2924	http://www.hawaii.gov
Idaho	1-800-VISIT-ID	http://www.state.id.us
Illinois	1-800-223-0121	http://www.state.il.us
Indiana	1-800-289-6646	http://www.ai.org
Iowa	1-800-345-IOWA	http://www.state.ia.us
Kansas	1-800-2KANSAS	http://www.ink.org
Kentucky	1-800-225-TRIP	http://www.state.ky.us
Louisiana	1-800-33GUMBO	http://www.state.la.us
Maine	1-800-553-9595	http://www.state.me.us
Maryland	1-800-543-1036	http://www.state.md.us
Mass.	1-800-447-MASS	http://www.state.ma.us
Michigan	1-888-784-7328	http://www.migov.state.mi.us
Minnesota	1-800-657-3700	http://www.state.mn.us
Mississippi	1-800-WARMEST	http://www.state.ms.us
Missouri	1-800-877-1234	http://www.ecodev.state.mo.us
Montana	1-800-VISITMT	http://www.mt.gov
Nebraska	1-800-228-4307	http://www.state.ne.us
Nevada	1-800-638-2328	http://www.state.nv.us
N. Hampshire	1-800-386-4664	http://www.state.nh.us
New Jersey	1-800-JERSEY7	http://www.state.nj.us
New Mexico	1-800-733-6396	http://www.state.nm.us
New York	1-800-CALLNYS	http://www.state.ny.us

United States Tourist Information, by State

State	Phone	Web Site
N. Carolina	1-800-VISITNC	http://www.state.nc.us
N. Dakota	1-800-HELLO-ND	http://www.state.nd.us
Ohio	1-800-BUCKEYE	http://www.state.oh.us
Oklahoma	1-800-652-6552	http://www.state.ok.us
Oregon	1-800-547-7842	http://www.state.or.us
Pennsylvania	1-800-VISITPA	http://www.state.pa.us
Rhode Isl.	1-800-556-2484	http://www.state.ri.us
S.Carolina	1-800-346-3634	http://www.state.sc.us
S. Dakota	1-800-SDAKOTA	http://www.state.sd.us
Tennessee	1-800-TENN200	http://www.state.tn.us
Texas	1-800-88888TX	http://www.state.tx.us
Utah	1-800-200-1160	http://www.state.ut.us
Vermont	1-800-VERMONT	http://www.state.vt.us
Virginia	1-800-VISITVA	http://www.state.va.us
Washington	1-800-544-1800	http://www.wa.gov
W. Virginia	1-800-CALLWVA	http://www.state.wv.us
Wisconsin	1-800-432-8747	http://www.state.wi.us
Wyoming	1-800-CALLWYO	http://www.state.wy.us

Getting from Here to There
Driving Distances Between Major U.S. Cities, in Miles

	Atlanta	Boston	Chicago	Cincinnati
Atlanta,GA	-	1,037	674	440
Boston, MA	1,037	-	963	840
Chicago, IL	674	963	-	287
Cincinnati, OH	440	840	287	-
Cleveland, OH	672	628	335	244
Dallas TX	795	1,748	917	920
Denver, CO	1,398	1,949	996	1,164
Detroit, MI	699	695	266	259
Houston, TX	789	1,804	1,067	1,029
Indianapolis, IN	493	906	181	106
Kansas City, MO	798	1,391	499	591
Los Angeles, CA	2,182	2,979	2,054	2,179
Memphis, TN	371	1,296	530	468
Milwaukee, WI	761	1,050	87	374
Minneapolis, MN	1,068	1,368	405	692
New Orleans, LA	479	1,507	912	786
New York, NY	841	206	802	647
Omaha, NE	986	1,412	459	693
Philadelphia, PA	741	296	738	567
Pittsburgh, PA	687	561	452	287
Portland OR	2,601	3,046	2,083	2,333
St. Louis, MO	541	1,141	289	340
San Francisco, CA	2,496	3,095	2,142	2,362
Seattle, WA	2,618	2,976	2,013	2,300
Tulsa, OK	772	1,537	683	736
Washington, DC	608	429	671	481

*Chicago was acquired from indians in 1795
and began to grow after the 1825 opening of the
Erie Canal. A third of the city was destroyed in
a fire in 1871. Today, it is home to 2.7 million
Americans and boasts 95 colleges and universities, 123 hospitals, and 9 TV stations.*

Driving Distances, in Miles, Cont'd.

	Cleveland	Dallas	Denver	Des Moines
Atlanta, GA	672	795	1,398	870
Boston, MA	628	1,748	1,949	1,280
Chicago, IL	335	917	996	327
Cincinnati, OH	244	920	1,164	571
Cleveland, OH	-	1,159	1,321	652
Dallas TX	1,159	-	781	684
Denver, CO	1,321	781	-	669
Detroit, MI	170	1,143	1,253	584
Houston, TX	1,273	243	1,019	905
Indianapolis, IN	294	865	1,058	465
Kansas City, MO	779	489	600	195
Los Angeles, CA	2,367	1,387	1,059	1,727
Memphis, TN	712	452	1,040	599
Milwaukee, WI	422	991	1,029	361
Minneapolis, MN	740	936	841	252
New Orleans, LA	1,030	496	1,273	978
New York, NY	473	1,552	1,771	1,119
Omaha, NE	784	644	537	132
Philadelphia, PA	413	1,452	1,691	1,051
Pittsburgh, PA	129	1,204	1,411	763
Portland OR	2,418	2,009	1,238	1,786
St. Louis, MO	529	630	857	333
San Francisco, CA	2,467	1,753	1,235	1,815
Seattle, WA	2,348	2,078	1,307	1,749
Tulsa, OK	925	257	681	443
Washington, DC	346	1,319	1,616	984

Denver owes its beginnings to gold and silver. It was first settled by prospectors and miners in 1858, and its early growth was fueled by the mining industry. Perched at an altitude of 5,282 feet, it is the cultural, financial, and industrial center of the Rocky Mountain region.

Driving Distances, in Miles, Cont'd.

	Detroit	Houston	Indianapolis	Kansas City
Atlanta, GA	699	789	493	798
Boston, MA	695	1,804	906	1,391
Chicago, IL	266	1,067	181	499
Cincinnati, OH	259	1,029	106	591
Cleveland, OH	170	1,273	294	779
Dallas TX	1,143	243	865	489
Denver, CO	1,253	1,019	1,058	600
Detroit, MI	-	1,265	278	743
Houston, TX	1,265	-	987	710
Indianapolis, IN	278	987	-	485
Kansas City, MO	743	710	485	-
Los Angeles, CA	2,311	1,538	2,073	1,589
Memphis, TN	713	561	435	451
Milwaukee, WI	353	1,142	268	537
Minneapolis, MN	671	1,157	586	447
New Orleans, LA	1,045	356	796	806
New York, NY	637	1,608	713	1,198
Omaha, NE	716	865	587	201
Philadelphia, PA	573	1,508	633	1,118
Pittsburgh, PA	287	1,313	353	838
Portland OR	2,349	2,205	1,227	1,809
St. Louis, MO	513	779	235	257
San Francisco, CA	2,399	1,912	2,256	1,835
Seattle, WA	2,279	2,274	2,194	1,839
Tulsa, OK	909	478	631	248
Washington, DC	506	1,375	558	1,043

Detroit was founded by the French in 1701. It was later controlled by the British before the U.S. took posession in 1796. In 1805, fire destroyed the settlement, but it was reborn and incorporated in 1824. Its modern life began with the dawn of auto manufacturing in 1899.

Driving Distances, in Miles, Cont'd.

	Los Angeles	Louisville	Memphis	Milwaukee
Atlanta, GA	2,182	382	371	761
Boston, MA	2,979	941	1,296	1,050
Chicago, IL	2,054	292	530	87
Cincinnati, OH	2,179	101	468	374
Cleveland, OH	2,367	345	712	422
Dallas TX	1,387	819	452	991
Denver, CO	1,059	1,120	1,040	1,029
Detroit, MI	2,311	360	713	353
Houston, TX	1,538	928	561	1,142
Indianapolis, IN	2,073	111	435	268
Kansas City, MO	1,589	520	451	537
Los Angeles, CA	-	2,108	1,817	2,087
Memphis, TN	1,817	367	-	612
Milwaukee, WI	2,087	379	612	-
Minneapolis, MN	1,889	697	826	332
New Orleans, LA	1,883	685	390	994
New York, NY	2,786	748	1,100	889
Omaha, NE	1,595	687	652	493
Philadelphia, PA	2,706	668	1,000	825
Pittsburgh, PA	2,426	388	752	539
Portland OR	959	2,320	2,259	2,010
St. Louis, MO	1,845	263	285	363
San Francisco, CA	379	2,349	2,125	2,175
Seattle, WA	1,131	2,305	2,290	1,940
Tulsa, OK	1,452	659	401	757
Washington, DC	2,631	582	867	758

Los Angeles, with its Hollywood district, is the motion picture capital of the world. It was founded by the Spanish in 1781 and captured by the U.S. in 1846. Today, it employs 1.6 million people and offers 192 universities and colleges, 822 hospitals, and 21 TV stations.

Driving Distances, in Miles, Cont'd.

	Minneapolis	New Orleans	New York	Omaha
Atlanta, GA	1,068	479	841	986
Boston, MA	1,368	1,507	206	1,412
Chicago, IL	405	912	802	459
Cincinnati, OH	692	786	647	693
Cleveland, OH	740	1,030	473	784
Dallas TX	936	496	1,552	644
Denver, CO	841	1,273	1,771	537
Detroit, MI	671	1,045	637	716
Houston, TX	1,157	356	1,608	865
Indianapolis, IN	586	796	713	587
Kansas City, MO	447	806	1,198	201
Los Angeles, CA	1,889	1,883	2,786	1,595
Memphis, TN	826	390	1,100	652
Milwaukee, WI	332	994	889	493
Minneapolis, MN	-	1,214	1,207	357
New Orleans, LA	1,214	-	1,311	1,007
New York, NY	1,207	1,311	-	1,251
Omaha, NE	357	1,007	1,251	-
Philadelphia, PA	1,143	1,211	100	1,183
Pittsburgh, PA	857	1,070	368	895
Portland OR	1,678	2,505	2,885	1,654
St. Louis, MO	552	673	948	449
San Francisco, CA	1,940	2,249	2,934	1,683
Seattle, WA	1,608	2,574	2,815	1,638
Tulsa, OK	695	647	1,344	387
Washington, DC	1,076	1,078	233	1,116

Many of New York's buildings reach a quarter mile high. Arguably the center of the human world, the city includes five burroughs: Brooklyn, Statten Island, Queens, the Bronx, and Manhattan. It was the main point of entry for immigrants throughout much of America's history and remains culturally diverse.

Driving Distances, in Miles, Cont'd.

	Philadelphia	Pittsburgh	Portland	St. Louis
Atlanta, GA	741	687	2,601	541
Boston, MA	296	561	3,046	1,141
Chicago, IL	738	452	2,083	289
Cincinnati, OH	567	287	2,333	340
Cleveland, OH	413	129	2,418	529
Dallas TX	1,452	1,204	2,009	630
Denver, CO	1,691	1,411	1,238	857
Detroit, MI	576	287	2,349	513
Houston, TX	1,508	1,313	2,205	779
Indianapolis, IN	633	353	2,227	235
Kansas City, MO	1,118	838	1,809	257
Los Angeles, CA	2,706	2,426	959	1,845
Memphis, TN	1,000	752	2,259	285
Milwaukee, WI	825	539	2,010	363
Minneapolis, MN	1,143	857	1,678	552
New Orleans, LA	1,211	1,070	2,505	673
New York, NY	100	368	2,885	948
Omaha, NE	1,183	895	1,654	449
Philadelphia, PA	-	288	2,821	868
Pittsburgh, PA	288	-	2,535	588
Portland OR	2,821	2,535	-	2,060
St. Louis, MO	868	588	2,060	-
San Francisco, CA	2,866	2,578	636	2,089
Seattle, WA	2,751	2,465	172	2,081
Tulsa, OK	1,264	984	1,913	396
Washington, DC	133	221	2,754	793

Hosting the Continental Congress in 1774, Philadelphia was one of the centers of development of America's independence and government. The city was first settled by Swedes in 1638; the Dutch played a role in its early days, as did English and Scottish Quakers.

Driving Distances, in Miles, Cont'd.

	Salt Lake City	San Francisco	Seattle	Toledo
Atlanta, GA	1,878	2,496	2,618	640
Boston, MA	2,343	3,095	2,976	739
Chicago, IL	1,390	2,142	2,013	232
Cincinnati, OH	1,610	2,362	2,300	200
Cleveland, OH	1,715	2,467	2,348	111
Dallas TX	1,242	1,753	2,078	1,084
Denver, CO	504	1,235	1,307	1,218
Detroit, MI	1,647	2,399	2,279	59
Houston, TX	1,438	1,912	2,274	1,206
Indianapolis, IN	1,504	2,256	2,194	219
Kansas City, MO	1,086	1,835	1,839	687
Los Angeles, CA	715	379	1,131	2,276
Memphis, TN	1,535	2,125	2,290	654
Milwaukee, WI	1,423	2,175	1,940	319
Minneapolis, MN	1,186	1,940	1,608	637
New Orleans, LA	1,738	2,249	2,574	986
New York, NY	2,182	2,934	2,815	578
Omaha, NE	931	1,683	1,638	681
Philadelphia, PA	2,114	2,866	2,751	514
Pittsburgh, PA	1,826	2,578	2,465	228
Portland OR	767	636	172	2,315
St. Louis, MO	1,337	2,089	2,081	454
San Francisco, CA	752	-	808	2,364
Seattle, WA	836	808	-	2,245
Tulsa, OK	1,172	1,760	1,982	850
Washington, DC	2,047	2,799	2,684	447

San Francisco was incorporated in 1846 but did not become a major city until the California Gold Rush of 1849. Seattle followed a similar pattern, booming during the Alaska Gold Rush of 1897. Both cities are cultural centers now, featuring ballets, symphonies, and universities.

Driving Distances, in Miles, Cont'd.

	Tulsa	Washington, DC
Atlanta, GA	772	608
Boston, MA	1,537	429
Chicago, IL	683	671
Cincinnati, OH	736	481
Cleveland, OH	925	346
Dallas, TX	257	1,319
Denver, CO	681	1,616
Detroit, MI	909	506
Houston, TX	478	1,375
Indianapolis, IN	631	558
Kansas City, MO	248	1,043
Los Angeles, CA	1,452	2,631
Memphis, TN	401	867
Milwaukee, WI	757	758
Minneapolis, MN	695	1,076
New Orleans, LA	647	1,078
New York, NY	1,344	233
Omaha, NE	387	1,116
Philadelphia, PA	1,264	133
Pittsburgh, PA	984	221
Portland OR	1,913	2,754
St. Louis, MO	396	793
San Francisco, CA	1,760	2,799
Seattle, WA	1,982	2,684
Tulsa, OK	-	1,189
Washington, DC	1,189	-

In 1790, George Washington chose a site along the Potomac River for our nation's capital city. Named for him, Washington DC has remained the center of the United States federal government and has been enhanced over the years with many mounments, museums, and parks.

International Travel

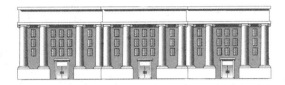

A Home Away From Home
U.S. Embassies Abroad

Country	City	Telephone
Angola	Luanda	[244] (2) 346-418/ 345-481
Argentina	Buenos Aires	[54] (1) 777-4533
Armenia	Yerevan	3742-151-144
Australia	Sydney	[61] (2) 373-9200
Austria	Vienna	[43] (1) 313-39
Azerbaijan	Baku	(9) (9412) 98-03-35
Bahrain	Manama	(973) 273-300
Bangladesh	Dhaka	[880] (2) 884700-22
Belarus	Minsk	(375) (172) 31-50-00
Belize	Belize City	[501] (2) 77161
Belgium	Brussels	[32] (2) 508-2111
Bolivia	La Paz	[591] (2) 430251
Bosnia/Herzegovina	Sarajevo	[387] (71) 445-700
Botswana	Gaborone	[267] 353-982
Brazil	Brasilia	[55] (61) 321-7272
Brunei	Bandar Seri Begawan	[673] (2) 229-670
Bulgaria	Sofia	[359] (2) 980-5241
Burkina Faso	Ouagadougou	[226] 30-67-23
Burundi	Bujumbura	[257] 22-34-54
Camaroon	Yaounde	(237) 23-40-14
Cambodia	Phnom Penh	(855) 23-426-436
Canada	Ottowa	(613) 238-5335
Cape Verde	Praia	[238] 61-56-16
Chile	Santiago	[56] (2) 232-2600

U.S. Embassies Abroad, *Continued*

Country	City	Telephone
China	Beijing	[86] (10) 6532-3831
Colombia	Bogota	[57] (1) 315-0811
Congo, Republic of	Brazzaville	(242) 83-20-70
Costa Rica	San Jose	(506) 220-3939
Cote D' Ivoire	Abidjan	(225) 21-09-79
Croatia	Zagreb	[385] (1) 455-55-00
Cyprus	Nicosia	[357] (2) 776400
Czech Republic	Prague	[420] (2) 5732-066
Denmark	Copenhagen	[45] (31) 42-31-44
Djibouti	Djibouti	[253] 35-39-95
Dominican Republic	Santo Domingo	(809) 221-2171
Ecuador	Quito	[593] (2) 562-890
Egypt	Cairo	[20] (2) 355-7371
El Salvador	San Salvador	(503) 278-4444
Eritrea	Asmara	[291] (1) 120004
Estonia	Tallinn	[372] (6) 312-021
Ethiopia	Addis Aababa	[251] (1) 550-666
Fiji	Suva	[679] 314-466
Finland	Helsinki	[358] (9) 171 931
France	Paris	[33] (1) 4312-2222
Gabon	Libreville	[241] 762003
Gambia, The	Banjul	(220) 392-856
Germany	Bonn	[49] (228) 3391
Ghana	Accra	[233] (21) 775348
Great Britain	London	[44] (171) 499.9000
Greece	Athens	[30] (1) 721-2951
Grenada	St. George's	(809) 444-1173
Guatemala	Guatemala City	[502] (2) 31-15-41
Guinea-Bissau	Bissau	[245] 25-2273
Guyana	Georgetown	[592] (2) 54900
Haiti	Port au Prince	[509] 22-0354
Honduras	Tegucigalpa	[504] 36-9320
Hong Kong	Hong Kong	(852)25239011
Hungary	Budapest	[36] (1) 267-4400

U.S. Embassies Abroad, Continued

Country	City	Telephone
India	New Delhi	[91] (11) 688-9033
Indonesia	Jakarta	(62-21)344-2211
Iraq	Baghdad	[964] (1) 719-6138/9
Ireland	Dublin	[353] (1) 44-1232-328239
Isreal	Tel Aviv	[972] (3) 5197575
Italy	Rome	(39) (6) 46741
Jamaica	Kingston	(809) 929-4850
Japan	Tokyo	[81] (3) 3224-5000
Jordan	Amman	[962] (6) 820-101
Kazakstan	Almaty	[7] (3272) 63-39-05
Kenya	Nairobi	[254] (2) 334141
Korea	Seoul	[82] (2) 397-4114
Kuwait	Kuwait	[965] 539-5307
Kyrgyzstan	Bishkek	[7] (3312) 22-29-20
Laos	Vientiane	[856] (21) 212581
Latvia	Riga	[371] 721-0005
Lebanon	Beirut	[961] (1) 402-200
Lesotho	Maseru	[266] 312-666
Liberia	Monrovia	[231] 226-370
Lithuania	Vilnius	(370-2) 223-031
Luxembourg	Luxembourg	[352] 460123
Macedonia	Skopje	[389] (91) 116-180
Madagascar	Antananarivo	[261] (2) 212-57
Malaysia	Kuala Lumpur	[60] (3) 248-9011
Mali	Bamako	[223] 225470
Malta	Valletta	[356] 235-960
Marshall Islands	Majuro	(692) 247-4011
Mauritania	Nouakchott	[222] (2) 526-60
Mauritius	Port Louis	[230] 208-2347
Mexico	Mexico City	[52] (5) 209-9100
Milawi	Lilongwe	[265] 783-166
Micronesia	Kolonia	[691] 320-2187
Moldova	Chisinau	373 (2) 23-37-72

U.S. Embassies Abroad, *Continued*

Country	City	Telephone
Mongolia	Ulaanbaatar	[976] (1) 329095
Morocco	Rabat	[212] (7) 76-22-65
Mozambique	Maputo	[258] (1) 49-27-97
New Zealand	Wellington	[64] (4) 472-2068
Namibia	Windhoek	[264] (61) 221-601
Nepal	Kathmandu	[977] (1) 411179
Netherlands	Hague	[31] (70) 310-9209
Nicaragua	Managua	(505)2666010
Niger	Niamey	[227] 72-26-61
Nigeria	Lagos	[234] (1) 261-0097
Norway	Oslo	[47] 22-44-85-50
Oman	Muscat	(968) 698-989
Pakistan	Islamabad	[92] (51) 826161
Palau	Koror	(680) 488-2920
Panama	Panama City	[507] 227-1777
Papua New Guinea	Port Moresby	(675) 321-1455
Paraguay	Asuncion	[595] (21) 213-715
Peru	Lima	[51] (1) 434-3000
Philippines	Manila	[63] (2) 523-1001
Poland	Warsaw	[48] (22) 628-3041
Portugal	Lisbon	[351] (1) 727-3300
Russia	Moscow	[7] (095) 252-2451
Qatar	Doha	(974) 864701
Samoa	Apia	(685) 21-631
Saudi Arabia	Riyadh	[966] (1) 488-3800
Senegal	Dakar	[221] 823-4296
Serbia/Montenegro	Belgrade	[381] (11) 645-655
Sierra Leone	Freetown	[232] (22) 226-481
Singapore	Singapore	(65) 338-0251
Slovakia	Bratislava	[421] (7) 533-0861
Slovenia	Ljubljana	[386] (61) 301-427/ 472/485
Spain	Madrid	[81] (3) 3224-5000
Sri Lanka	Colombo	[94] (1) 448007

U.S. Embassies Abroad, Continued

Country	City	Telephone
Sudan	Khartoum	249-11-774611
Suriname	Paramaribo	[597] 472900
Swaziland	Mbabane	[268] 46441/5
Sweden	Stockholm	[46] (8) 783-5300
Switzerland	Bern	031/357 72 34
Syria	Damascus	[963] (11) 333-2814
Tajikistan	Dushanbe	[7] (3772) 21-03-56
Tanzania	Dar Es Salaam	[255] (51) 666010
Thailand	Bangkok	(662) 205-4000
Togo	Lome	[228] 21-77-17
Tunisia	Tunis	[216] (1) 782-566
Turkey	Ankara	[90] (312) 468-6110
Turkmenistan	Ashgabat	[9] (9312) 35-00-45
Uganda	Kampala	[256] (41) 259792
Ukrane	Kiev	[380] (44) 244-7345
United Arab Emirates	Abu Dhabi	[971] (2) 436-691
Uruguay	Montevideo	(598-2) 408-7777
Uzbekistan	Tashkent	[7] (3712) 77-14-07
Venezuela	Caracas	[58] (2) 977-2011
Vietnam	Hanoi	[84] (4) 8431500
Yemen	Sanaa	[967] (1) 238-843/52
Zambia	Lusaka	[260] (1) 250-955
Zimbabwe	Harare	[263] (4) 794-521

*For a complete listing of embassies and consular offices, including their addresses and fax numbers, log onto the U.S. State Department's web site: **www.state.gov***

Traveling the World
Flying Distances Between Cities, in Miles

	Bangkok	Beijing	Berlin	Cairo
Bangkok	-	2,046	5,352	4,523
Beijing	2,046	-	4,584	4,698
Berlin	5,352	4,584	-	1,797
Cairo	4,523	4,698	1,797	-
Cape Town	6,300	8,044	5,961	4,480
Caracas	10,555	8,950	5,238	6,342
Chicago	8,570	6,604	4,414	6,141
Hong Kong	1,077	1,217	5,443	5,066
Honolulu	6,609	5,077	7,320	8,848
London	5,944	5,074	583	2,185
Los Angeles	7,637	6,250	5,782	7,520
Madrid	6,337	5,745	1,165	2,087
Melbourne	4,568	5,643	9,918	8,675
Mexico City	9,793	7,753	6,056	7,700
Montreal	8,338	6,519	3,740	5,427
Moscow	4,389	3,607	1,006	1,803
New York	8,669	6,844	3,979	5,619
Paris	5,877	5,120	548	1,998
Rio de Janeiro	9,994	10,768	6,209	6,143
Rome	5,494	5,063	737	1,326
San Francisco	7,931	5,918	5,672	7,466
Singapore	883	2,771	6,164	5,137
Stockholm	5,089	4,133	528	2,096
Tokyo	2,865	1,307	5,557	5,958
Warsaw	5,033	4,325	322	1,619
Washington, DC	8,807	6,942	4,181	5,822

*Beijing is the second largest city in China after
Shanghai. The nation's capital, it has been an
administrative center since the Zhou dynasty
(1027-256 B.C.). Beijing's two ancient sections --
the Forbidden City and the Imperial City -- are
surrounded by residential and industrial areas.*

Flying Distances, in Miles, Cont'd.

	Cape Town	Caracas	Chicago	Hong Kong
Bangkok	6,300	10,555	8,570	1,077
Beijing	8,044	8,950	6,604	1,217
Berlin	5,961	5,238	4,414	5,443
Cairo	4,480	6,342	6,141	5,066
Cape Town	-	6,366	8,491	7,376
Caracas	6,366	-	2,495	10,165
Chicago	8,491	2,495	-	7,797
Hong Kong	7,376	10,165	7,797	-
Honolulu	11,535	6,021	4,256	5,556
London	5,989	4,655	3,958	5,990
Los Angeles	9,969	3,632	1,745	7,240
Madrid	5,308	4,346	4,189	6,558
Melbourne	6,425	9,717	9,673	4,595
Mexico City	8,519	2,234	1,690	8,788
Montreal	7,922	2,438	745	7,736
Moscow	6,279	6,177	4,987	4,437
New York	7,803	2,120	714	8,060
Paris	5,786	4,732	4,143	5,990
Rio de Janeiro	3,781	2,804	5,282	11,009
Rome	5,231	5,195	4,824	5,774
San Francisco	10,248	3,902	1,859	6,905
Singapore	6,008	11,402	9,372	1,605
Stockholm	6,423	5,471	4,331	5,063
Tokyo	9,154	8,808	6,314	1,791
Warsaw	5,935	5,559	4,679	5,147
Washington, DC	7,895	2,047	596	8,155

Cape Town, with its natural scenic beauty and fine beaches, is a popular vacation resort. The city's landscape is dominated by Table Mountain and Table Bay, a large artificial harbor built to handle the active shipping commerce of gold, diamond, and citrus fruit exports.

Flying Distances, in Miles, Cont'd.

	Honolulu	Lima	London	Los Angeles
Bangkok	6,609	12,244	5,944	7,637
Beijing	5,077	10,349	5,074	6,250
Berlin	7,320	6,896	583	5,782
Cairo	8,848	7,726	2,185	7,520
Cape Town	11,535	6,072	5,989	9,969
Caracas	6,021	1,707	4,655	3,632
Chicago	4,256	3,775	3,958	1,745
Hong Kong	5,556	11,418	5,990	7,240
Honolulu	-	5,947	7,240	2,557
London	7,240	6,316	-	5,439
Los Angeles	2,557	4,171	5,439	-
Madrid	7,872	5,907	785	5,848
Melbourne	5,505	8,059	10,500	7,931
Mexico City	3,789	2,639	5,558	1,542
Montreal	4,918	3,970	3,254	2,427
Moscow	7,047	7,862	1,564	6,068
New York	4,969	3,639	3,469	2,451
Paris	7,449	6,370	214	5,601
Rio de Janeiro	8,288	2,342	5,750	6,330
Rome	8,040	6,750	895	6,326
San Francisco	2,398	4,518	5,367	347
Singapore	6,726	11,689	6,747	8,767
Stockholm	6,875	7,166	942	5,454
Tokyo	3,859	9,631	5,959	5,470
Warsaw	7,366	7,215	905	5,922
Washington, DC	4,838	3,509	3,674	2,300

Already bustling at the time the Romans occupied it in the first century A.D., London has a long, rich history and offers many sites to see, including Big Ben, the Tower of London, and Buckingham Palace. As Great Britain's capital, it is one of the world's cultural and financial centers.

Flying Distances, in Miles, Cont'd.

	Madrid	Melbourne	Mexico City	Montreal
Bangkok	6,337	4,568	9,793	8,338
Beijing	5,745	5,643	7,753	6,519
Berlin	1,165	9,918	6,056	3,740
Cairo	2,087	8,675	7,700	5,427
Cape Town	5,308	6,425	8,519	7,922
Caracas	4,346	9,717	2,234	2,438
Chicago	4,189	9,673	1,690	745
Hong Kong	6,558	4,595	8,788	7,736
Honolulu	7,872	5,505	3,789	4,918
London	785	10,500	5,558	3,254
Los Angeles	5,848	7,931	1,542	2,427
Madrid	-	10,758	5,643	3,448
Melbourne	10,758	-	8,426	10,395
Mexico City	5,643	8,426	-	2,317
Montreal	3,448	10,395	2,317	-
Moscow	2,147	8,950	6,676	4,401
New York	3,593	10,359	2,090	331
Paris	655	10,430	5,725	3,432
Rio de Janeiro	5,045	8,226	4,764	5,078
Rome	851	9,929	6,377	4,104
San Francisco	5,803	7,856	1,887	2,543
Singapore	7,080	3,759	10,327	9,203
Stockholm	1,653	9,630	6,012	3,714
Tokyo	6,706	5,062	7,035	6,471
Warsaw	1,427	9,598	6,337	4,022
Washington, DC	3,792	10,180	1,885	489

According to Aztec records, the ancient city of Tenochtitlan, which is today's Mexico City, was founded in 1325. It is the second largest city of the world, after Tokyo. More than half of Mexico's industrial output is produced in or near Mexico City, the nation's capital.

Flying Distances, in Miles, Cont'd.

	Moscow	New Delhi	New York	Paris
Bangkok	4,389	1,813	8,669	5,877
Beijing	3,607	2,353	6,844	5,120
Berlin	1,006	3,598	3,979	548
Cairo	1,803	2,758	5,619	1,998
Cape Town	6,279	5,769	7,803	5,786
Caracas	6,177	8,833	2,120	4,732
Chicago	4,987	7,486	714	4,143
Hong Kong	4,437	2,339	8,060	5,990
Honolulu	7,047	7,412	4,969	7,449
London	1,564	4,181	3,469	214
Los Angeles	6,068	7,011	2,451	5,601
Madrid	2,147	4,530	3,593	655
Melbourne	8,950	6,329	10,359	10,430
Mexico City	6,676	9,120	2,090	5,725
Montreal	4,401	7,012	331	3,432
Moscow	-	2,698	4,683	1,554
New York	4,683	7,318	-	3,636
Paris	1,554	4,102	3,636	-
Rio de Janeiro	7,170	8,753	4,801	5,684
Rome	1,483	3,684	4,293	690
San Francisco	5,885	7,691	2,572	5,577
Singapore	5,228	2,571	9,534	6,673
Stockholm	716	3,414	3,986	1,003
Tokyo	4,660	3,638	6,757	6,053
Warsaw	721	3,277	4,270	852
Washington, DC	4,876	7,500	205	3,840

The original Paris was on the Ile de la Cite, an island in the Seine River. It grew in a roughly circular shape and was enclosed in a series of defending walls, which are now wide boulevards. The art and architecture surrounding the visitor are among the city's many attractions.

Flying Distances, in Miles, Cont'd.

	Rio de Janeiro	Rome	San Francisco	Singapore
Bangkok	9,994	5,494	7,931	883
Beijing	10,768	5,063	5,918	2,771
Berlin	6,209	737	5,672	6,164
Cairo	6,143	1,326	7,466	5,137
Cape Town	3,781	5,231	10,248	6,008
Caracas	2,804	5,195	3,902	11,402
Chicago	5,282	4,824	1,859	9,372
Hong Kong	11,009	5,774	6,905	1,605
Honolulu	8,288	8,040	2,398	6,726
London	5,750	895	5,367	6,747
Los Angeles	6,330	6,326	347	8,767
Madrid	5,045	851	5,803	7,080
Melbourne	8,226	9,929	7,856	3,759
Mexico City	4,764	6,377	1,887	10,327
Montreal	5,078	4,104	2,543	9,203
Moscow	7,170	1,483	5,885	5,228
New York	4,801	4,293	2,572	9,534
Paris	5,684	690	5,577	6,673
Rio de Janeiro	-	5,707	6,613	9,785
Rome	5,707	-	6,259	6,229
San Francisco	6,613	6,259	-	8,448
Singapore	9,785	6,229	8,448	-
Stockholm	6,683	1,245	5,399	5,936
Tokyo	11,532	6,142	5,150	3,300
Warsaw	6,455	820	5,854	5,843
Washington, DC	4,779	4,497	2,441	9,662

Rio de Janeiro was Brazil's capital from 1763 until 1960, and remains a cultural, tourist, and manufacturing center. Set between spectacular mountains and the South Atlantic Ocean, its lush forests surround sparkling beaches, making it one of the world's most beautiful cities.

Flying Distances, in Miles, Cont'd.

	Stockholm	Tehran	Tokyo	Vienna
Bangkok	5,089	3,391	2,865	5,252
Beijing	4,133	3,490	1,307	4,648
Berlin	528	2,185	5,557	326
Cairo	2,096	1,234	5,958	1,481
Cape Town	6,423	5,241	9,154	5,656
Caracas	5,471	7,320	8,808	5,372
Chicago	4,331	6,502	6,314	4,698
Hong Kong	5,063	3,843	1,791	5,431
Honolulu	6,875	8,070	3,859	7,632
London	942	2,743	5,959	771
Los Angeles	5,454	7,682	5,470	6,108
Madrid	1,653	2,978	6,706	1,128
Melbourne	9,630	7,826	5,062	9,790
Mexico City	6,012	8,184	7,035	6,320
Montreal	3,714	5,880	6,471	4,009
Moscow	716	1,532	4,660	1,043
New York	3,986	6,141	6,757	4,234
Paris	1,003	2,625	6,053	645
Rio de Janeiro	6,683	7,374	11,532	6,127
Rome	1,245	2,127	6,142	477
San Francisco	5,399	7,362	5,150	5,994
Singapore	5,936	4,103	3,300	6,035
Stockholm	-	2,173	5,053	780
Tokyo	5,053	4,775	-	5,689
Warsaw	494	1,879	5,689	347
Washington, DC	4,183	6,341	6,791	4,438

Tokyo is home to more than 30 million people, making it the world's largest urban area. The city's heart is the Imperial Palace, which is surrounded by the Kasumigaseki government district, the Marunouchi business district, and the Keihin Industrial Region. The city's tremendous economy employs 8 million workers.

Flying Distances, in Miles, Cont'd.

	Warsaw	Wshington, DC
Bangkok	5,033	8,807
Beijing	4,325	6,942
Berlin	322	4,181
Cairo	1,619	5,822
Cape Town	5,935	7,895
Caracas	5,559	2,047
Chicago	4,679	596
Hong Kong	5,147	8,155
Honolulu	7,366	4,838
London	905	3,674
Los Angeles	5,922	2,300
Madrid	1,427	3,792
Melbourne	9,598	10,180
Mexico City	6,337	1,885
Montreal	4,022	489
Moscow	721	4,876
New York	4,270	205
Paris	852	3,840
Rio de Janeiro	6,455	4,779
Rome	820	4,497
San Francisco	5,854	2,441
Singapore	5,843	9,662
Stockholm	494	4,183
Tokyo	5,347	6,791
Warsaw	-	4,472
Washington, DC	4,472	-

Warsaw developed around the castle of the dukes of Masovia along the Wisla (Vistula) River in the 14th century. Occupied by Sweden, Prussia, Russia, and Germany, it has had a violent history. Rebuilding since WWII includes the restored Old City on the medieval market square surrounded by Renaissance and baroque houses.

10. Entertainment

See also 'Sports.'

Movies & Videos

TV & Radio

Computers & the Internet

Music

Reading

Performing Arts

Games

Leisure Activities & Sports

Spectator Sports

Movies & Videos

Voting with Our Wallets

Top Grossing Movies, in Millions of Dollars

Rank	Movie	U.S. Ticket Sales
1.	Titanic, 1997 [1]	579
2.	Star Wars, 1977	461
3.	E.T., 1982	400
4.	Jurassic Park, 1993	357
5.	Forrest Gump, 1994	330
6.	The Lion King, 1993	313
7.	Return of the Jedi, 1983	307
8.	Independence Day, 1996	306
9.	The Empire Strikes Back, 1980	290
10.	Home Alone, 1990	285
11.	Jaws, 1975	260
12.	Batman, 1989	251
13.	Men in Black, 1997	250
14.	Raiders of the Lost Ark, 1981	242
15.	Twister, 1996	242
16.	Beverly Hills Cop, 1984	235
17.	The Lost World, Jurassic Park, 1997	229
18.	Ghostbusters, 1984	221
19.	Mrs. Doubtfire, 1993	219
20.	Ghost, 1990	218
21.	Alladin, 1992	217
22.	Back to the Future, 1985	211
23.	Terminator 2: Judgement Day, 1991	204
24.	Indiana Jones and the Last Crusade, 1989	197
25.	Gone with the Wind, 1939	194

[1] *Still in release at the time of this publication*
www.movieweb.com

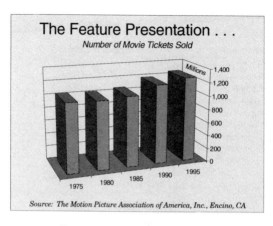

The Feature Presentation . . .
Number of Movie Tickets Sold

Millions | 1,400
1,200
1,000
800
600
400
200
0

1975   1980   1985   1990   1995

Source: The Motion Picture Association of America, Inc., Encino, CA

Between 1975 and 1995, the number of movie theaters in America nearly doubled, growing from 15 thousand to 28 thousand. Meanwhile, the drive-in theater was dying a slow death, dwindling from four thousand to a lonely one thousand nationwide.

Top Selling Movie Videos

1. The Lion King
2. Snow White
3. Aladdin
4. Jurassic Park
5. Beauty & the Beast
6. Independence Day
7. Toy Story
8. Poccahontas
9. Forrest Gump
10. Mrs. Doubtfire

Source: Paul Kagan Associates

TV & Radio

We're Tuned In
TV Shows with Highest All Time Ratings

Program	Broadcast Date
M*A*S*H -- last episode	2/28/83
Dallas -- Who Shot J.R.?	11/21/80
Roots-Pt. 8	1/30/77
Super Bowl XVI	1/24/82
Super Bowl XVII	1/30/83
XVII Winter Olympics	2/23/94
Super Bowl XX	1/26/86
Gone With the Wind-Pt. 1	11/7/76
Gone With the Wind-Pt. 2	11/8/76
Super Bowl XII	1/15/78

Source: Nielsen Media Research

Nielsen Media Research reports that 74% of American households had multiple TV sets in 1996, up from 50% in 1980.

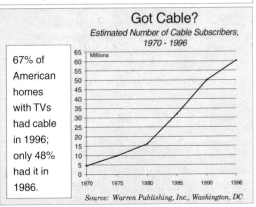

Got Cable?
Estimated Number of Cable Subscribers, 1970 - 1996

67% of American homes with TVs had cable in 1996; only 48% had it in 1986.

Source: Warren Publishing, Inc., Washington, DC

*American households
average 49 hours of TV
viewing each week.*

What We Watch on TV

*Top Rated Regular
Series Programs
1950 - 1997*

Year	Top Program	Year	Top Program
1996-97	E.R.	1972-73	All in the Family
1995-96	E.R.	1971-72	All in the Family
1994-95	Seinfeld	1970-71	Marcus Welby, MD
1993-94	Home Improvement	1969-70	Laugh-In
1992-93	60 Minutes	1968-69	Laugh-In
1991-92	60 Minutes	1967-68	Andy Griffith
1990-91	Cheers	1966-67	Bonanza
1989-90	Roseanne	1965-66	Bonanza
1988-89	Roseanne	1964-65	Bonanza
1987-88	Bill Cosby Show	1963-64	Beverly Hillbillies
1986-87	Bill Cosby Show	1962-63	Beverly Hillbillies
1985-86	Bill Cosby Show	1961-62	Wagon Train
1984-85	Dynasty	1960-61	Gunsmoke
1983-84	Dallas	1959-60	Gunsmoke
1982-83	60 Minutes	1958-59	Gunsmoke
1981-82	Dallas	1957-58	Gunsmoke
1980-81	Dallas	1956-57	I Love Lucy
1979-80	60 Minutes	1955-56	$64,000 Question
1978-79	Laverne & Shirley	1954-55	I Love Lucy
1977-78	Laverne & Shirley	1953-54	I Love Lucy
1976-77	Happy Days	1952-53	I Love Lucy
1975-76	All in the Family	1951-52	Godfrey's Talent Scout
1974-75	All in the Family	1950-51	Texaco Star Theater
1973-74	All in the Family		

Source: Nielsen Media Research

TV Parental Guidelines

 All Children. Animated or live action, designed to be appropriate for all children.

 Directed to Older Children, age 7 and above. More appropriate for children who have learned to distinguish reality from make-believe.

 General Audience. Most parents would find suitable for all ages, though not specifically designed for children.

 Parental Guidance Suggested. May contain some material that parents would find unsuitable for younger children. May contain moderate voilence (V), suggestive sexual situation (S), infrequent coarse language (L), or some suggestive dialog (D).

 Parents Strongly Cautioned. May contain material parents would find unsuitable for children under 14. May contain intense violence (V), intense sexual situations (S), strong coarse language (L), or intensly suggestive dialog (D).

 Mature Audience Only. Designed to be viewed by adults; may be unsuitable for children under age 17. Contains graphic violence (V), explicit sexual activity (S), and/or crude indecent language (L).

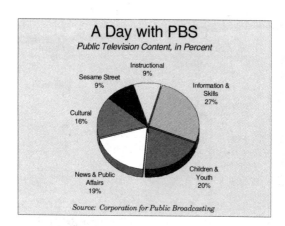

A Day with PBS

Public Television Content, in Percent

Instructional 9%

Sesame Street 9%

Information & Skills 27%

Cultural 16%

Children & Youth 20%

News & Public Affairs 19%

Source: Corporation for Public Broadcasting

There were 351 Public Broad-casting Stations in America in 1995, up from 290 in 1980. They recieve 18% of their $1.9 billion dollar budget from the Federal government, 29% from state and local government, 23% from subscribers, and 27% from businesses, foundations, and other sources.

Source: Corp. for Public Broadcasting

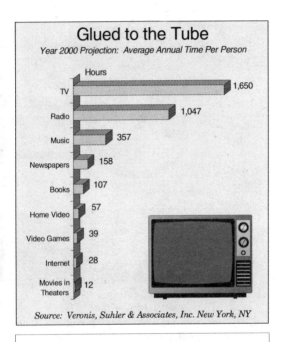

Glued to the Tube
Year 2000 Projection: Average Annual Time Per Person

Hours

	Hours
TV	1,650
Radio	1,047
Music	357
Newspapers	158
Books	107
Home Video	57
Video Games	39
Internet	28
Movies in Theaters	12

Source: Veronis, Suhler & Associates, Inc. New York, NY

Americans' Favorite Pastimes

1. Reading
2. Watching TV
3. Fishing
4. Spending time with family
5. Gardening
6. Team sports
7. Golf
8. Walking
9. Going to movies
10. Swimming

Source: Louis Harris & Associates

There are more than 10,000 radio stations in America. In addition to those shown in the chart below, there are 515 Spanish and ethnic radio stations, as well as 474 adult standard stations, and 348 urban black stations. 314 stations use a top-40 format, 91 are easy listening, and 65 classify themselves as variety. 54 are devoted to jazz and new age music, while 41 play only classical music and 30 call themselves preteen.

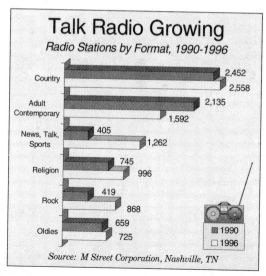

Talk Radio Growing
Radio Stations by Format, 1990-1996

Format	1990	1996
Country	2,452	2,558
Adult Contemporary	2,135	1,592
News, Talk, Sports	405	1,262
Religion	745	996
Rock	419	868
Oldies	659	725

Source: M Street Corporation, Nashville, TN

Computers & the Internet

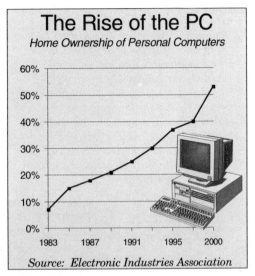

The Rise of the PC
Home Ownership of Personal Computers

Source: *Electronic Industries Association*

Pushing Buttons
Households with Various Electronics

Device	House-holds	Device	House-holds
Television	98%	Computer Printer	38%
Radio	98%	Cellular Phone	34%
Telephone	93%	Pager	28%
Cordless Phone	66%	Car Alarm	27%
Answering Machine	65%	Camcorder	26%
Stereo System	54%	PC & CD-ROM	21%
Home CD Player	49%	Modem	19%
Personal Computer	40%	Caller-ID Equip.	18%

Source: Consumer Electronics Mfg. Association, 1996

Confusing Terms Made Simple

The **Internet** is a worldwide collection of networks which transfer information from computer to computer via telephone and high speed data lines. This 'network of networks' has been called the *Information Superhighway.*

Using the Internet you can find, view, and print information and graphics from **web sites,** which are groups of related documents written in HyperText Markup Language (**HTML**). Think of web sites as interesting places you can visit when you travel on the information superhighway.

The vast, ever-growing set of web sites is refered to as the **World Wide Web**. This name is appropriate, as a seemingly unlimited number of **hyperlinks** enable the user to jump from one web site to another.

To get on the Internet, you need a **server** (an on ramp to the information superhighway). A server is a service vendor providing a software program that lets your computer read the HTML files that make up web sites, and use the hyperlinks that allow you to move from site to site. These servers are also responsible for maintaining high speed communication lines for their customers' use. For this they charge a fee.

The program by which you access the Internet is the **browser**. (Think of a browser as the vehicle which carries you up the on ramp and onto the highway.) In some cases this is loaded onto your computer as part of the software provided by your server. In other cases, it resides with the server, and is made available for your use each time you need it.

Internet Services
Descriptions of Commonly Used Internet Services

Service	Description
E-mail	Direct communication between two individuals via computer is called electronic mail, or e-mail. You must use the exact address for the person you wish to reach. E-mail addresses have three parts: a name, a service, and a domain. For example, to reach the president of the United States, type *president@whitehouse.gov* *President* is the name, *whitehouse* is the server, and *gov* is the domain. Other common domains are *com,* for businesses, *ed,* for educational institutions, and *org,* for other organizations.
FAQs	Frequently asked questions files have answers to many questions of internet beginners.
FTP	File transfer protocol is a method of transferring files to your computer from specific sites, usually servers on the Internet.
Search Engines	Often provided by your server, search engines allow you to search for a specific web site when you don't know its address. Simply type in a topic, or several key words that would be found on the site you are looking for. Use the help menu to learn how to refine your searches.
Newsgroups	Newsgroups are typically devoted to specific topics. You can read the information available, or post your own information or questions.
The World Wide Web	Begun as a method for scientists in Switzerland to share information, the world wide web has evolved into a varied collection of graphics, audio, text, animation and video files. You can access these files, called web sites, if you know their exact name (web addresses begin with *http//:www.*), or by using a search engine.

Music

Making Beautiful Music
The Musical Instruments Americans Play

- Clarinet 4%
- Trumpet 3%
- Violin 3%
- Keyboard 4%
- Saxophone 4%
- Organ 4%
- Flute 6%
- Drums 7%
- Piano 39%
- Guitar 26%

Source: National Assoc. of Music Merchants

Dabbling in the Arts
Percent Engaged in at Least Once During the Year

	Total	Male	Female
Needlework	25	5	43
Buying Art Work	22	22	22
Photography	12	13	10
Painting	10	9	10
Pottery Work	8	8	9
Modern Dancing	8	8	8
Creative Writing	7	7	8
Playing Classical Music	4	3	5

Source: U.S. National Endowment for the Arts

Top Selling U.S. Albums

1. Thriller, M. Jackson
2. Greatest Hits, Eagles
3. Rumours, Fleetwood Mac
4. Led Zepplin IV
5. Boston, Boston
6. The Bodyguard, Whitney Houston
7. Born in the USA, Bruce Springsteen
8. Jagged Little Pill, Alanis Morrissette
9. Cracked Rear View, Hootie & the Blowfish
10. Hotel California, Eagles

Source: Recording Ind. of Am.

Top Grossing Concert Tours

1. Rolling Stones, 94
2. Pink Floyd, 94
3. Rolling Stones, 89
4. The Eagles, 94
5. New Kids on the Block, 90
6. U2, 92
7. The Eagles, 95
8. Barbara Streisand, 94
9. Grateful Dead, 94
10. Elton John/Billy Joel, 94

Source: Pollstar

Top Selling Classical Albums in U.S.

1. *Tchaikovsky: Piano Concerto No.1.,* Van Cliburn
2. *The Three Tenors Concert,* Carreras, Domingo, Pavarotti
3. *Fantasia,* Philadelphia Orchestra
4. *Perhaps Love,* Placido Domingo
5. *Tchaikovsky: 1812 Overture / Capriccio Italien,* Minneapolis Symphony Orchestra
6. *Strauss Waltzes,* Mantovani
7. *Switched-On Bach,* Walter Carlos
8. *2001: A Space Odyssey,* Berlin Phil. Orchestra
9. *O Sole Mio,* Pavarotti
10. *Rachmininoff: Piano Concerto No. 3,* Van Cliburn

Source: Recording Industry of America

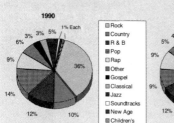

The Music We Buy
Music Purchases, 1990 - 1996

1990

1% Each
5%
3%
3%
6%
9%
14%
12%
10%
36%

Legend:
- Rock
- Country
- R & B
- Pop
- Rap
- Other
- Gospel
- Classical
- Jazz
- Soundtracks
- New Age
- Children's

1996

1% Each
3%
4%
3%
5%
9%
9%
12%
15%
33%

Source: Recording Industry Association of America, Inc., Washington, DC

Rock music leads sales, but country is growing fast.

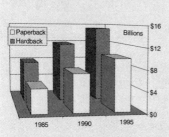

Book Buying
Consumer Expenditures for Books

- □ Paperback
- ■ Hardback

Billions

$16
$12
$8
$4
$0

1985   1990   1995

Americans bought 2.2 billion books in 1995, up from 1.8 billion in 1985.

Source: Book Industry Study Group, Inc.

Reading

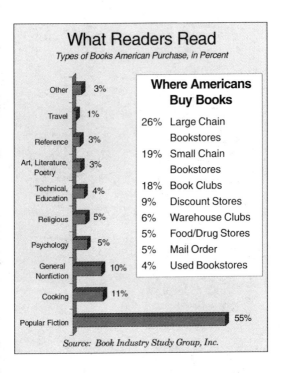

What Readers Read

Types of Books American Purchase, in Percent

- Other — 3%
- Travel — 1%
- Reference — 3%
- Art, Literature, Poetry — 3%
- Technical, Education — 4%
- Religious — 5%
- Psychology — 5%
- General Nonfiction — 10%
- Cooking — 11%
- Popular Fiction — 55%

Where Americans Buy Books

26%	Large Chain Bookstores
19%	Small Chain Bookstores
18%	Book Clubs
9%	Discount Stores
6%	Warehouse Clubs
5%	Food/Drug Stores
5%	Mail Order
4%	Used Bookstores

Source: Book Industry Study Group, Inc.

28% of Americans say reading is their favorite leisure time activity.
Source: Louis Harris & Associates

U.S. Daily Newspapers with Largest Circulation

1. Wall Street Journal
2. USA Today
3. New York Times
4. Los Angeles Times
5. Washington Post
6. New York Daily News
7. Chicago Tribune
8. Long Island Newsday
9. Houston Chronicle
10. Chicago Sun-Times

Source: Editor and Publisher

In the 1920s, there were more than 2,000 daily newspapers in the U.S., with a circulation totaling 27.8 million. In 1996, there were fewer dailies (1,520), but nearly 57 million readers.

U.S. Sunday Newspapers with Largest Circulation

1. New York Times
2. Los Angeles Times
3. Washington Post
4. Chicago Tribune
5. New York Daily News
6. Philadelphia Inquirer
7. Detroit Free Press and News
8. Dallas Morning News
9. Boston Sunday Globe
10. Houston Chronicle

Source: Editor and Publisher, 1997

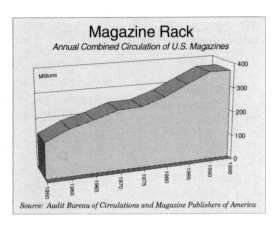

Magazine Rack

Annual Combined Circulation of U.S. Magazines

Millions

Source: Audit Bureau of Circulations and Magazine Publishers of America

Top 10 Magazines, by Ad Revenue	**Top 10 Magazines, by Paid Circulation**
1. People	1. NRTA/AARP Bulletin
2. Sports Illustrated	2. Modern Maturity
3. Time	3. Reader's Digest
4. TV Guide	4. TV Guide
5. Newsweek	5. National Geographic
6. Better Homes & Gardens	6. Better Homes & Gardens
7. PC Magazine	7. Family Circle
8. Business Week	8. Good Housekeeping
9. U.S. News & World Report	9. Ladies' Home Jrnl.
10. Forbes	10. Woman's Day
Source: Publishers Information Bureau	*Source: Audit Bureau of Circulations*

Performing Arts

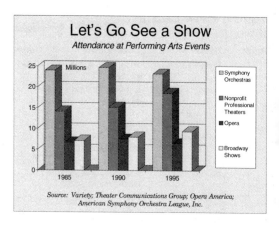

Let's Go See a Show
Attendance at Performing Arts Events

Millions

Symphony Orchestras

Nonprofit Professional Theaters

Opera

Broadway Shows

1985   1990   1995

Source: Variety; Theater Communications Group; Opera America; American Symphony Orchestra League, Inc.

Longest Running Broadway Plays

1. Cats
2. A Chorus Line
3. Oh Calcutta
4. Les Miserables
5. Phantom of the Opera
6. 42nd Street
7. Grease
8. Fiddler on the Roof
9. Life with Father
10. Tobacco Road

Source: League of American Theaters and Producers

Broadway ticket prices have climbed from $10.76 for a straight play and $13.76 for a musical in 1975 to $54.72 and $69.16, respectively, in 1996.

Games

Winning at Five Card Draw
Winning Poker Hands

Rank	Hand	Description	Odds
1.	Royal Flush	10, J, Q, K, A, all of same suit	1:649,739
2.	Straight Flush	5 in sequence, all of same suit	1:64,973
3.	Four of a Kind	4 of same value, 1 extra	1:4,164
4.	Full House	3 cards of one value, 2 of another	1:693
5.	Flush	5 of same suit	1:506
6.	Straight	5 in sequence, different suits	1:254
7.	Three of a Kind	3 of same value, 2 extra	1:46
8.	Two Pair	2 pairs of same value, 1 extra	1:20
9.	One Pair	2 of same value, 3 extra	1:1.37
10.	High Card	high card in hand with no combination	1:1

Most Landed on Monopolies in Monopoly

1.	Railroads	Short Line, Penn, B & O, Reading
2.	Oranges	Tennessee, St. James, New York
3.	Reds	Kentucky, Illinois, Indiana,
4.	Yellows	Atlantic, Marvin Gardens, Ventnor
5.	Greens	Pennsylvania, Pacific, N. Carolina
6.	Lt. Purples	States, St. Charles, Virginia
7.	Lt. Blues	Connecticut, Oriental, Vermont
8.	Utilities	Water Works, Electric Co.
9.	Dk. Blues	Park Place, Boardwalk
10.	Dk. Purples	Baltic, Mediterranean

Two-Letter Scrabble® Words

aa	ef	la	ox
ad	eh	li	oy
ae	el	lo	pa
ag	em	ma	pe
ah	en	me	pi
ai	er	mi	re
al	es	mm	sh
am	et	mo	si
an	ex	mu	so
ar	fa	my	ta
as	go	na	ti
at	ha	ne	to
aw	he	no	uh
ax	hi	nu	um
ay	hm	od	un
ba	ho	oe	up
be	id	of	us
bi	if	oh	ut
bo	in	om	we
by	is	on	wo
da	it	op	xi
de	jo	or	xu
do	ka	os	ya
		ow	ye

Leisure Activities & Sports

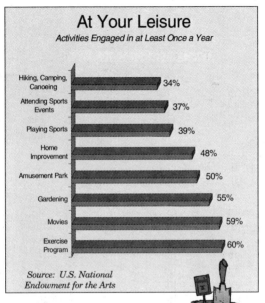

At Your Leisure
Activities Engaged in at Least Once a Year

- Hiking, Camping, Canoeing — 34%
- Attending Sports Events — 37%
- Playing Sports — 39%
- Home Improvement — 48%
- Amusement Park — 50%
- Gardening — 55%
- Movies — 59%
- Exercise Program — 60%

Source: U.S. National Endowment for the Arts

Getting Our Hands Dirty
Lawn & Garden Activities, in Percent Households

	1991	1993	1995
Lawn Care	62	54	53
Indoor Houseplants	42	31	30
Flower Gardening	41	39	38
Vegetable Gardening	31	26	28
Herb Gardening	9	8	8

Source: U.S. National Endowment for the Arts

Top Amusement Parks, by Attendance

1. Disneyland, CA
2. The Magic Kingdom at Walt Disney World, FL
3. Epcot at Walt Disney World, FL
4. Disney-MGM Studios at Walt Disney World, FL
5. Universal Studios, FL
6. Universal Studios, CA
7. Sea World, FL
8. Busch Gardens, FL
9. Six Flags, NJ
10. Sea World, CA

Source: Amusement Business

Weekend Warriors
Top 20 Sports Activities

1.	Walking	11.	Golf
2.	Swimming	12.	Aerobics
3.	Bicycling	13.	Running/jogging
4.	Weight Training	14.	Volleyball
5.	Camping	15.	Softball
6.	Bowling	16.	Hunting
7.	Fishing	17.	Baseball
8.	Billiards	18.	Tennis
9.	Basketball	19.	Touch Football
10.	Hiking	20.	Soccer

Source: National Sporting Goods Assoc., Mt. Prospect, IL

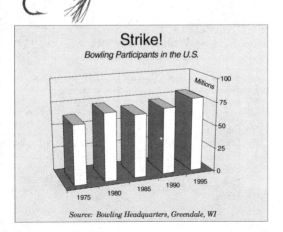

Gone Fishing
Fishing & Hunting Licenses

Millions

40
35
30
25
20
15
10
5
0

1980   1985   1990   1995

☐ Fishing Licenses   ▨ Hunting Licenses

Source: U.S. Fish and Wildlife Service

Strike!
Bowling Participants in the U.S.

Millions

100
75
50
25
0

1975   1980   1985   1990   1995

Source: Bowling Headquarters, Greendale, WI

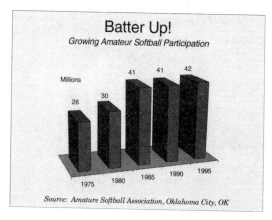

Batter Up!
Growing Amateur Softball Participation

Millions

26 — 1975
30 — 1980
41 — 1985
41 — 1990
42 — 1995

Source: Amature Softball Association, Oklahoma City, OK

It's a Team Sport
Amateur Softball Teams, in Thousands

	1975	1980	1985	1990	1995
Adult Teams	66	110	152	188	187
Youth Teams	9	18	31	46	74

Source: Amateur Softball Association, Oklahoma City, OK

A softball's core is made of a mixture of cork or rubber, a long fiber kapok, or polyurethane. This is wrapped with fine quality yarn and covered with real or synthetic cowhide.
Source: The Worth Book of Softball

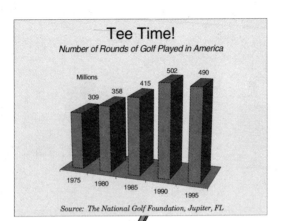

Tee Time!
Number of Rounds of Golf Played in America

Millions

309	358	415	502	490
1975	1980	1985	1990	1995

Source: The National Golf Foundation, Jupiter, FL

The number of golfers in America increased from 13 million in 1975 to 25 million in 1995.

Nowhere to Play?
Number and Type of U.S. Golf Facilities

	1975	1980	1985	1990	1995
Total	11,370	12,005	12,346	12,846	14,074
Municipal	1,586	1,794	1,912	2,012	2,259
Private	4,770	4,839	4,861	4,810	4,324
Daily Fee	5,014	5,372	5,573	6,024	7,491

Source: The National Golf Foundation, Jupiter, FL

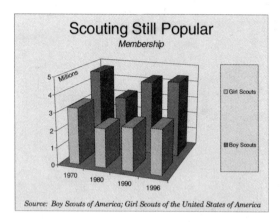

Scouting Still Popular
Membership

Millions

Girl Scouts

Boy Scouts

1970   1980   1990   1996

Source: Boy Scouts of America; Girl Scouts of the United States of America

Scouting Trends
Members, in Thousands

	1975	1980	1985	1990	1995
Boys	3,933	3,207	3,755	4,293	4,399
Adults	1,385	1,110	1,090	1,155	1,230
Girls	2,723	2,250	2,172	2,480	2,584
Adults	511	534	630	788	807

Of the 214 astronauts since 1959, 125 were Boy Scouts in their youth.

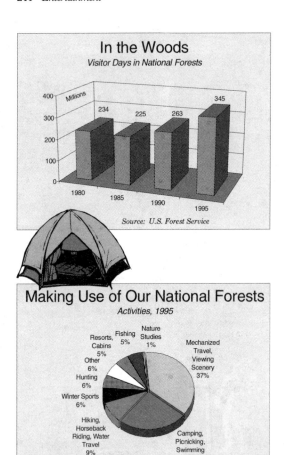

In the Woods
Visitor Days in National Forests

Millions

1980	1985	1990	1995
234	225	263	345

Source: U.S. Forest Service

Making Use of Our National Forests
Activities, 1995

Resorts, Cabins 5%
Fishing 5%
Nature Studies 1%
Other 6%
Hunting 6%
Winter Sports 6%
Hiking, Horseback Riding, Water Travel 9%
Mechanized Travel, Viewing Scenery 37%
Camping, Picnicking, Swimming 25%

Source: U.S. Forest Service

*U.S. national parks
average 264 million
visits a year.*

Most Visited National Parks

1. Great Smokey Mountains National Park
2. Grand Canyon National Park
3. Yosemite National Park
4. Olympic National Park
5. Yellowstone National Park
6. Rocky Mountain National Park
7. Acadia National Park
8. Grand Teton National Park
9. Zion National Park
10. Mammoth Cave National Park

Source: National Park Service

Best-Kept Secrets:
National Parks That Aren't Crowded

1. Cumberland Island Nat. Seashore, GA
2. Voyageurs National Park, MN
3. Grant-Kohrs Ranch Nat. Historic Site, MT
4. Great Basin National Park, NV
5. North Cascades National Park, WA
6. Channel Islands National Park, CA
7. Lassen Volcanic National Park, CA
8. Aniakchak Nat. Mon. and Preserve, AK

Source: National Park Service

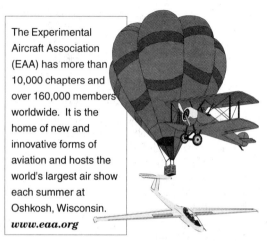

The Experimental Aircraft Association (EAA) has more than 10,000 chapters and over 160,000 members worldwide. It is the home of new and innovative forms of aviation and hosts the world's largest air show each summer at Oshkosh, Wisconsin.
www.eaa.org

The Soaring Society of America, founded in 1932, enjoys a membership exceeding 16,000 glider pilots. Some fly for recreation, while others compete in international contests.
www.ssa.org

Into the Wild Blue Yonder
Number of U.S. Pilots, in Thousands

Year	Student	Private	Com-mercial	Airline	% Women
1970	196	304	187	34	4.0
1980	200	357	183	70	6.4
1985	147	311	152	83	6.1
1990	128	299	149	108	5.8
1995	101	261	134	124	6.0

Source: U.S. Federal Aviation Administration
www.faa.gov

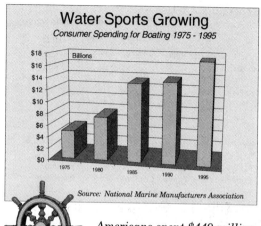

Water Sports Growing
Consumer Spending for Boating 1975 - 1995

Source: National Marine Manufacturers Association

Americans spent $449 million on fishing licenses in 1995, up from $363 million in 1990.
Source: U.S. Fish & Wildlife Service

Boating Growing More Popular
Recreational Boats Owned, in Millions

	1975	1985	1995
Total	9.7	13.8	17.1
Outboard	5.7	7.4	7.8
Inboard	.8	1.4	2.6
Sailboats	.8	1.2	1.4
Canoes	2.4	1.8	2.3
Rowboats, Other	(1)	1.8	3.0

(1) Included in Canoes

Source: National Marine Manufacturers Association

Spectator Sports

Spectators Are Us
Attendance at Professional Sporting Events, in Thousands

	1985	**1990**	**1995**
Major League Baseball	47,742	55,512	51,288
Horseracing	73,346	63,803	42,065[1]
Greyhound Racing	28,853	28,660	28,003[2]
Pro Basketball	11,534	18,586	19,883
National League Football	14,058	17,666	14,772[3]
National Hockey League	11,621	12,344	15,658

[1] *1994*   [2] *1992*   [3] *1993*

Sources: National League of Professional Baseball Clubs; The American League of Professional Baseball Clubs; National Basketball Assoc.; National Football League; Assoc. of Racing Commissioners International

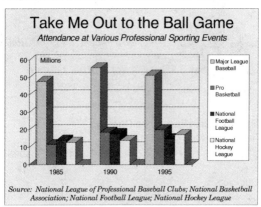

Take Me Out to the Ball Game
Attendance at Various Professional Sporting Events

Source: National League of Professional Baseball Clubs; National Basketball Association; National Football League; National Hockey League

Attendance at NBA basketball games averages 16,060; at NFL football games, the average is 62,352.

11. And the Winner Is . . .

Pulitzer Prizes

Nobel Prizes

Academy Awards

Emmy Awards

Tony Awards

Grammy Awards

Miss America

Pulitzer Prizes

Pulitzer Prizes were established by the will of Joseph Pulitzer, publisher of the New York World. *They have been awarded annually since 1917.*

Pulitzer Prizes in Letters

Pulitzer Winners for Fiction, 1990-1998

Year	Winner	Work
1990	Oscar Hijuelos	*The Mambo Kings Play Songs of Love*
1991	John Updike	*Rabbit at Rest*
1992	Jane Smiley	*A Thousand Acres*
1993	Robert Olen Butler	*A Good Scent From a Strange Mountain*
1994	E. Annie Proulx	*The Shipping News*
1995	Carol Shields	*The Stone Diaries*
1996	Richard Ford	*Independence Day*
1997	Steven Millhauser	*Martin Dresser: The Tale of an American Dreamer*
1998	Phillip Roth	*American Pastoral*

Pulitzer Winners for General Nonfiction, 1990-1998

Year	Winner	Work
1990	Dale Maharidge and Michael Williamson	*And Their Children After Them*
1991	Bert Holldobler and Edward O. Wilson	*The Ants*
1992	Daniel Yergin	*The Prize: The Epic Quest for Oil*
1993	Garry Wills	*Lincoln at Gettysburg*
1994	David Remnick	*Lenin's Tomb: The Last Days of the Soviet Empire*

Pulitzer Winners for General Nonfiction, Continued

Year	Winner	Work
1995	Jonathan Weiner	*The Beak of the Finch: A Story of Evolution in Our Time*
1996	Tina Rosenberg	*The Haunted Land: Facing Europe's Ghosts After Communism*
1997	Richard Kluger	*Ashes to Ashes: America's Hundred Year Cigarette War*
1998	Jared Diamond	*Guns, Germs and Steel: The Fates of Human Societies*

Pulitzer Winners for History, 1990-1998

Year	Winner	Work
1990	Stanley Karnow	*In Our Image: America's Empire in the Philippines*
1991	Laurel Thatcher Ulrich	*A Midwife's Tale: The Life of Martha Ballard*
1992	Mark E. Neely Jr.	*The Fate of Liberty: Abraham Lincoln and Civil Liberties*
1993	Gordon S. Wood	*The Radicalism of the American Revolution*
1995	Doris Kearns Goodwin	*No Ordinary Time: Franklin and Eleanor Roosevelt: The Home Front in World War II*
1996	Alan Taylor	*William Cooper's Town: Power and Persuasion on the Frontier of the Early American Republic*
1997	Jack N. Rakove	*Original Meanings: The Making of the Constitution*
1998	Edward J. Larson	*Summer for the Gods: The Scopes Trial and America's Continuing Debate Over Science and Religion*

Pulitzer Prizes in Letters, Continued
Pulitzer Winners for American Poetry, 1990-1998

Year	Winner	Work
1990	Charles Simic	*The World Doesn't End*
1991	Mona Van Duyn	*Near Changes*
1992	James Tate	*Selected Poems*
1993	Louise Glück	*The Wild Iris*
1994	Yusef Komunyakaa	*Neon Vernacular*
1995	Philip Levine	*The Simple Truth*
1996	Jorie Graham	*The Dream of the Unified Field*
1997	Lisel Mueller	*Alive and Together*
1998	Charles Wright	*Black Zodiac*

Pulitzer Winners for Biography or Autobiography, 1990-1998

Year	Winner	Work
1990	Sebastian de Grazia	*Machiavelli in Hell*
1991	Steven Naifeh and Gregory White Smith	*Jackson Pollock: An American Saga*
1992	Lewis B. Puller Jr.	*Fortunate Son: The Healing of a Vietnam Vet*
1993	David McCullough	*Truman*
1994	David Levering Lewis	*W.E.B. DuBois: Biography of a Race, 1868-1919*
1995	Joan D. Hedrick	*Harriet Beecher Stowe: A Life*
1996	Jack Miles	*God: A Biography*
1997	Frank McCourt	*Angela's Ashes: A Memoir*
1998	Katherine Graham	*Personal History*

Pulitzer Winners for Drama, 1990-1998

Year	Winner	Work
1990	August Wilson	*The Piano Lesson*
1991	Neil Simon	*Lost in Yonkers*
1992	Robert Schenkkan	*The Kentucky Cycle*
1993	Tony Kushner	*Angels in America: Millennium Approaches*
1994	Edward Albee	*Three Tall Women*
1995	Horton Foote	*The Young Man From Atlanta*
1996	Jonathan Larson	*Rent*
1998	Paula Vogel	*How I Learned to Drive*

Pulitzer Prizes in Music

Pulitzer Winners for Music, 1990-1998

Year	Winner	Work
1990	Mel Powell	*Duplicates: A Concerto for Two Pianos and Orchestra*
1991	Shulamit Ran	*Symphony*
1992	Wayne Peterson	*The Face of the Night, The Heart of the Dark*
1993	Christopher Rouse	*Trombone Concerto*
1994	Gunther Schuller	*Of Reminiscences and Reflections*
1995	Morton Gould	*Stringmusic*
1996	George Walker	*Lilacs*
1997	Wynton Marsalis	*Blood on the Fields*
1998	Aaron Jay Kernis	*String Quartet No.2, Musica Instrumentalis*

Pulitzer Prizes in Journalism

Pulitzer Winners for National Reporting, 1990-1998

Year	Winner	Newspaper
1990	Ross Anderson	
	Bill Dietrich	
	Mary Ann Gwinn	
	Eric Nalder	Seattle Times
1991	Marjie Lundstrom	
	Rochelle Sharpe	Gannett News Service
1992	Jeff Taylor	
	Mike McGraw	Kansas City Star
1993	David Maraniss	Washington Post
1994	Eileen Welsome	Albuquerque Tribune
1995	Tony Horwitz	Wall Street Journal
1996	Alix M. Freedman	Wall Street Journal
1997	Staff	Wall Street Journal
1998	Russell Carollo	Dayton Daily News
	Jeff Nesmith	

Pulitzer Winners for International Reporting, 1990-1998

Year	Winner	Newspaper
1989	Glenn Frankel	Washington Post
	Bill Keller	New York Times
1990	Nicholas D. Kirstof	
	Sheryl WuDunn	New York Times
1991	Caryle Murphy	Washington Post
	Serge Schmemann	New York Times
1992	Patrick J. Sloyan	Newsday (NY)
1993	John F. Burns	New York Times
	Roy Gutman	Newsday (NY)
1994	Staff	Dallas Morning News
1995	Mark Fritz	AP
1996	David Rohde	Christian Science Monitor
1997	Brooks Atkinson	New York Times
1998	Staff	New York Times

Pulitzer Winners for Beat Reporting, 1990-1998

Year	Winner	Newspaper
1991	Natalie Angier	New York Times
1992	Deborah Blum	Sacramento Bee
1993	Paul Ingrassia	
	Joseph B. White	Wall Street Journal
1994	Eric Freedman	
	Jim Mitzelfeld	Detroit News
1995	David Shribman	Boston Globe
1996	Bob Keeler	Newsday (Long Island, NY)
1997	Byron Acohido	Seattle Times
1998	Linda Greenhouse	New York Times

Pulitzer Winners for Feature Writing, 1990-1998

Year	Winner	Newspaper
1990	Dave Curtin	CO. Spr. Gazette Telegraph
1991	Sheryl James	St. Petersburg Times
1992	Howell Raines	New York Times
1993	George Lardner Jr.	Washington Post
1994	Isabel Wilkerson	New York Times
1995	Ron Suskind	Wall Street Journal
1996	Rick Bragg	New York Times
1997	Lisa Pollack	Baltimore Sun
1998	Thomas French	St. Petersburg Times

Pulitzer Winners for Feature Photography, 1990-1998

Year	Winner	Newspaper
1990	David C. Turnley	Detroit Free Press
1991	William Snyder	Dallas Morning News
1992	John Kaplan	Block Newspapers, Toledo, OH
1993	Associated Press staff	
1994	Kevin Carter	New York Times
1995	Associated Press staff	
1996	Stephanie Welsh	Newhouse News Service
1997	A. Zemlianichenko	AP
1998	Clarence Williams	Los Angeles Times

Pulitzer Prizes in Journalism, Continued

Pulitzer Winners for Editorial Writing, 1990-1998

Year	Winner	Newspaper
1990	Thomas J. Hylton	Pottstown (PA) Mercury
1991	Ron Casey, Harold Jackson, Joey Kennedy	Birmingham (AL) News
1992	Maria Henson	Lexington (KY) Herald-Leader
1993	No award	
1994	R. Bruce Dold	Chicago Tribune
1995	Jeffrey Good	St. Petersburg (FL) Times
1996	Robert B. Semple Jr.	New York Times
1997	Michael Gartner	Ames (IA) Daily Tribune
1998	Bernard L. Stein	Riverdale (NY) Press

Pulitzer Winners for Editorial Cartooning, 1990-1998

Year	Winner	Newspaper
1990	Tom Toles	Buffalo News
1991	Jim Borgman	Cincinnati Enquirer
1992	Signe Wilkinson	Philadelphia Daily News
1993	Stephen R. Benson	Arizona Republic
1994	Michael P. Ramirez	Commercial Appeal, Memphis, TN
1995	Mike Luckovich	Atlanta Constitution
1996	Jim Morin	Miami Herald
1997	Walt Handelsman	New Orleans Times-Picayune
1998	Stephen P. Breen	Asbury Park Press, (Neptune NJ)

www.pulitzer.org

Nobel Prizes

Nobel Prize Winners
Nobel Winners for Peace, 1990-1997

Year	Winner	Nationality
1990	Mikhail S. Gorbachev	USSR
1991	Aung San Suu Kyi	Myanmarese
1992	Rigoberta Menchú	Guatemalan
1993	Frederik W. de Klerk	South African
	Nelson Mandela	South African
1994	Yasir Arafat	Palestinian
	Shimon Peres	Israeli
	Yitzhak Rabin	Israeli
1995	Joseph Rotblat	Polish-British
1996	Bishop Carlos Ximenes Belo	Timorese
	José Ramos-Horta	Timorese
1997	International Campaign to Ban Landmines	
	Jody Williams	U.S.

Nobel Winners for Economic Science, 1990-1997

Year	Winner	Nationality
1990	Harry M. Markowitz	U.S.
	William F. Sharpe	U.S.
	Merton H. Miller	U.S.
1991	Ronald H. Coase	British-U.S.
1992	Gary S. Becker	U.S.
1993	Robert W. Fogel	U.S.
	Douglass C. North	U.S.
1994	John C. Harsanyi	U.S.
	John F. Nash	U.S.
1995	Robert E. Lucas Jr.	U.S.
1996	James A. Mirrlees	British
	William Vickrey	Canadian-U.S.
1997	Robert C. Merton	U.S.
	Myron S. Scholes	Canadian-U.S.

Nobel Winners for Literature, 1990-1997

Year	Winner	Nationality
1990	Octavio Paz	Mexican
1991	Nadine Gordimer	South African
1993	Toni Morrison	U.S.
	Derek Walcott	West Indian
1994	Kenzaburo Oe	Japanese
1995	Seamus Heaney	Irish
1996	Wislawa Szymborska	Polish
1997	Dario Fo	Italian

Nobel Winners for Physics, 1990-1997

Year	Winner	Nationality
1990	Richard E. Taylor	Canadian
	Jerome I. Friedman	U.S.
	Henry W. Kendall	U.S.
1991	Pierre-Giles de Gennes	French
1992	Georges Charpak	Polish-French
1993	Joseph H. Taylor	U.S.
	Russell A. Hulse	U.S.
1994	Bertram N. Brockhouse	Canadian
	Clifford G. Shull	U.S.
1995	Martin Perl	U.S.
	Frederick Reines	U.S.
1996	David M. Lee	U.S.
	Douglas D. Osheroff	U.S.
	Robert C. Richardson	U.S.
1997	Steven Chu	U.S.
	William D. Phillips	U.S.
	Claude Cohen-Tannoudji	Algerian-French

www.nobel.se

1997 Nobel Prize winners were awarded a gold medal and approximately $1 million.

Nobel Winners for Physiology or Medicine, 1990-1997

Year	Winner	Nationality
1990	Joseph E. Murray	U.S.
	E. Donnall Thomas	U.S.
1991	Edwin Neher	German
	Bert Sakmann	German
1992	Edmond H. Fisher	U.S.
	Edwin G. Krebs	U.S.
1993	Phillip A. Sharp	U.S.
	Richard J. Roberts	British
1994	Alfred G. Gilman	U.S.
	Martin Rodbell	U.S.
1995	Edward B. Lewis	U.S.
	Eric F. Wieschaus	U.S.
	Christiane Nuesslein-Volhard	German
1996	Peter C. Doherty	Australian
	Rolf M. Zinkernagel	Swiss
1997	Stanley B. Prusiner	U.S.

Nobel Winners for Chemistry, 1990-1997

Year	Winner	Nationality
1990	Elias James Corey	U.S.
1991	Richard R. Ernst	Swiss
1992	Rudolph A. Marcus	Canadian-U.S.
1993	Kary B. Mullis	U.S.
	Michael Smith	British-Canadian
1994	George A. Olah	U.S.
1995	Paul Crutzen	Dutch
	Mario Molina	Mexican-U.S.
	Sherwood Rowland	U.S.
1996	Harold W. Kroto	British
	Robert F. Curl Jr.	U.S.
	Richard E. Smalley	U.S.
1997	Paul D. Boyer	U.S.
	John E. Walker	British
	Jens S. Skou	Danish

Academy Awards

Taking Home an Oscar

Academy Awards for Best Picture and Best Director

	Best Picture	**Best Director**
1990	*Dances With Wolves*	Kevin Costner, *Dances With Wolves*
1991	*The Silence of the Lambs*	Jonathan Demme, *The Silence of the Lambs*
1992	*Unforgiven*	Clint Eastwood, *Unforgiven*
1993	*Schindler's List*	Steven Spielberg, *Schindler's List*
1994	*Forrest Gump*	Robert Zemeckis, *Forrest Gump*
1995	*Braveheart*	Mel Gibson, *Braveheart*
1996	*The English Patient*	Anthony Minghella, *The English Patient*
1997	*Titanic*	James Cameron, *Titanic*

Academy Awards for Acting in a Leading Role

	Best Actor	**Best Actress**
1990	Jeremy Irons, *Reversal of Fortune*	Kathy Bates, *Misery*
1991	Anthony Hopkins, *The Silence of the Lambs*	Jodie Foster, *The Silence of the Lambs*
1992	Al Pacino, *Scent of a Woman*	Emma Thompson, *Howards End*
1993	Tom Hanks, *Philadelphia*	Holly Hunter, *The Piano*
1994	Tom Hanks, *Forrest Gump*	Jessica Lange, *Blue Sky*
1995	Nicolas Cage, *Leaving Las Vegas*	Susan Sarandon, *Dead Man Walking*
1996	Geoffrey Rush, *Shine*	Frances McDormand, *Fargo*
1997	Jack Nicholson, *As Good As It Gets*	Helen Hunt, *As Good As It Gets*

Academy Awards for Acting in a Supporting Role

	Best Supporting Actor	**Best Supporting Actress**
1990	Joe Pesci, *Goodfellas*	Whoopi Goldberg, *Ghost*
1991	Jack Palance, *City Slickers*	Mercedes Ruehl, *The Fisher King*
1992	Gene Hackman, *Unforgiven*	Marisa Tomei, *My Cousin Vinny*
1993	Tommy Lee Jones, *The Fugitive*	Anna Paquin, *The Piano*
1994	Martin Landau, *Ed Wood*	Dianne Wiest, *Bullets Over Broadway*
1995	Kevin Spacey, *The Usual Suspects*	Mira Sorvino, *Mighty Aphrodite*
1996	Cuba Gooding Jr., *Jerry Maguire*	Juliette Binochet, *The English Patient*
1997	Robin Williams, *Good Will Hunting*	Kim Basinger, *LA Confidential*

www.oscar.com

Titanic received eleven academy awards in 1997 -- tying the record set by Ben-Hur in 1960.

Emmy Awards

The Best of Prime Time Television

Emmy Awards -- Best Shows

	Drama Series	Comedy Series	Mini Series	TV Movie
94-95	*NYPD Blue*	*Frasier*	*Joseph*	*Indictment: McMartin Trial*
95-96	*E.R.*	*Frasier*	*Gulliver's Travels*	*Truman*
96-97	*Law & Order*	*Frasier*	*Prime Suspect; Errors of Judgement*	*Miss Evers' Boys*

Emmy Awards -- Best Actor

	Drama Series	Comedy Series
94-95	Mandy Patinkin, *Chicago Hope*	Kelsey Grammer, *Frasier*
95-96	Dennis Franz, *NYPD Blue*	John Lithgow *Third Rock From the Sun*
96-97	Dennis Franz, *NYPD Blue*	John Lithgow *Third Rock from the Sun*

Emmy Awards -- Best Actress

	Drama Series	Comedy Series
94-95	Kathy Baker, *Picket Fences*	Candice Bergen, *Murphy Brown*
95-96	Kathy Baker, *Picket Fences*	Helen Hunt, *Mad About You*
96-97	Gillian Anderson, *The X Files*	Hlelen Hunt, *Mad About You*

Source: The Academy of Television Arts and Sciences
www.emmys.org

Tony Awards

Stars of the Stage

Tony Awards -- Best Play & Best Director

	Best Play	Best Director
1995	*Love! Valor! Compassion!,* by Terrence McNally	Gerald Gutierrez, *Heiress*
1996	*Master Class,* by Terrence McNally	Gerald Gutierrez, *A Delicate Balance*
1997	*The Last Night of Ballyhoo,* by Alfred Uhry	Anthony Page, *A Doll's House*
1998	*Art,* by Yasmina Reza	Garry Hynes, *The Beauty Queen of Leenane*

Tony Awards -- Best Actor & Actress in Plays

	Best Actor	Best Actress
1995	Ralph Fiennes, *Hamlet*	Cherry Jones, *The Heiress*
1996	George Grizzard, *A Delicate Balance*	Zoe Caldwell, *Master Class*
1997	Christopher Plummer, *Barrymore*	Janet McTeer, *A Doll's House*
1998	Anthony LaPaglia, *A View from the Bridge*	Marie Mullen *The Beauty Queen of Leenane*

Tony Awards -- Best Musical & Director

	Best Musical	Best Director
1995	*Sunset Boulevard*	Harold Prince, *Show Boat*
1996	*Rent*	George C. Wolfe, *Bring in 'da Noise, Bring in 'da Funk*
1997	*Titanic*	Walter Bobbie, *Chicago*
1998	*The Lion King*	Julie Taymor, *The Lion King*

Tony Awards -- Best Actor & Actress in Musicals

	Best Actor	Best Actress
1995	Mathew Broderick, *How to Succeed in Business Without Really Trying*	Glenn Close, *Sunset Boulevard*
1996	Nathan Lane, *A Funny Thing Happened on the Way to the Forum*	Donna Murphy, *The King and I*
1997	James Naughton, *Chicago*	Bebe Neuwirth, *Chicago*
1998	Alan Cumming, *Cabaret*	Natasha Richardson, *Cabaret*

www.tonys.org

According to the League of American Theaters and Producers, the 1997-1998 season was the best ever for Broadway -- with a total national attendance of 26.8 million and gross ticket sales exceeding $1.3 billion.

Grammy Awards

America's Favorite Music
Grammy Award Winning Records

Year	Artist	Record
1997	Shawn Colvin	Sunny Came Home
1996	Eric Clapton	Change the World
1995	Seal	Kiss From a Rose
1994	Sheryl Crow	All I Wanna Do
1993	Whitney Houston	I Will Always Love You
1992	Eric Clapton	Tears in Heaven
1991	Natalie Cole, with Nat "King" Cole	Unforgettable
1990	Phil Collins	Another Day in Paradise
1989	Bette Midler	Wind Beneath My Wings
1988	Bobby McFerrin	Don't Worry, Be Happy
1987	Paul Simon	Graceland
1986	Steve Winwood	Higher Love
1985	USA for Africa	We Are the World
1984	Tina Turner	What's Love Got to Do With It
1983	Michael Jackson	Beat It
1982	Toto	Rosanna
1981	Kim Carnes	Bette Davis Eyes
1980	Christopher Cross	Sailing
1979	The Doobie Brothers	What a Fool Believes
1978	Billy Joel	Just the Way You Are
1977	Eagles	Hotel California
1976	George Benson	This Masquerade
1975	Captain & Tennille	Love Will Keep Us Together
1974	Olivia Newton-John	I Honestly Love You
1973	Roberta Flack	Killing Me Softly With His Song
1972	Roberta Flack	The First Time Ever I Saw Your Face
1971	Carole King	It's Too Late
1970	Simon & Garfunkel	Bridge Over Troubled Water
1969	5th Dimension	Aquarius/Let the Sunshine In
1968	Simon & Garfunkel	Mrs. Robinson
1967	5th Dimension	Up, Up and Away

Grammy Award Winning Records, Continued

Year	Artist	Record
1966	Frank Sinatra	Strangers in the Night
1965	Herb Alpert	A Taste of Honey
1964	Stan Getz, Astrud Gilberto	The Girl From Ipanema
1963	Henry Mancini	The Days of Wine and Roses
1962	Tony Bennett	I Left My Heart in San Francisco
1961	Henry Mancini	Moon River
1960	Percy Faith	Theme From a Summer Place
1959	Bobby Darin	Mack the Knife
1958	Domenico Modugno	Nel Blu Dipinto Di Blu (Volare)

More Great Music

Grammy Award Winning Albums

Year	Artist	Album
1997	Bob Dylan	Time Out of Mind
1996	Celine Dion	Falling Into You
1995	Allanis Morissette	Jaged Little Pill
1994	Tony Bennett	MTV Unplugged
1993	Whitney Houston	The Bodyguard
1992	Eric Clapton	Unplugged
1991	Natalie Cole, with Nat "King" Cole	Unforgettable
1990	Quincy Jones	Back on the Block
1989	Bonnie Raitt	Nick of Time
1988	George Michael	Faith
1987	U2	The Joshua Tree
1986	Paul Simon	Graceland
1985	Phil Collins	No Jacket Required
1984	Lionel Richie	Can't Slow Down
1983	Michael Jackson	Thriller
1982	Toto	Toto IV
1981	John Lennon, Yoko Ono	Double Fantasy
1980	Christopher Cross	Christopher Cross

Grammy Award Winning Albums, Continued

Year	Artist	Album
1979	Billy Joel	52nd Street
1978	Bee Gees	Saturday Night Fever
1977	Fleetwood Mac	Rumours
1976	Stevie Wonder	Songs in the Key of Life
1975	Paul Simon	Still Crazy After All These Years
1974	Stevie Wonder	Fulfillingness' First Finale
1973	Stevie Wonder	Innervisions
1972	George Harrison & Friends	Concert for Bangla Desh
1971	Carole King	Tapestry
1970	Simon & Garfunkel	Bridge Over Troubled Water
1969	Blood Sweat and Tears	Blood, Sweat and Tears
1968	Glen Campbell	By the Time I Get to Phoenix
1967	The Beatles	Sgt. Pepper's Lonely Hearts Club Band
1966	Frank Sinatra	A Man and His Music
1965	Frank Sinatra	September of My Years
1964	Stan Getz, Astrud Gilberto	Getz/Gilberto
1963	Barbra Streisand	The Barbra Streisand Album
1962	Vaughn Meader	The First Family
1961	Judy Garland	Judy at Carnegie Hall
1960	Bob Newhart	Button Down Mind
1959	Frank Sinatra	Come Dance With Me
1958	Henry Mancini	The Music From Peter Gunn

Source: The Academy of Recording Arts and Sciences
www.grammy.com

In addition to those listed above, Grammys are given in specific categories such as Jazz, Blues, and Country. During the 40th Annual Grammy Awards in February of 1998, a total of 92 awards were presented.

Miss America

Here She Is . . .
Miss America Winners

Year	Winner	Home Town
1998	Kate Schindle	Evanston, Illinois
1997	Tara Dawn Holland	Overland Park, Kansas
1996	Shawntel Smith	Muldrow, Oklahoma
1995	Heather Whitestone	Birmingham, Alabama
1994	Kimberly Aiken	Columbia, South Carolina
1993	Leanza Cornett	Jacksonville, Florida
1992	Carolyn Suzanne Sapp	Honolulu, Hawaii
1991	Marjorie Vincent	Oak Park, Illinois
1990	Debbye Turner	Columbia, Missouri
1989	Gretchen Carlson	Anoka, Minnesota
1988	Kaye Lani Rae Rafko	Monroe, Michigan
1987	Kellye Cash	Memphis, Tennessee
1986	Susan Akin	Meridian, Mississippi
1985	Sharlene Wells	Salt Lake City, Utah
1984	Vanessa Williams [1]	Milwood, New York
	Suzette Charles	Mays Landing, New Jersey
1983	Debra Maffett	Anaheim, California
1982	Elizabeth Ward	Russellville, Arkansas
1981	Susan Powell	Elk City, Oklahoma
1980	Cheryl Prewitt	Ackerman, Mississippi
1979	Kylene Barker	Galax, Virginia
1978	Susan Perkins	Columbus, Ohio
1977	Dorothy K. Benham	Edina, Minnesota
1976	Tawney Elaine Godin	Yonkers, New York
1975	Shirley Cothran	Fort Worth, Texas
1974	Rebecca Ann King	Denver, Colorado
1973	Terry Anne Meeuwsen	DePere, Wisconsin
1972	Laurie Lea Schaefer	Columbus, Ohio
1971	Phyllis Ann George	Denton, Texas
1970	Pamela Anne Eldred	Birmingham, Michigan
1969	Judith Anne Ford	Belvidere, Illinois
1968	Debra Dene Barnes	Moran, Kansas
1967	Jane Anne Jayroe	Laverne, Oklahoma
1966	Deborah Irene Bryant	Overland Park, Kansas
1965	Vonda Kay Van Dyke	Phoenix, Arizona

1 Resigned July 23, 1984

12. Sports

See also 'Entertainment.'

Baseball

Basketball

Bowling

Boxing

Chess

Cycling

Dog Racing

Fishing

Football

Golf

Hockey

Horseracing

Hydroplane
 Racing

Motor Racing

Skating & Skiing

Soccer

Tennis

Track & Field

Wrestling

Yacht Racing

The Big League
Professional Baseball Champions, 1967 - 1997

Year	American League	National League	World Series
1967	Boston	St. Louis	St. Louis
1968	Detroit	St. Louis	Detroit
1969	Baltimore	New York	New York
1970	Baltimore	Cincinnati	Baltimore
1971	Baltimore	Pittsburgh	Pittsburgh
1972	Oakland	Cincinnati	Oakland
1973	Oakland	New York	Oakland
1974	Oakland	Los Angeles	Oakland
1975	Boston	Cincinnati	Cincinnati
1976	New York	Cincinnati	Cincinnati
1977	New York	Los Angeles	New York
1978	New York	Los Angeles	New York
1979	Baltimore	Pittsburgh	Pittsburgh
1980	Kansas City	Philadelphia	Philadelphia
1981	New York	Los Angeles	Los Angeles
1982	Milwaukee	St. Louis	St. Louis
1983	Baltimore	Philadelphia	Baltimore
1984	Detroit	San Diego	Detroit
1985	Kansas City	St. Louis	Kansas City
1986	Boston	New York	New York
1987	Minnesota	St. Louis	Minnesota
1988	Oakland	Los Angeles	Oakland
1989	Oakland	San Francisco	Oakland
1990	Oakland	Cincinnati	Cincinnati
1991	Minnesota	Atlanta	Minnesota
1992	Toronto	Atlanta	Toronto
1993	Toronto	Philadelphia	Toronto
1994			No series
1995	Cleveland	Atlanta	Atlanta
1996	New York	Atlanta	New York
1997	Cleveland	Florida	Florida

Source: Office of the Commissioner of Baseball

Heavy Hitters
Professional Baseball Batting Champions, 1977 - 1997

Year	American League	Team	National League	Team
1987	Boggs	Boston	Gwynn	San Diego
1988	Boggs	Boston	Gwynn	San Diego
1989	Puckett	Minnesota	Gwynn	San Diego
1990	Brett	Kansas City	McGee	St. Louis
1991	Franco	Texas	Pendleton	Atlanta
1992	Martinez	Seattle	Sheffield	San Diego
1993	Olerud	Toronto	Galaraga	Colorado
1994	O'Neill	New York	Gwynn	San Diego
1995	Martinez	Seattle	Gwynn	San Diego
1996	Rodriguez	Seattle	Gwynn	San Diego
1997	Thomas	Chicago	Gwynn	San Diego

Detroit's Tiger Stadium has the longest American League home run distance: 440' to center field. For the National League, it's Coors Field, home of the Rockies, at 415'.

Cy Young Award Winners

American League		National League	
1990	Bob Welch	1990	Doug Drabek
1991	Roger Clemens	1991	Tom Glavine
1992	Dennis Eckersley	1992	Greg Maddux
1993	Jack McDowell	1993	Greg Maddux
1994	David Cone	1994	Greg Maddux
1995	Randy Johnson	1995	Greg Maddux
1996	Pat Hentgen	1996	John Smoltz
1997	Roger Clemens	1997	Pedro Martinez

All-Star Baseball Game Winners

1970	National	1980	National	1989	American
1971	American	1981	National	1990	American
1972	National	1982	National	1991	American
1973	National	1983	American	1992	American
1974	National	1984	National	1993	American
1975	National	1985	National	1994	National
1976	National	1986	American	1995	National
1978	National	1987	National	1996	American
1979	National	1988	American	1997	National

NCAA Baseball Champions

1980	Arizona	1989	Wichita State
1981	Arizona State	1990	Georgia
1982	Miami, FL	1991	LSU
1983	Texas	1992	Pepperdine
1984	Cal. St. Fullerton	1993	LSU
1985	Miami, FL	1994	Oklahoma
1986	Arizona	1995	Cal. St. Fullerton
1987	Stanford	1996	LSU
1988	Stanford	1997	LSU

Little League World Series Winners

1980	Taiwan	1989	Trumbull, CT
1981	Taiwan	1990	Chinese Taipei
1982	Kirkland, WA	1991	Chinese Taipei
1983	Marietta, GA	1992	Long Beach, CA
1984	South Korea	1993	Long Beach, CA
1985	South Korea	1994	Venezuela
1986	Taiwan	1995	Taiwan
1987	Chinese Taipei	1996	Taiwan
1988	Chinese Taipei	1997	Mexico

Hoop Leaders
NBA Champions, 1968 - 1998

Year	Eastern Div.	Western Div.	Champion
1967-68	Boston	Los Angeles	Boston
1968-69	Boston	Los Angeles	Boston
1969-70	New York	Los Angeles	New York
1970-71	Baltimore	Milwaukee	Milwaukee
1971-72	New York	Los Angeles	Los Angeles
1972-73	New York	Los Angeles	New York
1973-74	Boston	Milwaukee	Boston
1974-75	Washington	Golden State	Golden State
1975-76	Boston	Phoenix	Boston
1976-77	Philadelphia	Portland	Portland
1977-78	Washington	Seattle	Washington
1978-79	Washington	Seattle	Seattle
1979-80	Los Angeles	Philadelphia	Los Angeles
1980-81	Boston	Houston	Boston
1981-82	Philadelphia	Los Angeles	Los Angeles
1982-83	Philadelphia	Los Angeles	Philadelphia
1983-84	Boston	Los Angeles	Boston
1984-85	Boston	L.A. Lakers	Los Angeles
1985-86	Boston	Houston	Boston
1986-87	Boston	Los Angeles	Los Angeles
1987-88	Detroit	Los Angeles	Los Angeles
1988-89	Detroit	Los Angeles	Detroit
1989-90	Detroit	Portland	Detroit
1990-91	Chicago	Los Angeles	Chicago
1991-92	Chicago	Portland	Chicago
1992-93	Chicago	Phoenix	Chicago
1993-94	New York	Houston	Houston
1994-95	Orlando	Houston	Houston
1995-96	Chicago	Seattle	Chicago
1996-97	Chicago	Utah	Chicago
1997-98	Chicago	Utah	Chicago

Source: National Basketball Association
www.nba.com

NBA Scoring Champions
Points Scored, Average

1987	Michael Jordan	3,041	37.1
1988	Michael Jordan	2,868	35.0
1989	Michael Jordan	2,633	32.5
1990	Michael Jordan	2,753	33.6
1991	Michael Jordan	2,580	31.5
1992	Michael Jordan	2,404	30.1
1993	Michael Jordan	2,541	32.6
1994	David Robinson	2,383	29.8
1995	Shaquille O'Neal	2,315	29.3
1996	Michael Jordan	2,465	30.4
1997	Michael Jordan	2,431	29.6
1998	Michael Jordan	2,357	28.7

The average salary for NBA players increased from $130,000 in 1977 to $2.3 million in 1997.

The Best of the Best
NBA Most Valuable Player & Rookie of the Year Winners

Year	MVP/Team	Rookie/Team
1986	Larry Bird, Boston	Patrick Ewing, New York
1987	Magic Johnson, Chicago	Chuck Person, Indiana
1988	Michael Jordan, Chicago	Mark Jackson, New York
1989	Magic Johnson, Los Angeles	Mitch Richmond, Golden St.
1990	Magic Johnson, Los Angeles	David Robinson, San Antonio
1991	Michael Jordan, Chicago	Derrick Coleman, N. Jersey
1992	Michael Jordan, Chicago	Larry Johnson, Charoltte
1993	Charles Barkley, Phoenix	Shaquille O'Neal, Orlando
1994	Hakeem Olajuwon, Houston	Chris Webber, Golden State
1995	David Robinson, San Antonio	Grant Hill, Detroit
		Jason Kidd, Dallas
1996	Michael Jordan, Chicago	Damon Stoudamire, Toronto
1997	Karl Malone, Utah	Alan Iverson, Philadelphia
1998	Michael Jordan, Chicago	Tim Duncan, San Antonio

NCAA Division 1 Mens' Basketball Champs

1981	Indiana	1990	UNLV
1982	North Carolina	1991	Duke
1983	North Carolina St.	1992	Duke
1984	Georgetown	1993	North Carolina
1985	Villanova	1994	Arkansas
1986	Louisville	1995	UCLA
1987	Indiana	1996	Kentucky
1988	Kansas	1997	Arizona
1989	Michigan	1998	Kentucky

National Invitation Tournament Winners

1981	Tulsa	1990	Vanderbilt
1982	Bradley	1991	Stanford
1983	Fresno State	1992	Virginia
1984	Michigan	1993	Minnesota
1985	UCLA	1994	Villanova
1986	Ohio State	1995	Virginia Tech
1987	S. Mississippi	1996	Nebraska
1988	Connecticut	1997	Michigan
1989	St. John's	1998	Minnesota

NCAA Division 1 Women's Basketball Champs

1983	USC	1991	Tennessee
1984	USC	1992	Stanford
1985	Old Dominion	1993	Texas Tech
1986	Texas	1994	North Carolina
1987	Tennessee	1995	Connecticut
1988	Louisiana Tech	1996	Tennessee
1989	Tennessee	1997	Tennessee
1990	Stanford	1998	Tennessee

Bowlers Bring Home the Bucks

PBA Leading Money Winners

Year	Top Money Winner	Winnings
1990	Amleto Monacelli	$204,775
1991	David Ozio	$225,585
1992	Marc McDowell	$174,215
1993	Walter Ray Williams, Jr.	$296,370
1994	Norm Duke	$273,753
1995	Mike Aulby	$219,792
1996	Walter Ray Williams, Jr.	$241,330
1997	Walter Ray Williams, Jr.	$211,544

American Bowling Congress Masters Tournament Winners		Tournament of Champions Winners	
1982	Joe Berardi	1982	Mike Durbin
1983	Mike Lastowski	1983	Joe Berardi
1984	Earl Anthony	1984	Mike Durbin
1985	Steve Wunderlich	1985	Mark Williams
1986	Mark Fahy	1986	Marshall Holman
1987	Rick Steelsmith	1987	Pete Weber
1988	Del Ballard, Jr.	1988	Mark Williams
1989	Mike Aulby	1989	Del Ballard, Jr.
1990	Chris Warren	1990	Dave Ferraro
1991	Doug Kent	1991	David Ozio
1992	Ken Johnson	1992	Marc McDowell
1993	Norm Duke	1993	George Branham
1994	Steve Fehr	1994	Norm Duke
1995	Mike Aulby	1995	Mike Aulby
1996	Ernie Schlegel	1996	Dave D'Entremont
1997	Jason Queen	1997	John Gant

Source: Professional Bowlers Association
www.pbatour.com

Heavyweight Champions of the World
Heavyweight Boxing Champions

Year	Champion	Title
1990	James Douglas	WBA, WBC, IBF
	Evander Holyfield	WBA, WBC, IBF
1992	Riddick Bowe	WBA, IBF, WBC
	Lennox Lewis	WBC
1993-1994	Evander Holyfield	WBA, IBF
1994	Michael Moorer	WBA, IBF
	Oliver McCall	WBC
	George Foreman	WBA, IBF
1995	Bruce Seldon	WBA
	Frank Bruno	WBC
	Frans Botha	IBF
1996	Mike Tyson	WBC, WBA
	Michael Moorer	IBF
	Evander Holyfield	WBA
1997	Lennox Lewis	WBC

World Chess Champions

1960-61	Mikhail Tal, USSR	
1961-63	Mikhail Botvinnik, USSR	
1963-69	Tigran Peetrosian, USSR	
1969-72	Boris Spassky, USSR	
1972-75	Bobby Fischer, US	
1975-85	Anotoly Karpov, USSR	
1985-93	Gary Kasparov, USSR/Russia	
1993-	Gary Kasparov, Russia (PCA)	
	Anotoly Karpov, Russia (FIDE)	

Source: Federation Internationale de Eschecs
www.fide.com

United States Chess Champions

1986   Yasser Seirwan
1987   Tie - Joel Benjamin,
       Nick DeFirmian
1988   Michael Wilder
1989   Tie - Stuart Rachels,
       Yasser Seirwan,
       Roman Dzindzichashvili
1990   Lev Albert
1991   Gata Kamsky
1992   Patrick Wolff
1993   Tie - Alexander Shabaloz,
       Alex Yermolinsky
1994   Boris Gulko
1995   Patrick Wolff
1996   Alex Yermolinsky
1997   Joel Benjamin

Source: U.S. Chess Federation
www.uschess.com

Tour de France Winners

1990   Greg Lemond, US
1991   Miguel Indurain, Spain
1992   Miguel Indurain, Spain
1993   Miguel Indurain, Spain
1994   Miguel Indurain, Spain
1995   Miguel Indurain, Spain
1996   Bjarne Riis, Demnark
1997   Jan Ulrich, Germany

Source: Tour de France
www.letour.fr

Greyhounds race at speeds of up to 45 mph.

Fast Dogs

Greyhound Racing Records -- Speed

Distance	Dog	Time	Date
5/16 mi.	P's Ban Tee	29.46	1997
3/8 mi.	P's Rambling	36.43	1987
7/16 mi.	Runaround Sue	42.57	1991

Other Greyhound Racing Records

Record		Dog	Date
Most Wins, Career	143	JR's Ripper	
Most Wins, Year	63	JJ Doc Richard	1995
Winning Streak	29	Berry Impressive	1995
Most Starts	351	Twilite Review	93-98

The "winningest litter" in greyhound racing was born in 1969 to Westy Whizzer and Flying Sipper, known as the "Whiz Kids." Their pups went on to win 399 races.

Born to Run

Top Ranked Sires & Dams, 1997

Dogs	Bitches
Hb's Commander	Steves Stones
Oshkosh Racey	Panama Pee Wee
Mi Designer	ML Hello Dolly
Wigwam Wag	Rema Bellmard
Trouper Zeke	Riley's Marymary
Bara Buzz	Dakota Penny
EJ's Douglas	RL Dalley

Source: Nat. Greyhound Assoc.
www.nga.jc.net

There are 55 greyhound tracks in America, with an attendance of more than 27 million annually. To find out about adopting a greyhound, call 1-800-366-1472.

Iditarod Dog Sled Race Winners

1973	Dick Wilmarth	1986	Susan Butcher
1974	Carl Huntington	1987	Susan Butcher
1975	Emmitt Peters	1988	Susan Butcher
1976	Gerald Riley	1989	Joe Runyan
1977	Rick Swenson	1990	Susan Butcher
1978	Dick Mackey	1991	Rick Swenson
1979	Rick Swenson	1992	Martin Buser
1980	Joe May	1993	Jeff King
1981	Rick Swenson	1994	Martin Buser
1982	Rick Swenson	1995	Doug Swingley
1983	Rick Mackey	1996	Jeff King
1984	Dean Osmar	1997	Martin Buser
1985	Libby Riddles	1998	Jeff King

Source: Iditarod   ***www.dogsled.com***

Now That's a Dog

Westminster Kennel Club Best-In-Show Winners

Year	Dog	Breed
1986	Ch. Marjetta National Acclaim	Pointer
1987	Ch. Covy Tucker Hill's Manhattan	German Shepherd
1988	Ch. Great Elms Prince Charming II	Pomeranian
1989	Ch. Royal Tudor's Wild as the Wind	Doberman
1990	Ch. Wendessa Crown Prince	Pekingese
1991	Ch. Whisperwind on a Carousel	Poodle
1992	Ch. Registry's Lonesome Dove	Fox Terrier
1993	Ch. Salilyn's Condor	Eng. Springer Spaniel
1994	Ch. Chidley Willum	Norwich Terrier
1995	Ch. Galeforce Post Script	Scottish Terrier
1996	Ch. Clussex Country Sunrise	Clumber Spaniel
1997	Ch. Parsifal Di Casa Netzer	Standard Schnauzer
1998	Ch. Fairewood Frolic	Norwich Terrier

Source: Westminster Kennel Club   ***ww.akc.org***

Anglers Everywhere Are Jealous
Largest Freshwater Fish Caught in the World

Species	Weight	Angler	Location	Date
Barramundi	63 lbs. 2 oz.	Barnsley	Australia	1991
Bass, lrgmth.	22 lbs. 4 oz.	Perry	GA	1932
Bass, peacock	27 lbs.	Lawson	Brazil	1994
Bass, rock	3 lbs.	Gulgin	Canada	1974
Bass, smlmth	10 lbs. 14 oz.	Gorman	KY	1969
Bass, Suwannee	3 lbs. 14 oz.	Everett	FL	1985
Bass, white	6 lbs. 13 oz.	Sprouse	VA	1989
Bass, whtrk.	25 lbs. 8 oz.	Hobby	GA	1995
Bass, yellow	2 lbs. 4 oz.	Stalker	IN	1977
Bluegill	4 lbs. 12 oz.	Hudson	AL	1950
Bowfin	21 lbs. 8 oz.	Harmon	SC	1980
Buffalo, bigmth.	70 lbs. 5 oz.	Sisk	LA	1980
Buffalo, black	55 lbs. 8 oz.	McLain	TN	1984
Buffalo, smlmth.	68 lbs. 8 oz.	Dolezal	AR	1984
Bullhead, brn.	5 lbs. 11 oz.	Bengis	FL	1995
Bullhead, ylw.	4 lbs. 4 oz.	Williams	AZ	1984
Burbot	18 lbs. 4 oz.	Courtemanche	MI	1980
Carp	75 lbs. 11 oz.	Gugten	France	1987
Catfish, blue	109 lbs. 4 oz.	Lijewski	SC	1991
Catfish, channel	58 lbs.	Whaley	SC	1964
Catfish, flthd.	91 lbs. 4 oz.	Rogers	TX	1982
Catfish, white	18 lbs. 14 oz.	Miller	FL	1991
Char, Arctic	32 lbs. 9 oz.	Ward	Canada	1981
Crappie, white	5 lbs. 3 oz.	Bright	MS	1957
Dolly Varden	18 lbs. 9 oz.	Evans	AK	1993
Dorado	51 lbs. 5 oz.	Giudice	Argentina	1984
Drum	54 lbs. 8 oz.	Hull	TN	1972
Gar, alligator	279 lbs.	Valverde	TX	1951
Gar, Florida	21 lbs. 3 oz.	Sabol	FL	1981
Gar, longnose	50 lbs. 5 oz.	Miller	TX	1954
Gar, shortnose	5 lbs. 12 oz.	Willmert	IL	1995
Gar, spotted	9 lbs. 12 oz.	Rivard	TX	1994
Grayling, Arctic	5 lbs. 15 oz.	Branson	Canada	1967
Inconnu	53 lbs.	Hudnall	AK	1986
Kokanee	9 lbs. 6 oz.	Kuhn	Canada	1988
Muskellunge	67 lbs. 8 oz.	Johnson	WI	1949

Species	Weight	Angler	Location	Date
Muskellunge, tgr.	51 lbs. 3 oz.	Knobla	MI	1919
Perch, Nile	191 lbs. 8 oz.	Davison	Kenya	1991
Perch, white	4 lbs. 12 oz.	Small	ME	1949
Perch, yellow	4 lbs. 3 oz.	Abbot	NJ	1865
Pickerel, chain	9 lbs. 6 oz.	McQuaig	GA	1961
Pike, northern	55 lbs. 1 oz.	Louis	Germany	1986
Redhorse, grtr.	9 lbs. 3 oz.	Wilson	NY	1985
Redhorse, slvr.	11 lbs. 7 oz.	Long	WI	1985
Salmon, Atl.	79 lbs. 2 oz.	Henriksen	Norway	1928
Salmon, chnk.	97 lbs. 4 oz.	Anderson	AK	1985
Salmon, chum	32 lbs.	Thynes	AK	1985
Salmon, coho	33 lbs. 4 oz.	Lifton	NY	1989
Salmon, pink	13 lbs. 1 oz.	Higaki	Canada	1992
Salmon, scky.	15 lbs. 3 oz.	Roach	AK	1987
Sauger	8 lbs. 12 oz.	Fischer	ND	1971
Shad, Am.	11 lbs. 4 oz.	Thibodo	MA	1986
Sturgeon	224 lbs. 13 oz.	Lehne	Kazakstan	1993
Sturgeon, wht.	468 lbs.	Pallotta	CA	1983
Sunfish, grn.	2 lbs. 2 oz.	Dilley	MO	1971
Sunfish, rdbrst.	1 lb. 12 oz.	Buchanan	FL	1984
Sunfish, rdr.	5 lbs. 3 oz.	White	CA	1994
Tigerfish, giant	97 lbs.	Houtmans	Zaire	1988
Tilapia	6 lbs. 5 oz.	Smith	Costa Rica	1995
Trout, Apache	5 lb. 3 oz.	Baldwin	AZ	1991
Trout, brook	14 lbs. 8 oz.	Cook	Canada	1916
Trout, brown	40 lbs. 4 oz.	Collins	AR	1992
Trout, bull	32 lbs.	Higgins	ID	1949
Trout, cutthroat	41 lbs.	Skimmerhorn	NV	1925
Trout, golden	11 lbs.	Reed	WY	1948
Trout, lake	66 lbs. 8 oz.	Harback	Canada	1991
Trout, rainbow	42 lbs. 2 oz.	Robert	AK	1970
Trout, tiger	20 lbs. 13 oz.	Friedland	WI	1978
Walleye	25 lbs.	Harper	TN	1960
Warmouth	2 lbs. 7 oz.	Dempsey	FL	1985
Whitefish, lk.	14 lbs. 6 oz.	Laycock	Canada	1984
Whitefish, mt.	5 lbs. 6 oz.	Bell	Canada	1988
Whitefish, rnd.	6 lbs.	Ristori	Canada	1984
Zander	25 lbs. 2 oz.	Tennison	Sweden	1986

Source: International Game Fish Association, 1997

The One That Didn't Get Away

Largest Saltwater Fish Caught in the World

Species	Weight	Angler	Location	Date
Albacore	88 lbs. 2 oz.	Dickemann	Canary	1977
Amberjack, grt.	155 lbs. 10 oz.	Dawson	Bermuda	1981
Barracuda, grt.	85 lbs.	Helfrich	Kiribati	1992
Barracuda, Mex.	21 lbs.	Kent	Cst. Rica	1987
Barracuda, Pac.	7 lbs. 11 oz.	Kingsmill	CA	1994
Bass, blk. sea	9 lbs. 8 oz.	Mizelle Jr.	VA	1987
		Stallings	VA	1990
Bass, brd. snd.	13 lbs. 3 oz.	Halal	CA	1988
Bass, giant sea	563 lbs. 8 oz.	McAdam Jr.	CA	1968
Bass, redeye	8 lbs. 12 oz.	Davis	FL	1995
Bass, striped	78 lbs. 8 oz.	McReynolds	NJ	1982
Bluefish	31 lbs. 12 oz.	Hussey	NC	1972
Bonefish	19 lbs.	Batchelor	S. Africa	1962
Bonito, Atl.	18 lbs. 4 oz.	Higgs	Azores	1953
Bonito, Pac.	14 lbs. 12 oz.	Rilling	Mexico	1980
Cabezon	23 lbs.	Hunter	WA	1990
Cobia	135 lbs. 9 oz.	Goulding	Australia	1985
Cod, Atl.	98 lbs. 12 oz.	Bielevich	NH	1969
Cod, Pac.	30 lbs.	Vaughn	AK	1984
Conger	133 lbs. 4 oz.	Evans	England	1995
Dolphin	87 lbs.	Salazar	Cst. Rica	1976
Drum, black	113 lbs. 1 oz.	Townsend	DE	1975
Drum, red	94 lbs. 2 oz.	Deuel	NC	1984
Eel, Am.	9 lbs. 4 oz.	Pennick	NJ	1995
Eel, mrbld.	36 lbs. 1 oz.	van Nooten	S. Africa	1984
Flounder, smr.	22 lbs. 7 oz.	Nappi	NY	1975
Flounder, sthrn.	20 lbs. 9 oz.	Mungin	FL	1983
Grouper, Wrsw.	436 lbs. 12 oz.	Haeusler	FL	1985
Halibut, Atl.	255 lbs. 4 oz.	Manley	MA	1989
Halibut, Cal.	53 lbs. 4 oz.	Harmon	CA	1988
Halibut, Pac.	395 lbs.	Golat	Bering S.	1995
Jack, crevalle	57 lbs. 5 oz.	Nicolson	Angola	1992
Jack, horse-eye	24 lbs. 8 oz.	Schnau	FL	1982

Species	Weight	Angler	Location	Date
Jack, Pac. crvl.	29 lbs. 8 oz.	Snody	Cst. Rica	1994
Jewfish	680 lbs.	Joyner	FL	1961
Kawakawa	29 lbs.	Nakamura	Mexico	1986
Lingcod	69 lbs.	Romer	Canada	1992
Mackerel, cero	17 lbs. 2 oz.	Mills	FL	1986
Mackerel, king	90 lbs.	Thomton	FL	1976
Mackerel, Sp.	13 lbs.	Cranton	NC	1987
Marlin, Atl. bl.	1,402 lbs. 2 oz.	Amorim	Brazil	1992
Marlin, black	1,560 lbs.	Glassell Jr.	Peru	1953
Marlin, Pac. blue	1,376 lbs.	de Beaubien	HI	1982
Marlin, striped	494 lbs.	Boniface	N. Zealand	1986
Marlin, wht.	181 lbs. 14 oz.	Coser	Brazil	1979
Permit	53 lbs. 4 oz.	Brooker	FL	1994
Pollack, Euro.	27 lbs. 6 oz.	Milkins	England	1986
Pollock	50 lbs.	Lekang	Norway	1995
Pompano, Afr.	50 lbs. 8 oz.	Sargent	FL	1990
Roosterfish	114 lbs.	Sackheim	Mexico	1960
Runner, blue	8 lbs. 7 oz.	Windecker	TX	1995
Runner, rnbw.	37 lbs. 9 oz.	Pfleger	Mexico	1991
Sailfish, Atl.	141 lbs. 1 oz.	Neves	Angola	1994
Sailfish, Pac.	221 lbs.	Stewart	Ecuador	1947
Seabass, wht.	83 lbs. 12 oz.	Baumgardner	Mexico	1953
Seatrout, sptd.	17 lbs. 7 oz.	Carson	FL	1995
Shark, bigeye thrshr.	802 lbs.	North	N. Zealand	1981
Shark, bgns.	369 lbs. 14 oz.	Rohrlach	N. Guinea	1993
Shark, blue	437 lbs.	Hyde	Australia	1976
Shark, grt. hmrhd.	991 lbs.	Ogle	FL	1982
Shark, Grnlnd.	1,708 lbs. 9 oz.	Nordtvedt	Norway	1987
Shark, mn-etng. wht.	2,664 lbs.	Dean	Australia	1959
Shark, porbeagle	507 lbs.	Bennet	Scotland	1993
Shark, shrtfn. mako	1,115 lbs.	Guillanton	Mauritius	1988
Shark, tiger	1,780 lbs.	Maxwell	SC	1964
Shark, tope	98 lbs. 8 oz.	Oakley	CA	1994
Sheepshead	21 lbs. 4 oz.	Deselle	LA	1982
Skipjack, black	26 lbs.	Hamaishi	Mexico	1991
Snapper, cubera	121 lbs. 8 oz.	Hebert	LA	1982

Species	Weight	Angler	Location	Date
Snapper, red	46 lbs. 8 oz.	Nichols	FL	1985
Snook	53 lbs. 10 oz.	Ponzi	Cst. Rica	1978
Spearfish, Med.	90 lbs. 13 oz.	Larkin	Portugal	1980
Swordfish	1,182 lbs.	Marron	Chile	1953
Tarpon	283 lbs. 4 oz.	Sebag	S. Leone	1991
Tautog	24 lbs.	Bell	VA	1987
Trevally, bigeye	18 lbs. 1 oz.	Mills	France	1990
Trevally, giant	145 lbs. 8 oz.	Mori	HI	1991
Tuna, Atl. bigeye	375 lbs. 8 oz.	Browne	MD	1977
Tuna, blackfin	42 lbs. 8 oz.	Snyder	FL	1995
Tuna, bluefin	1,496 lbs.	Fraser	Canada	1979
Tuna, longtail	79 lbs. 2 oz.	Simpson	Australia	1982
Tuna, Pac. bigeye	435 lbs.	Lee	Peru	1957
Tuna, skipjack	41 lbs. 14 oz.	Heinzen	Mauritius	1985
Tuna, s. blfn.	348 lbs. 5 oz.	Wood	N. Zealand	1981
Tuna, ylwfn.	388 lbs. 12 oz.	Wiesenhutter	Mexico	1977
Tunny, little	35 lbs. 2 oz.	Chatard	Algeria	1988
Wahoo	155 lbs. 8 oz.	Bourne	Bahamas	1990
Weakfish	19 lbs. 2 oz.	Rooney	NY	1984
		Thomas	DE	1989
Yellowtail, Cal.	79 lbs. 4 oz.	Walker	Mexico	1991
Yellowtail, sthrn.	114 lbs. 10 oz.	Godfrey	N. Zealand	1984

Source: International Game Fish Association, 1997

Fishing is one of Americans' favorite pastimes, and it is also an important business. America is fifth in the world in its annual catch of fish, bringing in more than 6.5 million tons. China leads the world, though, catching nearly 20 million tons of fish each year. Also ahead of the U.S. are Peru (9.3 tons), Japan (8.9 tons), and Chile (6.7 tons).

The Big Game

NFL Superbowl Results

	Year	Winner/Score	Opponent/Score
I	1967	Green Bay Packers, 35	Kansas City Chiefs, 10
II	1968	Green Bay Packers, 33	Oakland Raiders, 14
III	1969	New York Jets, 16	Baltimore Colts, 7
IV	1970	Kansas City Chiefs, 23	Minnesota Vikings, 7
V	1971	Baltimore Colts, 16	Dallas Cowboys, 13
VI	1972	Dallas Cowboys, 24	Miami Dolphins, 3
VII	1973	Miami Dolphins, 14	Washington Redskins, 7
VIII	1974	Miami Dolphins, 24	Minnesota Vikings, 7
IX	1975	Pittsburgh Steelers, 16	Minnesota Vikings, 6
X	1976	Pittsburgh Steelers, 21	Dallas Cowboys, 17
XI	1977	Oakland Raiders, 32	Minnesota Vikings, 14
XII	1978	Dallas Cowboys, 27	Denver Broncos, 10
XIII	1979	Pittsburgh Steelers, 35	Dallas Cowboys, 31
XIV	1980	Pittsburgh Steelers, 31	Los Angeles Rams, 19
XV	1981	Oakland Raiders, 27	Philadelphia Eagles, 10
XVI	1982	San Francisco 49ers, 26	Cincinnati Bengals, 21
XVII	1983	Washington Redskins, 27	Miami Dolphins, 17
XVIII	1984	Los Angeles Raiders, 38	Washington Redskins, 9
XIX	1985	San Francisco 49ers, 38	Miami Dolphins, 16
XX	1986	Chicago Bears, 46	New England Patriots, 10
XXI	1987	New York Giants, 39	Denver Broncos, 20
XXII	1988	Washington Redskins, 42	Denver Broncos, 10
XXIII	1989	San Francisco 49ers, 20	Cincinnati Bengals, 16
XXIV	1990	San Francisco 49ers, 55	Denver Broncos, 10
XXV	1991	New York Giants, 20	Buffalo Bills, 19
XXVI	1992	Washington Redskins, 37	Buffalo Bills, 24
XXVII	1993	Dallas Cowboys, 52	Buffalo Bills, 17
XXVIII	1994	Dallas Cowboys, 30	Buffalo Bills, 13
XXIX	1995	San Francisco 49ers, 49	San Diego Chargers, 26
XXX	1996	Dallas Cowboys, 27	Pittsburgh Steelers, 17
XXXI	1997	Green Bay Packers, 35	New England Patriots, 21

Quarterbacks in the NFL earned an average of $1.3 million in 1996 -- double their 1990 pay of $660,000.

College Bowl Games
College Bowl Game Results

	Rose Bowl		Orange Bowl	
Year	Winner	Opponent	Winner	Opponent
1990	Southern Cal	Michigan	Notre Dame	Colorado
1991	Washington	Iowa	Colorado	Notre Dame
1992	Washington	Michigan	Miami, FL	Nebraska
1993	Michigan	Washington	Florida State	Nebraska
1994	Wisconsin	UCLA	Florida State	Nebraska
1995	Penn State	Oregon	Nebraska	Miami, FL
1996	Southern Cal	Northwestern	Florida State	Notre Dame
1997	Ohio State	Arizona State	Nebraska	Virginia Tech

Heisman Trophy Winners

1988 Barry Sanders	1993 Charlie Ward
1989 Andre Ware	1994 Rashaan Salaam
1990 Ty Detmer	1995 Eddie George
1991 Desmond Howard	1996 Danny Wuerffel
1992 Gino Torretta	1997 Charles Woodson

Professional Golf Association Champions

1988	Jeff Sluman	1993	Paul Azinger
1989	Payne Stewart	1994	Nick Price
1990	Wayne Grady	1995	Steve Elkington
1991	John Daly	1996	Mark Brooks
1992	Nick Price	1997	Davis Love III

As of April of 1998, Greg Norman is the PGA's all-time leading money winner, with nearly $12 million. He is followed by Tom Kite, at $10.4 million and Fred Couples and Nick Price, each with more than $9 million.

Take It to the Bank

PGA Leading Money Winners

Year	Golfer	Winnings
1987	Curtis Strange	925,941
1988	Curtis Strange	1,147,644
1989	Tom Kite	1,395,278
1990	Greg Norman	1,165,477
1991	Corey Pavin	979,430
1992	Fred Couples	1,344,188
1993	Nick Price	1,478,557
1994	Nick Price	1,499,927
1995	Greg Norman	1,654,959
1996	Tom Lehman	1,780,159
1997	Tiger Woods	2,066,832

LPGA Leading Money Winners

Year	Golfer	Winnings
1987	Ayako Okamoto	466,034
1988	Sherri Turner	347,255
1989	Betsy King	654,132
1990	Beth Daniel	863,578
1991	Pat Bradley	763,118
1992	Dottie Mochrie	693,335
1993	Betsy King	595,992
1994	Laura Davies	687,201
1995	Annika Sorenstam	666,533
1996	Karrie Webb	1,002,000
1997	Annika Sorenstam	1,076,789

www.pga.com

U.S. Open Winners

1988	Curtis Strange
1989	Curtis Strange
1990	Hale Irwin
1991	Payne Stewart
1992	Tom Kite
1993	Lee Janzen
1994	Ernie Els
1995	Corey Pavin
1996	Steve Jones
1997	Ernie Els
1998	Lee Janzen

Source: U.S. Golf Assoc.

Masters Winners

1988	Sandy Lyle
1989	Nick Faldo
1990	Nick Faldo
1991	Ian Woosnan
1992	Fred Couples
1993	Bernhard Langer
1994	Jose M. Olazabal
1995	Ben Crenshaw
1996	Nick Faldo
1997	Tiger Woods
1998	Mark O'Meara

Source: PGA Tour

U.S. Women's Open Winners

1988	Liselotte Neuman
1989	Betsy King
1990	Besty King
1991	Meg Mallon
1992	Patty Sheehan
1993	Lauri Merten
1994	Patty Sheehan
1995	Annika Sorenstam
1996	Annika Sorenstam
1997	Alison Nicholas
1998	Se Ri Pak

Source: U.S. Golf Assoc.

British Open Winners

1988	Steve Ballesteros
1989	Mark Calcavecchia
1990	Nick Faldo
1991	Ian Baker-Finch
1992	Nick Faldo
1993	Greg Norman
1994	Nick Price
1995	John Daly
1996	Tom Lehman
1997	Justin Leonard
1998	Mark O'Meara

The Traveling Trophy
National Hockey League Stanley Cup Finalists

Year	Winner	Opponent
1967	Toronto	Montreal
1968	Montreal	St. Louis
1969	Montreal	St. Louis
1970	Boston	St. Louis
1971	Montreal	Chicago
1972	Boston	N.Y. Rangers
1973	Montreal	Chicago
1974	Philadelphia	Boston
1975	Philadelphia	Buffalo
1976	Montreal	Philadelphia
1977	Montreal	Boston
1978	Montreal	Boston
1979	Montreal	N.Y. Rangers
1980	N.Y. Islanders	Philadelphia
1981	N.Y. Islanders	Minnesota
1982	N.Y. Islanders	Vancouver
1983	N.Y. Islanders	Edmonton
1984	Edmonton	N.Y. Islanders
1985	Edmonton	Philadelphia
1986	Montreal	Calgary
1987	Edmonton	Philadelphia
1988	Edmonton	Boston
1989	Calgary	Montreal
1990	Edmonton	Boston
1991	Pittsburgh	Minnesota
1992	Pittsburgh	Chicago
1993	Montreal	Los Angeles
1994	N.Y. Rangers	Vancouver
1995	New Jersey	Detroit
1996	Colorado	Florida
1997	Detroit	Philadelphia
1998	Detroit	Washington

NHL salaries averaged $981,000 for the 1996-97 season. That represents a tenfold increase since 1980, when players were paid an average of $108,000.

Source: National Hockey League   ***www.nhl.com***

Hockey Greats
All-Time Leading Scorers

Player	Goals	Assists	Points
Wayne Gretzky	837	1,771	2,608
Gordie Howe	801	1,049	1,850
Marcel Dionne	731	1,040	1,771
Phil Esposito	717	873	1,590
Mark Messier	539	929	1,468
Stan Mikita	541	926	1,467
Bryan Trottier	524	901	1,425
Paul Coffey	372	1,038	1,410
Dale Hawerchuk	506	869	1,375
Mario Lemieux	563	809	1,372

Source: National Hockey League

Art Ross Trophy Winners
Highest Scorer in a Single Season

1986	Wayne Gretzky
1987	Wayne Gretzky
1988	Mario Lemieux
1989	Mario Lemieux
1990	Wayne Gretzky
1991	Wayne Gretzky
1992	Mario Lemieux
1993	Mario Lemieux
1994	Wayne Gretzky
1995	Jaromir Jagr
1996	Mario Lemieux
1997	Mario Lemieux
1998	Jaromir Jagr

Vezina Winners
Outstanding Goalie

1986	John Vanbiesbrouck
1987	Ron Hextall
1988	Grant Fuhr
1989	Patrick Roy
1990	Patrick Roy
1991	Ed Belfour
1992	Patrick Roy
1993	Ed Belfour
1994	Dominik Hasek
1995	Dominik Hasek
1996	Chris Chelios
1997	Brian Leetch
1998	Dominik Hasek

Fast Horses, Fast Riders
Kentucky Derby Winners

Year	Horse	Jockey
1989	Sunday Silence	P. Valenzuela
1990	Unbridled	C. Perret
1991	Strike the Gold	C. Antley
1992	Lil E. Tee	P. Day
1993	Sea Hero	J. Bailey
1994	Go for Gin	C. McCarron
1995	Thunder Gulch	G. Stevens
1996	Grindstone	J. Bailey
1997	Silver Charm	G. Stevens
1998	Real Quiet	K. Desormeaux

Preakness Winners

Year	Horse	Jockey
1989	Sunday Silence	P. Valenzuela
1990	Summer Squall	P. Day
1991	Hansel	J. Bailey
1992	Pine Bluff	C. McCarron
1993	Prairie Bayou	M. Smith
1994	Tabasco Cat	P. Day
1995	Timber Country	P. Day
1996	Louis Quatorze	P. Day
1997	Silver Charm	G. Stevens
1998	Real Quiet	K. Desormeaux

Belmont Stakes Winners

Year	Horse	Jockey
1989	Easy Goer	P. Day
1990	Go and Go	M. Kinane
1991	Hansel	J. Bailey
1992	A.P. Indy	E. Delahoussaye
1993	Colonial Affair	J. Krone
1994	Tabasco Cat	P. Day
1995	Thunder Gulch	G. Stevens
1996	Editor's Note	R. Douglas
1997	Touch Gold	C. McCarron
1998	Victory Gallup	G. Stevens

Harness Horse of the Year

1987 Mack Lobell
1988 Mack Lobell
1989 Matt's Scooter
1990 Beach Towel
1991 Precious Bunny
1992 Artsplace
1993 Staying Together
1994 Cam's Card Shark
1995 CR Kay Suzie
1996 Continentalvictory
1997 Malabar Man

Source: U.S. Trotting Assoc.
www.ustrotting.com

Triple Crown Winners

1919 Sir Barton
1930 Gallant Fox
1935 Omaha
1937 War Admiral
1941 Whirlaway
1943 Count Fleet
1946 Assault
1948 Citation
1973 Secretariat
1977 Seattle Slew
1978 Affirmed

Hydroplane Racing

American Power Boat Association Gold Cup Champions

Year	Boat	Driver
1987	Miller American	Chip Hanauer
1988	Miller American	Chip Hanauer
1989	Miss Budweiser	Tom D'Eath
1990	Miss Budweiser	Tom D'Eath
1991	Winston Eagle	Mark Tate
1992	Miss Budweiser	Chip Hanauer
1993	Miss Budweiser	Chip Hanauer
1994	Smokin' Joe's	Mark Tate
1995	Miss Budweiser	Chip Hanauer
1996	Pico's Am. Dream	Dave Villwock
1997	Miss Budweiser	Dave Villwock

Gentlemen, Start Your Engines!
Indianapolis 500 Winners

Year	Winner	Mph.
1967	A.J. Foyt Jr.	151.207
1968	Bobby Unser	152.882
1969	Mario Andretti	156.867
1970	Al Unser	155.749
1971	Al Unser	157.735
1972	Mark Donohue	162.962
1973	Gordon Johncock	159.036
1974	Johnny Rutherford	158.589
1975	Bobby Unser	149.213
1976	Johnny Rutherford	148.725
1977	A.J. Foyt Jr.	161.331
1978	Al Unser	161.363
1979	Rick Mears	158.899
1980	Johnny Rutherford	142.862
1981	Bobby Unser	139.084
1982	Gordon Johncock	162.029
1983	Tom Sneva	162.117
1984	Rick Mears	163.612
1985	Danny Sullivan	152.982
1986	Bobby Rahal	170.722
1987	Al Unser	162.175
1988	Rick Mears	144.809
1989	Emerson Fittipaldi	167.581
1990	Arie Luyendyk	185.981
1991	Rick Mears	176.457
1992	Al Unser Jr.	134.479
1993	Emerson Fittipaldi	157.207
1994	Al Unser Jr.	160.872
1995	Jacques Villeneuve	153.616
1996	Buddy Lazier	147.956
1997	Arie Luyendyk	145.857
1998	Eddie Cheever	145.155

Source: Indianapolis Motor Speedway
www.indy500.com   www.indyracingleague.com

Nascar Champions
Winston Cup and Daytona 500 Winners

Year	Winston Cup	Daytona 500	Speed
1967	Richard Petty	Mario Andretti	146.926
1968	David Pearson	Cale Yarborough	143.251
1969	David Pearson	Lee Roy Yarborough	160.875
1970	Bobby Isaac	Pete Hamilton	149.601
1971	Richard Petty	Richard Petty	144.456
1972	Richard Petty	A. J. Foyt	161.550
1973	Benny Parsons	Richard Petty	157.205
1974	Richard Petty	Richard Petty	140.894
1975	Richard Petty	Benny Parsons	153.649
1976	Cale Yarborough	David Pearson	152.181
1977	Cale Yarborough	Cale Yarborough	153.218
1978	Cale Yarborough	Bobby Allison	159.730
1979	Richard Petty	Richard Petty	143.977
1980	Dale Earnhardt	Buddy Baker	177.602
1981	Darrell Waltrip	Richard Petty	169.651
1982	Darrell Waltrip	Bobby Allison	153.991
1983	Bobby Allison	Cale Yarborough	155.979
1984	Terry Labonte	Cale Yarborough	150.994
1985	Darrell Waltrip	Bill Elliott	172.265
1986	Dale Earnhardt	Geoff Bodine	148.124
1987	Dale Earnhardt	Bill Elliott	176.263
1988	Bill Elliott	Bobby Allison	137.531
1989	Rusty Wallace	Darrell Waltrip	148.466
1990	Dale Earnhardt	Derrike Cope	165.761
1991	Dale Earnhardt	Ernie Irvan	148.148
1992	Alan Kulwicki	Davey Allison	160.256
1993	Dale Earnhardt	Dale Jarrett	154.972
1994	Dale Earnhardt	Sterling Marlin	156.931
1995	Jeff Gordon	Sterling Marlin	141.710
1996	Terry Labonte	Dale Jarrett	154.308
1997	Jeff Gordon	Jeff Gordon	148.295

www.nascar.com
www.daytonausa.com

American Motorcyclist Association Champions

Superbike

1995	Miguel Duhamel
1996	Doug Chandler
1997	Doug Chandler

250cc Grand Prix

1995	Rich Oliver
1996	Rich Oliver
1997	Rich Oliver

600cc SuperSport

1995	Miguel Duhamel
1996	Miguel Duhamel
1997	Miguel Duhamel

750cc SuperSport

1995	Tom Kipp
1996	Aaron Yates
1997	Jason Pridmore

SuperTwins

1995	Scott Zampach
1996	Matt Wait
1997	Eric Bostram

Grand National Dirt Track

1995	Scott Parker
1996	Scott Parker
1997	Scott Parker

883cc Dirt Track

1995	Mike Hacker
1996	Eric Bostrom
1997	Eric Bostrom

250cc Motocross

1995	Jeremy McGrath
1996	Jeff Emig
1997	Jeff Emig

125cc Motocross

1995	Steve Lamson
1996	Steve Lamson
1997	Ricky Carmichael

Supercross

1995	Jeremy McGrath
1996	Jeremy McGrath
1997	Jeff Emig

Source: American Motorcyclist Association

www.ama-cycle.org

World Motorcycle Racing Champions

Superbike

1995	Carl Fogarty
1996	Troy Corser
1997	John Kocinski

500cc

1995	Michael Doohan
1996	Michael Doohan
1997	Michael Doohan

250cc

1995	Max Biaggi
1996	Max Biaggi
1997	Max Biaggi

125cc

1995	Aoki Haruchika
1996	Aoki Haruchika
1997	Valentino Rossi

Source: Federation Internationale Motocycliste

www.dorna.com   www.superbike.it

Ice Skating

U.S. Figure Skating Champions

Year	Men	Women
1988	Brian Boitano	Debi Thomas
1989	Christopher Bowman	Jill Trenary
1990	Todd Eldredge	Jill Trenary
1991	Todd Eldredge	Tonya Harding
1992	Christopher Bowman	Kristi Yamaguchi
1993	Scott Davis	Nancy Kerrigan
1994	Scott Davis	NA
1995	Todd Eldredge	Nicole Bobek
1996	Rudy Galindo	Michelle Kwan
1997	Todd Eldredge	Tara Lipinski

World Figure Skating Champions

Year	Men	Women
1988	Brian Boitano, U.S.	Katarina Witt, E. Germany
1989	Kurt Browning, Canada	Midori Ito, Japan
1990	Kurt Browning, Canada	Jill Trenary, U.S.
1991	Kurt Browning, Canada	Kristi Yamaguchi, U.S.
1992	Viktor Petrenko, Ukraine	Kristi Yamaguchi, U.S.
1993	Kurt Browning, Canada	Oksana Baiul, Ukraine
1994	Elvis Stojko, Canada	Yuka Sato, Japan
1995	Elvis Stojko, Canada	Chen Lu, China
1996	Todd Eldredge, U.S.	Michelle Kwan, U.S.
1997	Elvis Stojko, Canada	Tara Lipinski, U.S.

At the age of 14, Tara Lipinski became the youngest ever U.S. figure skating champion and world figure skating champion in 1997.

Skiing - World Cup Alpine Champions

Men

Year	Champion	Country
1982	Phil Mahre	U.S.
1983	Phil Mahre	U.S.
1984	Pirmin Zurbriggen	Switzerland
1985	Marc Girardelli	Luxembourg
1986	Marc Girardelli	Luxembourg
1987	Pirmin Zurbriggen	Switzerland
1988	Pirmin Zurbriggen	Switzerland
1989	Marc Girardelli	Luxembourg
1990	Pirmin Zurbriggen	Switzerland
1991	Marc Girardelli	Luxembourg
1992	Paul Accola	Switzerland
1993	Marc Girardelli	Luxembourg
1994	Kjetil Andre Aamodt	Norway
1995	Alberto Tomba	Italy
1996	Lasse Kjus	Norway

Women

Year	Champion	Country
1982	Erika Hess	Switzerland
1983	Tamara McKinney	U.S.
1984	Erika Hess	Switzerland
1985	Michela Figini	Switzerland
1986	Maria Walliser	Switzerland
1987	Maria Walliser	Switzerland
1988	Michela Figini	Switzerland
1989	Vreni Schneider	Switzerland
1990	Petra Kronberger	Austria
1991	Petra Kronberger	Austria
1992	Petra Kronberger	Austria
1993	Anita Wachter	Austria
1994	Vreni Schneider	Switzerland
1995	Vreni Schneider	Switzerland
1996	Katja Seizinger	Germany

Soccer -- The Other Football

World Cup Champions

Year	Winner	Opponent	Site
1930	Uruguay	Argentina	Uruguay
1934	Italy	Czechoslovakia	Italy
1938	Italy	Hungary	France
1950	Uruguay	Brazil	Brazil
1954	W. Germany	Hungary	Switzerland
1958	Brazil	Sweden	Sweden
1962	Brazil	Czechoslovakia	Chile
1966	England	W. Germany	England
1970	Brazil	Italy	Mexico
1974	W. Germany	Netherlands	W. Germany
1978	Argentina	Netherlands	Argentina
1982	Italy	W. Germany	Spain
1986	Argentina	W. Germany	Mexico
1990	W. Germany	Argentina	Italy
1994	Brazil	Italy	U.S.
1998	France	Brazil	France

A New League: Major League Soccer

MLS Cup Winners

Year	Winner	Opponent
1996	Washington D.C. United	Los Angeles Galaxy
1997	Washington D.C. United	Colorado Rapids

Best of the U.S. Soccer Players

1997 MLS Awards

Award	Player
Most Valuable Player	Preki, Kansas City
Defender of the Year	Eddie Pope, Washington DC
Goalkeeper of the Year	Brad Friedel, Columbus
Rookie of the Year	Mike Duhaney, Tampa Bay

U.S. Open Champs
Women's Singles

1988	Steffi Graf
1989	Steffi Graf
1990	Gabriela Sabatini
1991	Monica Seles
1992	Monica Seles
1993	Steffi Graf
1994	A. Sanchez Vicario
1995	Steffi Graf
1996	Steffi Graf
1997	Martina Hingis

U.S. Open Champs
Men's Singles

1988	Mats Wilander
1989	Boris Becker
1990	Pete Sampras
1991	Stefan Edberg
1992	Stefan Edberg
1993	Pete Sampras
1994	Andre Agassi
1995	Pete Sampras
1996	Pete Sampras
1997	Patrick Rafler

In 1997, 16 year old Martina Hingis became the youngest to win the women's singles at Wimbledon since 1887.

Wimbledon Champs
Men's Singles

1988	Stefan Edberg
1989	Boris Becker
1990	Stefan Edberg
1991	Michael Stich
1992	Andre Agassi
1993	Pete Sampras
1994	Pete Sampras
1995	Pete Sampras
1996	Richard Krajicek
1997	Pete Sampras
1998	Pete Sampras

Wimbledon Champs
Women's Singles

1988	Steffi Graf
1989	Steffi Graf
1990	Martina Navratilova
1991	Steffi Graf
1992	Steffi Graf
1993	Steffi Graf
1994	Conchita Martinez
1995	Steffi Graf
1996	Steffi Graf
1997	Martina Hingis
1998	Jana Novotna

Going the Distance

Boston Marathon Winners

Year	Men	Time	Women	Time
1988	Ibrahim Hussein	2:08:43	Rosa Mota	2:24:30
1989	Abebe Mekonnen	2:09:06	I. Kristiansen	2:24:33
1990	Gelindo Bordin	2:08:19	Rosa Mota	2:25:24
1991	Ibrahim Hussein	2:11:06	Wanda Panfil	2:24:18
1992	Ibrahim Hussein	2:08:14	Olga Markova	2:23:43
1993	Cosmas Ndeti	2:09:33	Olga Markova	2:25:27
1994	Cosmas Ndeti	2:07:15	Uta Pippig	2:21:45
1995	Cosmas Ndeti	2:09:22	Uta Pippig	2:25:11
1996	Moses Tanui	2:09:15	Uta Pippig	2:27:12
1997	Lameck Aguta	2:10:34	Fatuma Roba	2:26:23
1998	Moses Tanui	2:07:34	Fatuma Roba	2:23:21

New York Marathon Winners

Year	Men	Time	Women	Time
1988	Steve Jones	2:08:20	Grete Waitz	2:28:17
1989	Juma Ikangaa	2:08:01	I. Kristiansen	2:25:30
1990	Douglas Wakiihuri	2:12:39	Wenda Panfil	2:30:45
1991	Salvador Garcia	2:09:28	Liz McColgan	2:27:00
1992	Willie Mtolo	2:09:29	Lisa Ondieki	2:24:40
1993	Andres Espinosa	2:10:04	Uta Pipig	2:26:24
1994	German Silva	2:11:21	Tegla Loroupe	2:27:37
1995	German Silva	2:10:00	Tegla Loroupe	2:28:06
1996	Giacomo Leone	2:09:54	Anuta Ctuna	2:28:18
1997	John Kague	2:08:12	Franziska Rochat	2:28:42

In 1998, Moses Tanui won the Boston Marathon with the third-fastest time in the race's 102-year history. The only faster times were recorded by the first and second place finishers in 1994: Cosmas Ndeti (2:07:15) and Andres Espinosa (2:07:19).

Track & Field All-Time Bests -- Running

Men's Records, as of October, 1997

Event	Athlete	Date	Record
Marathon	Dinsamo	4/17/98	2 hrs. 6 min. 50 sec.
25,000 m	Seko	3/22/81	1 hr. 13 min. 55.8 sec.
20,000 m	Barrios	3/30/91	56 min. 55.6 sec.
10,000 m	Tergat	8/22/97	26 min. 27.85 sec.
1 mile	Morcelli	9/5/93	3 min. 44.39 sec.
1,500 m	Morcelli	7/12/95	3 min. 27.37 sec.
1,000 m	Coe	7/11/81	2 min. 12.18 sec.
800 m	Kipketer	8/24/97	1 min. 41.11 sec.
400 m	Reynolds	8/17/88	43.29 sec.
200 m	Johnson	8/1/96	19.32 sec.
100 m	Bailey	7/27/96	9.84 sec.

Women's Records, as of October, 1997

Event	Athlete	Date	Record
Marathon	Kristiansen	4/21/85	2 hr. 21 min. 6 sec.
10,000 m	Junxia	9/8/93	29 min. 31.78 sec.
5,000 m	Ribeiro	7/22/95	14 min. 36.45 sec.
1 mile	Masterkova	8/4/96	4 min. 12.56 sec.
3,000 m	Junxia	9/13/93	8 min. 6.11 sec.
2,000 m	O'Sullivan	7/8/94	5 min. 25.36 sec.
1,500 m	Yunxia	9/11/93	3 min. 50.46 sec.
1,000 m	Masterkova	8/23/96	2 min. 28.98 sec.
800 m	Kratochvilova	7/26/93	1 min. 53.28 sec.
400 m	Koch	10/6/85	47.60 sec.
200 m	Griffith-Joyner	9/29/88	21.34 sec.
100 m	Griffith-Joyner	7/16/88	10.49 sec.

Source: International Amateur Athletic Federation

Track & Field All-Time Bests
Men's Records, as of October, 1997

Event	Athlete	Date	Record
110 m Hurdles	Jackson	8/20/93	12.91 sec.
400 m Hurdles	Young	8/6/92	46.78 sec.
High Jump	Solomayer	7/27/93	8' 1/2"
Long Jump	Powell	8/30/91	29' 4-1/2"
Triple Jump	Edwards	8/7/95	60' 1/4"
Pole Vault	Bubka	7/31/94	20' 1-3/4"
16 lb. Shot Put	Barnes	5/20/90	75' 10-1/4"
Discus	Schult	6/6/86	243'
Javelin	Zelezny	5/25/69	323'
16 lb. Hammer	Sedykh	8/30/86	284'
Decathlon	O'Brien	9/5/92	8,891 pts.

Women's Records, as of October, 1997

Event	Athlete	Date	Record
100 m Hurdles	Donkova	8/20/88	12.21 sec.
400 m Hurdles	Batten	8/11/95	52.61 sec.
High Jump	Kostadinova	8/30/87	6' 10-1/4"
Long Jump	Chistyakova	6/11/88	24' 8-1/4"
Triple Jump	Kravets	8/10/95	50' 10-1/4"
Pole Vault	George	2/20/97	14' 11"
Shot Put	Lisovskaya	6/7/87	74' 3"
Discus	Reinsch	6/9/88	252'
Javelin	Felke	9/9/88	262' 5"
Hammer	Kuzenkova	6/22/97	239' 8"
Decathlon	Joyner-Kersee	9/24/88	7,291 pts.

Source: International Amateur Athletic Federation

The National Collegiate Athletic Association (NCAA) sponsors 81 annual championships. 42 are for men, 36 for women, and three are coeducational.

NCAA Wrestling Champions

1980 Iowa	1989 Oklahoma State
1981 Iowa	1990 Oklahoma State
1982 Iowa	1991 Iowa
1983 Iowa	1992 Iowa
1984 Iowa	1993 Iowa
1985 Iowa	1994 Oklahoma State
1986 Iowa	1995 Iowa
1987 Iowa State	1996 Iowa
1988 Arizona State	1997 Iowa

Yacht Racing
America's Cup Winners

Year	Winner	Opponent	Score
1967	Intrepid	Dame Pattie	4-0
1970	Intrepid	Gretel II	4-1
1974	Courageous	Southern Cross	4-0
1977	Courageous	Australia	4-0
1980	Freedom	Australia	4-1
1983	Australia II	Liberty	4-3
1987	Stars & Stripes	Kookaburra III	4-0
1988	Stars & Stripes	New Zealand	2-0
1992	America II	Moro di Venezia	4-1
1995	Black Magic	Young America	5-0

13. Science & Technology

See also 'Money & Business' and 'The Environment.'

The Earth, Sun, Moon & Planets

Space Exploration

Formulas, Laws & Theories

Scientific Discoveries

Chemical Elements

Inventions

The Earth, Sun, Moon & Planets

The Earth's atmosphere is composed of 77% nitrogen, 21% oxygen, and 1% argon. Traces of carbon dioxide, hydrogen, neon, helium, krypton, and xenon are also present.

The Earth is made up of a dense core of magnetic material surrounded by a thick rock-like shell called the mantle. Covering the mantle is a thin crust that forms the base of continents and ocean floors.

EARTH

Min.Dist. from Sun:	91.4 million miles
Max.Dist. from Sun:	94.5 million miles
Radius:	3,959 miles
Rev. around Sun:	365.3 days
Orbital Velocity:	18.51 miles per second
1 Rotation:	24.0 hours
Area (sq. mi.):	196,938,800
Rank (size):	5
Mass:	6 sextillion, 588 quintillion short tons
Natural Satellites:	1
Average Temp.:	45 °F

THE SUN

Diameter:	8,64000 miles
Ave. Dist. from Earth:	92,980,000 miles
Mass (Earth = 1):	332,946
Density (Earth = 1):	0.26
Gravity (Earth = 1):	27.9
Ave. Surface Temp.:	10,000 °F

The Sun is a star that dominates our solar system due to its mass and gravitational effects. It is made up of mostly hydrogen. Near the center, the temperature is almost 29 million degrees Fahrenheit. The nuclei of the hydrogen atoms undergo nuclear fusion, releasing tremendous energy which is transported to the surface by radiation and the mixing of gasses.

Lights Out!
Upcoming Total Solar Eclipses

Date of Eclipse	Can Be Seen from
August 11, 1999	Europe, Middle East, India
June 21, 2001	Atlantic Ocean, Africa, Madagascar
December 4, 2002	South Africa, Indian Ocean, Australia
November 23, 2003	Antarctica
April 8, 2005	Northwest South America
March 29, 2006	Atlantic Ocean, Africa, Asia
August, 2008	Arctic Ocean, Asia
July 22, 2009	Asia, Pacific Ocean
July 11, 2010	Atlantic Ocean

THE MOON

Mean Dist. from Earth:	238,856 miles
Radius:	1,080 miles
Rev. around Earth:	27.322 days
Period of Phases:	27.322 days
Orbital Velocity:	2,300 miles per hour
Mass (Earth = 1):	0.0123
Density (Earth = 1):	0.61
Average Temp.:	-10 °F

The moon is the natural satellite of Earth. It is about 4.6 billion years old -- about the same age as Earth and probably the rest of the solar system. A current theory as to the moon's origin is that more than four billion years ago, Earth was struck by a planetesimal (an object the size of a small planet). The impact broke away chunks of Earth and the planetesimal and sent them into space, where the debris gathered to form the moon.

The moon has a harsh environment. Its temperatures range from 261 degrees Fahrenheit to -173, and its atmosphere is so thin that it can not be duplicated in a vacuum chamber. Its surface features three trillion craters -- some as large as 183 miles wide and 13,000 miles deep -- mountain peaks of 20,000 feet, and lava plains up to 750 miles wide.

Half of the moon is always in sunlight. The phases of the moon depend on how much of the half visible from Earth is sunlit.

Phases of the Moon

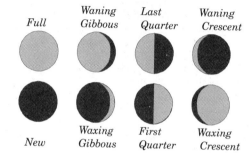

The Harvest Moon is the full moon nearest the fall equinox. It is so called because it is followed by several days when the moon rises just after sunset. This gives farmers in temperate latitudes extra hours of light in which to harvest their crops before the first frost.

The moon rotates on its own axis at the same rate at which it revolves around the Earth. Because of this, it always keeps the same face toward the Earth. We had our first look at the hidden side of the moon when the Soviet mission Lunik III photographed it in 1959.

MERCURY

Min. Dist. from Sun:	28.6 million miles
Max. Dist. from Sun:	43.4 million miles
Min. Dist. from Earth:	48 million miles
Max. Dist. from Earth:	138 million miles
Radius:	1,516 miles
Rev. around Sun:	87.97 Earth days
1 Rotation :	175.97 Earth days
Orbital Velocity:	29.75 miles per second
Rank (size):	8
Mass (Earth = 1):	0.0553
Density (Earth = 1):	0.98
Natural Satellites:	0
Average Temp.:	333 °F

Mercury is the closest planet to the Sun and has the greatest range of surface temperatures. The daytime highs reach 840 °F, while the nighttime lows can be -300 °F. Mariners 4 and 10 passed close to Mercury, photographing its surface and studying its atmosphere. The planet has a very thin atmosphere made up of hydrogen and helium thought to be gasses of wind from the Sun, temporarily concentrated around Mercury.

VENUS

Min. Dist. from Sun:	66.8 million miles
Max. Dist. from Sun:	67.7 million miles
Min. Dist. from Earth:	24 million miles
Max. Dist. from Earth:	162 million miles
Radius:	3,761 miles
Rev. around Sun:	224.7 Earth days
Orbital Velocity:	21.76 miles per second
1 Rotation :	116.75 Earth days (retrograde)
Rank (size):	6
Mass (Earth = 1):	0.8151
Density (Earth = 1):	0.94
Natural Satellites:	0
Average Temp.:	870 °F

*Every 19 months, Venus is the
closest planet to Earth. This is
due to its own orbit and that of
Earth. It is easy to observe from
Earth, because its thick white
cloud cover reflects sunlight,
making it very bright. The same
dense, cloudy atmosphere exerts
a pressure nearly 90 times that of
Earth's normal sea level pressure. The very hot surface
temperature -- caused by an
extreme greenhouse effect --
varies little from day to night,
due to its heavy cloud layer.*

MARS

Min. Dist. from Sun:	128.4 million miles
Max. Dist. from Sun:	154.8 million miles
Min. Dist. from Earth:	34 million miles
Max. Dist. from Earth:	249 million miles
Radius:	2,106 miles
Rev. around Sun:	686.98 Earth days
1 Rotation :	24 hrs. 41 min. 58 sec.
Orbital Velocity:	14.99 miles per second
Rank (size):	7
Mass (Earth = 1):	0.1075
Density (Earth = 1):	0.71
Natural Satellites:	2
Average Temp.:	-76 °F

Mars rotates on an axis which is inclined at 25 degrees from its orbital plane, giving the planet seasons. There are large green patches on the surface of Mars which were once thought to be vegetation. Mariner 4, however, found a complete lack of oxygen and water, making growth of plants as we know them virtually impossible. The mysterious green areas are now hypothesized to be volcanic salts, which vary in color with changes in temperature. Or, they could in fact be grey, which the human eye would see as green when next to the red areas on the surface of Mars.

JUPITER

Min. Dist. from Sun:	460.2 million miles
Max. Dist. from Sun:	507 million miles
Min. Dist. from Earth:	366 million miles
Max. Dist. from Earth:	602 million miles
Radius:	43,441 miles
Rev. around Sun:	11.86 Earth years
1 Rotation :	9 hrs. 55 min. 33 sec.
Orbital Velocity:	18.12 miles per second
Rank (size):	1
Mass (Earth = 1):	317.83
Density (Earth = 1):	0.24
Natural Satellites:	16
Average Temp.:	-160 °F

Jupiter, the largest of the planets, is a relatively liquid mass which rotates very quickly. One day on Jupiter is less than ten hours long. That means that a point on its equator travels at a speed of 22,000 miles per hour, compared to 1,000 m.p.h. at Earth's equator. The U.S. has studied Jupiter at close range with Voyagers 1 and 2, Pioneers 10, and 11, and Galileo, which released a probe into the planet's atmosphere, finding wind speeds exceeding 4,000 m.p.h. In 1994 we were able to observe a dramatic display when 21 large comet fragments collided with Jupiter, some with the force 100,000 times that of the largest nuclear bomb ever detonated.

SATURN

Min. Dist. from Sun:	837.4 million miles
Max. Dist. from Sun:	936 million miles
Min. Dist. from Earth:	48 million miles
Max. Dist. from Earth:	138 million miles
Radius:	36,184 miles
Rev. around Sun:	29.46 Earth years
1 Rotation :	10 hrs. 30 min. 2 sec.
Orbital Velocity:	5.99 miles per second
Rank (size):	2
Mass (Earth = 1):	95.16
Density (Earth = 1):	0.12
Natural Satellites:	18
Average Temp.:	-220 °F

*Saturn is the most distant planet
which can be seen by the naked eye.
It is similar in size to Jupiter, and
also like Jupiter, it rotates quickly --
making its daily spin in only about
ten hours. Scientists had discovered
ten of Saturn's satellites using
Earth-based methods, but Pioneer 11
discovered two more, and Voyagers 1
and 2 revealed another six. The ring
system, about 10 miles thick with a
diameter of 170,000 miles, was also
studied by Voyagers 1 and 2, and
was found to be much more complex
than previously thought.*

URANUS

Min. Dist. from Sun:	1,698.8 million miles
Max. Dist. from Sun:	1,876.2 million miles
Min. Dist. from Earth:	48 million miles
Max. Dist. from Earth:	138 million miles
Radius:	15,759 miles
Rev. around Sun:	84.01 Earth years
1 Rotation :	17 hrs. 14 min. 23 sec. (retrograde)
Orbital Velocity:	4.23 miles per second
Rank (size):	4
Mass (Earth = 1):	14.54
Density (Earth = 1):	0.24
Natural Satellites:	15
Average Temp.:	-320 °F

*Uranus has extreme seasons because
it is inclined at the dramatic angle of
98 degrees from its plane of orbit.
The sun, after rising at its north
pole, shines for 42 of our years, then
sets, putting the north pole in
darkness and winter for another 42
Earth years. Ten moons were
discovered during Voyager 2's flyby
in 1986, bringing the total known
satellites to 15. They all orbit in the
plane of the planet's equator, in
which there are also a series of rings.
These are not visible from Earth,
and were first observed in 1978 when
Uranus passed before a star.*

NEPTUNE

Min. Dist. from Sun:	2,770.1 million miles
Max. Dist. from Sun:	2,818.0 million miles
Min. Dist. from Earth:	2,676 million miles
Max. Dist. from Earth:	2,912 million miles
Radius:	15,301 miles
Rev. around Sun:	164.79 Earth years
1 Rotation :	16 hrs. 6 min. 37 sec.
Orbital Velocity:	3.38 miles per second
Rank (size):	3
Mass (Earth = 1):	17.15
Density (Earth = 1):	0.30
Natural Satellites:	8
Average Temp.:	-330 °F

Neptune has an atmosphere which appears to be blue, with scattered white clouds moving rapidly high above the surface, as seen by Voyager 2. The expedition also revealed six new satellites, five of which circle Neptune in a half day or less. The largest of the satellites is the moon Triton. It orbits Neptune in retrograde (reverse direction), which suggests that it was captured by Neptune's gravity. Along with its eight satellites, Neptune has at least three rings, made up of fine particles.

PLUTO

Min. Dist. from Sun:	2,762.5 million miles
Max. Dist. from Sun:	4,586.5 million miles
Min. Dist. from Earth:	2,668 million miles
Max. Dist. from Earth:	4,681 million miles
Radius:	707 miles
Rev. around Sun:	247.69 Earth years
1 Rotation :	6 days 9 hrs. 18 min (retrograde)
Orbital Velocity:	2.95 miles per second
Rank (size):	9
Mass (Earth = 1):	0.0021
Density (Earth = 1):	0.37
Natural Satellites:	1
Average Temp.:	-370 °F

Pluto is the smallest of the planets and is usually the farthest from the Earth and Sun. Though as yet unseen, its existence was hypothesized about 100 years ago to explain the orbital paths of Neptune and Uranus. Clyde Tombaugh at Lowell Observatory in Flagstaff, Arizona, first observed the planet in 1930, and the hypothesis was believed to be true. However, even considering the mass of Pluto's moon, discovered in 1978 by James Christy at the U.S. Naval Observatory, Pluto does not exert enough gravitational force to alter the orbits of Neptune and Uranus.

Space Exploration

Fly Me to the Moon . . .
Firsts in Space Exploration

Date	Spacecraft	First
1961	Vostok 1	1st manned orbital flight
1961	Mercury-Redstone 3	1st American in space (Shepard)
1962	Mercury-Atlas 6	1st American in orbit (Glenn)
1963	Vostok 6	1st woman in space (Tereshkova)
1965	Voskhod 2	1st space walk (Leonov)
1965	Gemini-Titan 4	1st American space walk (White)
1965	Gemini-Titan 6	1st U.S. space rendezvous (Gem. 7)
1966	Gemini-Titan 10	1st orbital docking
1968	Apollo-Saturn 8	1st lunar orbit, piloted reentry
1969	Apollo-Saturn 9	1st piloted flight of lunar module
1969	Apollo-Saturn 10	1st lunar module orbit of Moon
1969	Apollo-Saturn 11	1st Moon landing (Armstrong, Aldrin)
1971	Salyut	1st space station
1971	Soyuz 10	1st docking with space station
1971	Soyuz 11	1st crew to enter space station
1971	Apollo-Saturn 15	1st rover used on Moon
1973	Skylab 1	1st U.S. space station
1978	Soyuz 26, 27	1st multiple docking to a space station
1978	Soyuz 28	1st Czech in space (Remek)
1982	Columbia	1st reuse of space shuttle
1983	Challenger	1st U.S. woman in space (Ride)
1983	Challenger	1st U.S. black in space (Bluford)
1983	Columbia	1st Spacelab mission
1984	Challenger	1st satellite repair while in orbit
1984	Discovery	1st satellite retrieval
1986	Columbia	1st U.S. Rep. in space (Nelson)
1992	Endeavor	1st black woman in space (Jemison)
		1st married couple in space (Lee/Davis)
1993	Discovery	1st Hispanic woman in space (Ochoa)
1994	Discovery	1st Russian on U.S. shuttle (Krikalev)
1995	Soyuz	1st American aboard Russian craft
1995	Atlantis	1st docking with Mir space station

Source: National Aeronautics and Space Administration

The United States sent 235 men and women into space between 1961 and 1996. The world-wide total for the period is 370.

Going Places
Exploration of Other Planets -- Highlights

Launch Date	Spacecraft	Accomplishment
1962	Mariner 2	Passed within 22,000 mi. of Venus
1964	Mariner 4	Traveled behind Mars, photos
1969	Mariner 6	Within 2,000 mi. of Mars, photos
1971	Mariner 9	Orbited Mars, photos
1972	Pioneer 10	Passed Jupiter, left solar system
1973	Pioneer 11	Discovered additional ring of Saturn
1973	Mariner 10	Used gravity of Venus to reach Mercury
1975	Viking 1	Landed on Mars, 6 yrs. of research
1977	Viking 2	Landed on Mars, 3 yrs. of research
1977	Voyager 1	Reached Jupiter, neared Saturn
1977	Voyager 2	Reached Jupiter, Saturn, Uranus, Neptune
1978	Pioneer Venus 1	Entered Venus' orbit, 14 yrs.
1978	Pioneer Venus 2	Probes landed on Venus' surface
1989	Magellan	Orbited, mapped Venus
1989	Galileo	Released probe to Jupiter
1996	Mars Global Surveyor	Orbited, mapped Mars
1996	Mars Pathfinder	Landed, rover Sojourner conducted experiments
1997	Cassini	Scheduled to reach Saturn in 2004

Source: National Aeronautics and Space Administration

Formulas, Laws & Theories

How Big Is It?
Formulas to Calculate Area

Shape	Formula
Circle	Multiply diameter times π (3.14)
Rectangle	Multiply base times height
Sphere	The square of the radius times π (3.14), times 4
Square	Square the length of one side
Triangle	Multiply base times height, divide by 2

What Will Fit in It?
Formulas to Calculate Volume

Shape	Formula
Cone	Square of the radius of the base, multiply by π (3.14), multiply by the height, divide by 3
Cube	Cube the length of one side
Cylinder	Multiply the square of the radius of the base by π, (3.14), and multiply by height
Pyramid	Multiply the area of the base by the height, and divide by 3
Sphere	Multiply the cube of the radius by π (3.14), multiply by 4, and divide by 3

Newton's Laws of Motion

- *Inertia:* If no forces act on an object, the object will remain at rest or in motion at a constant velocity.

- *Acceleration:* A force on an object will accelerate the object at a rate proportional to the strength of the force and in the same direction as the force.

- *Action & Reaction:* An object experiences a force because it is interacting with another object. The force exerted by the first object on the second object is equal to the force exerted by the second object on the first object but in the opposite direction.

Light is a form of energy visible to the human eye. It is emitted by moving charged particles. The work of Albert Einstein led to an understanding of light as not only particles nor only waves, but a combination of both. The speed of light is 299,792.458 kilometers per second in a vacuum (186,282 statute miles per second). The brightness of light is measured in lumens -- units based on the brightness of a candle flame.

The speed of sound is usually defined as 1,088 feet per second. This is at sea level pressure, and at 32 degrees Fahrenheit. It travels at varying speeds according to the temperature and density of the media through which it moves. For example, while it takes sound five seconds to move through a mile of air, it travels a mile under water in one second.

Moving at the Speed of Sound

The Speed of Sound Through Various Media, in Feet per Second

Media	Speed
Air, 32 degrees F	1,088
Ice-cold vapor	4,708
Ice-cold water	4,938
Gold	5,717
Silver	8,656
Brick	11,960
Hardwood	12,620
Granite	12,960
Glass	16,410

From Gravitation to Relativity . . .

Early theories about gravitation include the Greek philosopher Aristotle's opinion (300 B.C.) that all things are made up of four components -- earth, air, fire and water -- and similar objects are drawn to each other. Hence objects with more earth in them are drawn to the Earth.

Later, 17th century Italian astronomer and physicist Galileo discovered that objects fall toward Earth with the same acceleration regardless of their weight.

Sir Isaac Newton developed a theory of mechanics and gravitation in 1687. His theory held that every object in the universe attracts every other object with a force that could be calculated by multiplying the two objects' masses and dividing by the square of the distance between them. This theory was accepted and used for many years.

Problems with Newton's theory became apparent when two observers measured the speed of a moving object. If the observers were also moving, in different directions or at different speeds, they did not perceive the same movement of the object. This suggested that speed was relative, not constant.

However, near the end of the 19th century, English physicist James Clerk Maxwell proposed a theory of electric and magnetic forces that found a constant speed -- the speed of light.

Albert Einstein, German born American physicist resolved the confusion with his theory of relativity in 1915. Relying on the constant of the speed of light, he

...To Quantum Physics

linked gravitation, acceleration, and four dimensional space-time (in which three dimensions represent space, and one represents time). Every object is described by a 'world line' that describes its position in time and space. When two lines intersect, an event takes place. This explained how two observers could see the same object moving at differing speeds. The space-time continuum, according to Einstein's theory, is curved in the neighborhood of massive objects (like planets). The world line of every object is a geodesic. This is the shortest distance between two points, but in curved space is not a straight line.

Since its introduction, Einstein's theory has been further developed and extended to include electromagnetic and cosmological applications. It also influenced the development of the quantum theory.

Quantum mechanics was first proposed by Max Planck in 1900. He theorized that all matter gives off or absorbs energy in distinct units called quanta. Applying the relativity theory improved the understanding of the structure of matter and of the atom. It showed that wave mechanics and matrix mechanics -- two theories used to explain electromagnetic particles and their behavior -- are simply different mathematical versions of the same theory. New fields of physics emerged, including solid-state physics, condensed matter physics, superconductivity, nuclear physics, and elementary particle physics -- all based on quantum mechanics.

The Evolution Theory

In the early 19th century, Jean Baptiste de Lamarck theorized that resemblances among certain species were the result of common ancestry.

In 1859, Charles Darwin published his theory of evolution in *On the Origin of Species by Means of Natural Selection.* Darwin reasoned that individuals of any species with qualities which make them more suited to their environments or better able to reproduce -- the most fit -- would leave more offspring. Those offspring would likely inherit many of those qualities. In this way, over time, the species would be modified to include the characteristics it most requires for survival.

At the beginning of the 20th century, the work of Austrian monk Gregor Mendel revealed that mutations -- or inheritable changes in genes -- could happen spontaneously. The theory of natural selection fell out of favor, as mutationism took hold.

Building on Mendel's work, a theory called population genetics developed. It held that when mutations occurred, they did not always spread through a population. The theory also developed the idea of the gene pool, or the genes available for inheritance in a generation. When a population is stable, the gene pool remains constant. When the gene pool shows sustained changes, evolution is occurring.

In the 1930s the research of American geneticist Theodsius Dobzhansky showed that genetics is compatible with Darwinian natural selection.

This led to a new theory of evolution called the synthetic theory. During its development, many exciting discoveries were made. German born zoologist Ernst Mayr showed that new species usually develop in isolation. Through studies of fossils, paleontologist George Simpson showed that rates and modes of evolution are correlated. Botanist G. Ledyard Stebbins showed that plants evolve in ways similar to animals. Perhaps the most exciting discovery of the period was in 1953, when American biochemist James Watson and British biophysicist Francis Crick revealed the structure of the genetic material DNA, beginning the study of evolution at the molecular level.

Evolution traces life to about 3.4 billion years ago, when single-celled organisms lived in water. They slowly evolved into multicellular plants and animals. The first land plants appeared about 400 million years ago, with animal life soon following them out of the water. Vertebrates rose from freshwater fish about 360 million years ago and developed into many forms. Five waves of mass extinctions are known to have eliminated species over the past 600 million years most notably the one that wiped out the dinosaurs 65 million years ago. Mammals survived, however, and continued to evolve. Human beings, through use of tools to control their environment, have proven uniquely able to adapt.

Scientific Discoveries

Who Discovered That?
Selected Scientific Discoveries

Discovery	Scientist	Nationality	Date
Adrenaline	Takamine	Japanese	1901
Anesthesia, ether	Long	U.S.	1842
Antiseptic surgery	Lister	English	1867
Aspirin	Dresser	German	1889
Atomic theory	Dalton	English	1803
Bacteria	Leeuwenhoek	Dutch	1676
Bleaching powder	Tennant	English	1798
Blood, circulation	Harvey	English	1628
Calculus	Newton	English	1670
Canning - food	Appert	French	1804
Combustion	Lavoisier	French	1777
Conditioned reflex	Pavlov	Russian	1914
DNA structure	Crick, Wilkins, Watson	English U.S.	1951
Electric resistance	Ohm	German	1827
Electric waves	Hertz	German	1888
Electrolysis	Faraday	English	1852
Electromagnetism	Oersted	Danish	1819
Electron	Thomson, J.	English	1897
Evolution	Darwin	English	1858
Falling bodies, law of	Galileo	Italian	1590
Geometry, analytic	Descartes	French	1619
Gold extraction	MacArthur, Forest	British	1887
Gravitation, law of	Newton	English	1687
Holograph	Gabor	British	1948
Human heart transplant	Barnard	S. African	1967
HIV	Montagnier, Gallo	French, U.S.	1984
Intelligence testing	Binet, Simon	French	1905
In vitro fertilization	Steptoe, Edwards	English	1978
Isotopes, theory of	Soddy	English	1912
Laser	Gould	U.S.	1957
Light, velocity of	Roemer	Danish	1675

Discovery	Scientist	Nationality	Date
Light, wave theory	Huygens	Dutch	1690
Motion, laws of	Newton	English	1687
Neutron	Chadwick	English	1932
Nitroglycerin	Sobrero	Italian	1846
Ozone	Schonbein	German	1840
Penicillin	Fleming	Scottish	1929
Periodic law and table of elements	Mendeleyev	Russian	1869
Planetary motion, laws	Kepler	German	1609
Positron	Anderson	U.S.	1932
Proton	Rutherford	N. Zealand	1919
Psychoanalysis	Freud	Austrian	1900
Quantum theory	Planck	German	1900
Radiocarbon dating	Libby	U.S.	1947
Relativity theory	Einstein	German	1905
Uranium fission theory	Hahn, Meitner, Strassmann	German German	1939
	Bohr	Danish	
	Fermi	Italian	
	Einstein, Pegram, Wheeler	U.S. U.S.	
Vaccine, measles	Enders, Peebles	U.S.	1954
Vaccine, polio	Salk	U.S.	1955
Vaccine, rabies	Pasteur	French	1885
Vaccine, smallpox	Jenner	English	1796
Vitamin A	McCollum, Davis	U.S.	1913
Vitamin B	McCollum	U.S.	1916
Vitamin C	Szent-Gyorgyi, King	U.S. U.S.	1928
Vitamin D	McCollum	U.S.	1922
Vitamin K	Dam, Doisy	U.S.	1935
X ray	Roentgen	German	1895

Chemical Elements

An Elemental Thing
Chemical Elements

Element	Symbol	Atomic Number	Atomic Weight
Actinium	Ac	89	227
Aluminum	Al	13	26.9815
Americium	Am	95	243
Antimony	Sb	51	121.75
Argon	Ar	18	39.948
Arsenic	As	33	74.9216
Astatine	At	85	210
Barium	Ba	56	137.34
Berkelium	Bk	97	249
Beryllium	Be	4	9.0122
Bismuth	Bi	83	208.980
Boron	B	5	10.811
Bromine	Br	35	79.904
Cadmium	Cd	48	112.40
Calcium	Ca	20	40.08
Californium	Cf	98	251
Carbon	C	6	12.01115
Cerium	Ce	58	140.12
Cesium	Cs	55	132.905
Chlorine	Cl	17	35.453
Chromium	Cr	24	51.996
Cobalt	Co	27	58.9332
Copper	Cu	29	63.546
Curium	Cm	96	24
Dysprosium	Dy	66	162.50*
Einsteinium	Es	99	254
Erbium	Er	68	167.26
Europium	Eu	63	151.96
Fermium	Fm	100	257
Fluorine	F	9	18.9984
Francium	Fr	87	223
Gadolinium	Gd	64	157.25
Gallium	Ga	31	69.72
Germanium	Ge	32	72.59
Gold	Au	79	196.967
Hafnium	Hf	72	178.49

Element	Symbol	Atomic Number	Atomic Weight
Hahnium	Ha	105	262
Hassium	Hs	108	265
Helium	He	2	4.0026
Holmium	Ho	67	164.930
Hydrogen	H	1	1.00797
Indium	In	49	114.82
Iodine	I	53	126.9044
Iridium	Ir	77	192.2
Iron	Fe	26	55.847
Krypton	Kr	36	83.80
Lanthanum	La	57	138.91
Lawrencium	Lr	103	262
Lead	Pb	82	207.19
Lithium	Li	3	6.939
Lutetium	Lu	71	174.97
Magnesium	Mg	12	24.312
Manganese	Mn	25	54.9380
Meitnerium	Mt	109	266
Mendelevium	Md	101	258
Mercury	Hg	80	200.59
Molybdenum	Mo	42	95.94
Neodymium	Nd	60	144.24
Neon	Ne	10	20.183
Neptunium	Np	93	237
Nickel	Ni	28	58.71
Nielsbohrium	Ns	107	262
Niobium	Nb	41	92.906
Nitrogen	N	7	14.0067
Nobelium	No	102	259
Osmium	Os	76	190.2
Oxygen	O	8	15.9994
Palladium	Pd	46	106.4
Phosphorus	P	15	30.9738
Platinum	Pt	78	195.09
Plutonium	Pu	94	242
Polonium	Po	84	210
Potassium	K	19	39.102
Praseodymium	Pr	59	140.907

Element	Symbol	Atomic Number	Atomic Weight
Promethium	Pm	61	147
Protactinium	Pa	91	231
Radium	Ra	88	226
Radon	Rn	86	222
Rhenium	Re	75	186.2
Rhodium	Rh	45	102.905
Rubidium	Rb	37	85.47
Ruthenium	Ru	44	101.07
Rutherfordium	Rf	104	261
Samarium	Sm	62	150.35
Scandium	Sc	21	44.956
Seaborgium	Sg	106	266
Selenium	Se	34	78.96
Silicon	Si	14	28.086
Silver	Ag	47	107.868
Sodium	Na	11	22.9898
Strontium	Sr	38	87.62
Sulfur	S	16	32.064
Tantalum	Ta	73	180.948
Technetium	Tc	43	99
Tellurium	Te	52	127.60
Terbium	Tb	65	158.924
Thallium	Tl	81	204.37
Thorium	Th	90	232.038
Thulium	Tm	69	168.934
Tin	Sn	50	118.69
Titanium	Ti	22	47.90
Tungsten	W	74	183.85
Uranium	U	92	238.03
Vanadium	V	23	50.942
Xenon	Xe	54	131.30
Ytterbium	Yb	70	173.04
Yttrium	Y	39	88.905
Zinc	Zn	30	65.37
Zirconium	Zr	40	91.22

Inventions

The Best Thing Since Sliced Bread
Selected Inventions

Invention	Inventor	Nationality	Date
Air conditioning	Carrier	U.S.	1911
Airplane with motor	Wright bros.	U.S.	1903
Automobile, experimental	Marcus	Austrian	1864
Automobile, gasoline	Daimler	German	1889
Automobile muffler	Pope	U.S.	1904
Balloon	Montgolfier	French	1783
Barometer	Toricelli	Italian	1643
Bicycle, modern	Starley	English	1885
Bifocal	Franklin	U.S.	1780
Carburetor, gasoline	Maybach	German	1893
Carpet sweeper	Bissel	U.S.	1876
Cash register	Ritty	U.S.	1879
Cassette, audio	Phillips Co.	U.S.	1963
Cassette, video	Sony	Japanese	1969
CAT scan	Hounsfield	English	1973
Cellophane	Brandenberger	Swiss	1908
Circuit breaker	Hilliard	U.S.	1925
Computer, electronic	Atanasoff, Berry	U.S.	1942
Computer, mini	Digital Corp.	U.S.	1960
Contraceptive, oral	Pincus, Rock	U.S.	1954
Cotton gin	Whitney	U.S.	1793
Diesel engine	Diesel	German	1895
Disc, compact	RCA	U.S.	1972
Disk, floppy	IBM	U.S.	1970
Disc, video	Phillips Co.	Dutch	1972
Dynamite	Nobel	Swedish	1866
Electric battery	Volta	Italian	1800

Invention	Inventor	Nationality	Date
Electric fan	Wheeler	U.S.	1882
Electrocardiograph	Einthoven	Dutch	1903
Engine, auto. transmission	Fottinger	German	1910
Engine, electric ignition	Benz	German	1883
Engine, gasoline	Brayton, Geo	U.S.	1872
Engine, jet	Whittle	English	1930
Fiberglass	Owens-Corning	U.S.	1930
Fiber optics	Kapany	English	1955
Gas lighting	Murdoch	Scottish	1792
Gasoline, high octane	Ipatieff	Russian	1930
Geiger counter	Geiger	German	1913
Glider	Cayley	English	1853
Gun, breechloader	Thornton	U.S.	1811
Gyroscope	Foucault	French	1852
Heart, artificial	Jarvik	U.S.	1982
Helicopter	Sikorsky	U.S.	1939
Lamp, incandescent	Edison	U.S.	1879
Lightning rod	Franklin	U.S.	1752
Linoleum	Walton	English	1860
Locomotive, electric	Vail	U.S.	1851
Machine gun	Gatling	U.S.	1861
Microphone	Berliner	U.S.	1877
Microprocessor	Intel Corp.	U.S.	1971
Microscope, compound	Janssen	Dutch	1590
Motor, AC	Tesla	U.S.	1892
Motor, DC	Davenport	U.S.	1837
Motorcycle	Daimler	German	1885
Movie machine	Jenkins	U.S.	1894
Movie, talking	Warner Bros.	U.S.	1927
Nylon	Dupont Corp.	U.S.	1937
Paper	Ts'ai	Chinese	105
Parachute	Blanchard	French	1785
Pen, ball point	Loud	U.S.	1888
Phonograph	Edison	U.S.	1877
Photo, color	Ives	U.S.	1892
Piano	Cristofori	Italian	1709

Invention	Inventor	Nationality	Date
Pin, safety	Hunt	U.S.	1849
Pistol	Colt	U.S.	1836
Radio beacon	Donovan	U.S.	1928
Radio, signals	Marconi	Italian	1895
Razor, electric	Shick	U.S.	1917
Razor, safety	Gillette	U.S.	1895
Record, LP	Goldmarck	U.S.	1947
Refrigerator car	David	U.S.	1868
Richter scale	Richter	U.S.	1935
Rifle, repeating	Spencer	U.S.	1860
Rubber, vulcanized	Goodyear	U.S.	1839
Sewing machine	Howe	U.S.	1846
Slide rule	Oughtred	English	1820
Steel, stainless	Brearley	English	1916
Stock ticker	Edison	U.S.	1870
Stove, electric	Hadaway	U.S.	1896
Submarine	Holland	U.S.	1891
Synthesizer	Moog	U.S.	1964
Tank, military	Swinton	English	1914
Tape recorder, magnetic	Poulsen	Danish	1899
Teflon	Dupont	U.S.	1938
Telegraph, magnetic	Morse	U.S.	1837
Telephone	Bell	U.S.-Scot	1876
Telescope	Lippershey	Neth.	1608
Television, color	Baird	Scottish	1928
Television, electronic	Farnsworth	U.S.	1927
Thermometer	Galileo	Italian	1593
Thermometer, mercury	Farenheit	German	1714
Tire, pneumatic	Dunlop	Scottish	1888
Toaster, automatic	Strite	U.S.	1918
Toilet, flush	Harrington	English	1589
Type, movable	Guttenberg	German	1447
Vacuum cleaner	Spangler	U.S.	1907
Velcro	De Mestral	Swiss	1948
Washer, electric	Fisher	U.S.	1901
X-ray tube	Coolidge	U.S.	1913

Companies Receiving the Most U.S. Patents

1. IBM
2. Cannon
3. Motorola
4. NEC
5. Hitachi
6. Mitsubishi Denki
7. Toshiba
8. Fujitsu
9. Sony
10. Matsushita
11. General Electric
12. Kodak
13. Xerox
14. Texas Instruments
15. Minnesota Mining
16. AT&T Corp.
17. Fuji Photo Film
18. Hewlett-Packard
19. Samsung Electronics
20. U.S. Phillips Corp.

Source: U.S. Patent and Trademark Office, 1996

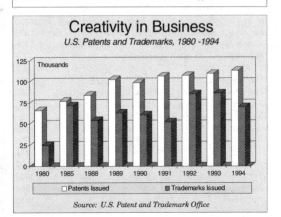

Creativity in Business
U.S. Patents and Trademarks, 1980 -1994

Thousands

	1980	1985	1988	1989	1990	1991	1992	1993	1994

□ Patents Issued   ▣ Trademarks Issued

Source: U.S. Patent and Trademark Office

14. The Environment

See also 'Weather' & 'Travel.'

Bodies of Water

Mountains

Volcanoes

Forests

Deserts

Animals

Pollution

Bodies of Water

As Deep as the Ocean
Area and Depth of the World's Oceans

Ocean	Area (square miles)	Average Depth (feet)	Deepest Point	Depth of Deepest Point
Pacific	64,186,300	12,925	Mariana Trench	35,840
Atlantic	33,420,000	11,730	Puerto Rico Trench	28,232
Indian	28,350,500	12,598	Java Trench	23,376
Arctic	5,105,700	3,407	Eurasia Basin	17,881

The world ocean covers 71% of the Earth's surface. Geographers divide it into four parts: Pacific, Atlantic, Indian, and Arctic. The water in the oceans contains salts (sodium and chlorine) from eroding continental rocks. It averages about 35 parts salt per 1,000 parts water. Ocean temperatures range from 79°F in tropical areas to 29.5°F in polar regions.

Where oceans meet continents, the continental shelf slopes gently seaward. It becomes steeper at about 660 feet and is called the continental slope. At 12,000 feet begins the continental rise, which is part of the ocean bottom. It continues to the abyssal plains of the ocean bottom, where there is a system of ridges and trenches.

As Wide as the Sea

Area and Depth of the World's Largest Seas, Gulfs, and Bays

Body of Water	Area (sq. mi.)	Depth (feet)
South China Sea	1,148,500	4,802
Caribbean Sea	971,400	8,448
Mediterranean Sea	969,100	4,926
Bering Sea	873,000	4,893
Gulf of Mexico	582,100	5,297
Sea of Okhotsk	537,500	3,192
Sea of Japan	391,100	5,468
Hudson Bay	281,900	305
East China Sea	256,600	620
Andaman Sea	218,100	3,667
Black Sea	196,100	3,906
Red Sea	174,900	1,764
North Sea	164,900	308
Baltic Sea	147,500	180
Yellow Sea	113,500	121
Persian Gulf	88,800	328
Gulf of California	59,100	2,375

The word 'sea' refers to bodies of saltwater which are partially landlocked.

World's Largest Natural Lakes
in Square Miles

1.	Caspian S.	143,244	11.	Great Slave	11,031
2.	Superior	31,700	12.	Erie	9,910
3.	Victoria	26,828	13.	Winnipeg	9,417
4.	Aral Sea	24,904	14.	Ontario	7,340
5.	Huron	23,000	15.	Balkhash	7,115
6.	Michigan	22,300	16.	Ladoga	6,835
7.	Tanganyika	12,700	17.	Chad	6,300
8.	Baykal	12,162	18.	Maracaibo	5,217
9.	Great Bear	12,096	19.	Onega	3,710
10.	Nyasa	11,150	20.	Eyre	3,600

North American Rivers

Major Rivers of North America (450 Miles or Longer)

River	Length (miles)	Source or Upper Limit	Outflow
Alabama	729	Gilmer Co., GA	Mobile R.
Albany	610	Ontario	James Bay
Altamaha-Apalachicola-Chattahoochee	524	Towns Co., GA	Gulf of Mexico
Arkansas	1,459	Lake Co., CO	Mississippi R.
Assiniboine	450	Saskatchewan	Red R.
Attawapiskat	465	Ontario	James Bay
Back (NWT)	605	Contwoyto Lake	Arctic Ocean
Brazos	923	Stonewall Co., TX	Gulf of Mexico
Canadian	906	Las Animas Co., CO	Arkansas R.
Churchill, Man.	1,000	Saskatchewan	Hudson Bay
Cimarron	600	Colfax County, NM	Arkansas R.
Colorado (AZ)	1,450	Rky. Mt. Natl. Pk., CO	Gulf of CA
Colorado (TX)	862	West Texas	Matagorda Bay
Columbia	1,243	British Columbia	Pacific Ocean
Columbia, Upper	890	British Columbia	Snake River
Coppermine (NWT)	525	Lac de Gras	Arctic Ocean
Cumberland	720	Letcher County, KY	Ohio R.
Fraser	850	Near Mt. Robson	Strait of Georgia
Gila	649	Catron County, NM	Colorado R.
Green (UT-WY)	730	Sublette Co., WY	Colorado R.
Hamilton (Lab.)	532	Lake Ashuanipi	Atlantic Ocean
James (ND-SD)	710	Wells County, ND	Missouri R.
Koyukuk	470	Endicott Mts., AK	Yukon R.
Kuskokwim	724	Alaska Range	Kuskokwim Bay
Liard	693	S. Yukon, Alaska	Mackenzie R.
Little Missouri	560	Crook Co., WY	Missouri R.
Mackenzie	1,025	N.W.T.	Arctic Ocean
Milk	625	Alberta	Missouri R.
Mississippi	2,340	Lake Itasca, MN	Mth. of SW Pass
Mississippi, Upr.	1,171	Lake Itasca, MN	Missouri R.

Major Rivers of North America, Continued

River	Length (miles)	Source or Upper Limit	Outflow
Mississippi-Missouri-Red Rock	3,710	Beaverhead Co., MT	Mth. of SW Pass
Missouri	2,315	Madison County, MT	Mississippi R.
Missouri-Red Rock	2,540	Beaverhead Co., MT	Mississippi R.
Mobile-Alabama-Coosa	774	Gilmer County, GA	Mobile Bay
Neosho	460	Morris County, KS	Arkansas R., OK
North Canadian	800	Union County, NM	Canadian R., OK
North Platte	618	Jackson County, CO	Platte R., NE
Ohio	981	Pittsburgh, PA	Mississippi R.
Ohio-Allegheny	1,310	Potter County, PA	Mississippi R.
Osage	500	East-central KS	Missouri R.
Ottawa	790	Lk. Capimitchigama	St. Lawrence R.
Ouachita	605	Polk Co., AR	Black R.
Peace	1,210	Stikine Mts., B.C.	Slave R.
Pecos	926	Mora Co., NM	Rio Grande
Pend Oreille-Clark Fork	531	Butte, MT	Columbia R.
Porcupine	569	Ogilvie Mts., AK	Yukon R., AK
Red (OK-TX-LA)	1,290	Curry Co., NM	Atchafalaya R.
Red River of the North	545	Wilkin Co., MN	Lake Winnipeg
Rio Grande	1,900	San Juan Co., CO	Gulf of Mexico
St. Lawrence	800	Lake Ontario	Atlantic Ocean
Santee-Wateree-Catawba	538	McDowell Co., NC	Atlantic Ocean
Saskatchewan, N.	800	Rocky Mts.	Saskatchewan R.
Saskatchewan, S.	865	Rocky Mts.	Saskatchewan R.
Severn (Ont.)	610	Sandy Lake	Hudson Bay
Smoky Hill	540	Cheyenne Co., CO	Kansas R., KS
Snake	1,038	Teton Co., WY	Columbia R., WA

Major Rivers of North America, Continued

River	Length (miles)	Source or Upper Limit	Outflow
Tanana	659	Wrangell Mts., AK	Yukon R.
Tennessee	652	Fr. Broad/Holston R.	Ohio R.
Tennessee-French Broad	886	Transylvania Co., NC	Ohio R.
Tombigbee	525	Prentiss Co., MS	Mobile R.
Wabash	512	Darke Co., OH	Ohio R.
Washita	500	Hemphill Co., TX	Red River, OK
White (AR-MO)	722	Madison Co., AR	Mississippi R.
Yellowstone	692	Park Co., WY	Missouri R.
Yukon	1,979	McNeil R., Yukon	Bering Sea

Source: U.S. Department of the Interior

World's Longest Rivers
in Miles

1.	Nile	4,160	12.	Parana	2,485
2.	Amazon	4,000	13.	Mississippi	2,340
3.	Chang	3,964	14.	Missouri	2,315
4.	Huang	3,395	15.	Murray-Darling	2,310
5.	Ob-Irtysh	3,362			
6.	Amur	2,744	16.	Volga	2,290
7.	Lena	2,734	17.	Purus	2,100
8.	Congo	2,718	18.	Madiera	2,013
9.	Mekong	2,600	19.	San Francisco	1,988
10.	Niger	2,590	20.	Yukon	1,979
11.	Yenisey	2,543			

Longest Rivers in North America
in Miles

1.	Mackenzie-Peace	2,635	6.	Rio Grande	1,760
2.	Mississippi	2,348	7.	Nelson	1,600
3.	Missouri	2,315	8.	Arkansas	1,459
4.	Yukon	1,979	9.	Colorado	1,450
5.	St. Lawrence	1,945	10.	Atchafalaya-Red	1,432

Longest Rivers in South America
in Miles

1.	Amazon	4,007
2.	Plata-Parana	2,485
3.	Madiera-Mamore	2,100
4.	Purus	1,993
5.	Sao Francisco	1,987

Longest Rivers in Asia
in Miles

1.	Yangze	3,915
2.	Yenisey-Anagara-Selenga	3,442
3.	Huang-Ho	3,395
4.	Ob-Irtysh	3,362
5.	Lena-Kerengal	2,734

Longest Rivers in Europe
in Miles

1.	Danube	1,766	6.	Meuse	590
2.	Rhine	850	7.	Ebro	580
3.	Elbe	725	8.	Rhone	505
4.	Loire	630	9.	Guadiana	500
5.	Tagus	627	10.	Seine	482

Waterfalls are sudden sheer descents of a stream or river over a steep drop in its bed.

A Long Way Down
The World's Highest Waterfalls

Fall	Total Drop in Feet	Location
Angel	3,212	Venezuela
Tugela	3,110	South Africa
Utigard	2,625	Norway
Mongefosssen	2,540	Norway
Yosemite	2,425	California
Ostre Mardola Foss	2,154	Norway
Tyssestrengane	2,120	Norway
Cuquenan	2,000	Venezuela
Sutherland	1,904	New Zealand
Kjellfossen	1,841	Norway

Quite a Shower
The World's Mightiest Waterfalls, by Volume of Water, in Cubic Meters per Second

Fall	Average Flow	Location
Boyoma	17,000	Congo (Zaire)
Khone	11,610	Laos
Niagara	5,830	Canada, U.S.
Grande	4,500	Uruguay
Paulo Afonso	2,890	Brazil
Urubupunga	2,750	Brazil
Iguacu	1,700	Argentina, Brazil
Maribondo	1,500	Brazil
Churchill	1,390	Canada
Kabalega	1,200	Uganda

Mountains

Most mountains are formed by geological processes involving plate tectonics. The massive plates which make up the Earth's crust move slowly over time and periodically collide with each other. The tremendous pressures exerted by the meeting of these plates trigger processes such as folding, in which portions of the crust are wrinkled and bulge upward; and lifting, in which a thick sheet of rock is thrust over another sheet. The results of this violent activity are mountains, ridges, ranges, and the valleys between them. Over time, erosion carves away the rough edges, vegetation grows, and the mountains become smoother and lower. In the United States, the newest -- and highest -- mountain ranges are in the West, such as the Rocky Mountains. The older and much lower mountains are in the East, such as the Appalachians and the Piedmonts.

North American Heights
Highest Mountains in North America

Mountain	Height in Feet	Location
McKinley	20,320	AK
Logan	19,850	Yukon
Citlaltepetl (Orizaba)	18,700	Mexico
St. Elias	18,008	AK-Yukon
Popocatépetl	17,930	Mexico
Foraker	17,400	AK
Iztaccihuatl	17,343	Mexico
Lucania	17,147	Yukon
King	16,971	Yukon
Steele	16,644	Yukon
Bona	16,550	AK
Blackburn	16,390	AK
Kennedy	16,286	AK
Sanford	16,237	AK
Vancouver	15,979	AK-Yukon
South Buttress	15,885	AK
Wood	15,885	Yukon
Churchill	15,638	AK
Fairweather	15,300	AK-BC
Zinantecatl (Toluca)	15,016	Mexico
Hubbard	15,015	AK-Yukon
Bear	14,831	AK
Walsh	14,780	Yukon

Icy Peaks
Highest Mountains in Antarctica

Mountain	Height in Feet
Vinson Massif	16,864
Tyree	16,290
Shinn	15,750
Gardner	15,375
Epperly	15,100

The first attempts to climb Mt. Everest, the world's tallest mountain, were made in the 1920s.

The first woman to reach the summit was Junko Tabei of Japan in 1975. The first climber to complete the ascent alone and without oxygen was Italian Reinhold Messner, in 1980.

The First to Climb to Mt. Everest's Peak

1. Edmund Hillary 5/29/53
2. Tenzeng Norgay 5/29/53
3. Jurg Marmet 5/23/56
4. Ernst Schmied 5/23/56
5. Hans-Rudolf von Gunten 5/24/56
6. Adolf Reist 5/24/56
7. Wang Fu-chou 5/25/60
8. Chu Ying-hua 5/25/60
9. Konbu 5/25/60
10. Nawang Gombu and James Whittaker 5/1/63

Great Heights of Asia

Highest Mountains in the Asian Mainland

Mountain	Height in Feet	Location
Everest	29,028	Nepal-Tibet
K2 (Godwin Austen)	28,250	Kashmir
Kanchenjunga	28,208	India-Nepal
Lhotse I (Everest)	27,923	Nepal-Tibet
Makalu I	27,824	Nepal-Tibet
Lhotse II (Everest)	27,560	Nepal-Tibet
Dhaulagiri	26,810	Nepal
Manaslu I	26,760	Nepal
Cho Oyu	26,750	Nepal-Tibet
Nanga Parbat	26,660	Kashmir

Peaks Along the Europe-Asia Border
Highest Mountains in Caucasus Mountains

Mountain	Height in Feet	Location
Elbrus	18,510	Russia
Shkara	17,064	Russia
Dykh Tau	17,054	Russia
Kashtan Tau	16,877	Russia
Dzhangi Tau	16,565	Russia

High Points of Europe
Highest Mountains in the Alps

Mountain	Height in Feet	Location
Mont Blanc	15,771	France-Italy
Monte Rosa	15,203	Switzerland
Dom	14,911	Switzerland
Liskamm	14,852	Italy-Switzerland
Weisshorn	14,780	Switzerland

Southeastern Mountains
Highest Mountains in Africa, Southeast Islands, Australia, & New Zealand

Mountain	Height in Feet	Location
Kilimanjaro	19,340	Tanzania
Kenya	17,058	Tanzania
Margherita Pk	16,763	Uganda-Zaire
Jaya	16,500	New Guinea
Trikora	15,585	New Guinea

Southern Peaks
Highest Mountains in South America

Mountain	Height in Feet	Location
Aconcagua	22,834	Argentina
Ojos del Salado	22,572	Argentina-Chile
Bonete	22,546	Argentina
Tupungato	22,310	Argentina-Chile
Pissis	22,241	Argentina

Volcanoes

Nearly 75% of the world's 540 active volcanoes are found in The Ring of Fire -- a zone running along the west coast of the Americas, down the east cost of Asia, to New Zealand.

Explosive Mountains

Volcanoes -- Active Since 1995 in Africa

Volcano	Location	Most Recent Eruption
Ol Doinyo Lengai	Tanzania	1996
Erta-Ale	Ethiopia	1995

Volcanoes -- Active Since 1995 in Antarctica

Volcano	Location	Most Recent Eruption
Erebus	Ross Island	1995

Volcanoes -- Active Since 1995 in Asia-Oceana

Volcano	Location	Most Recent Eruption
Kliuchevskoi	Russia	1995
Semeru	Java, Indonesia	1995
Merapi	Java, Indonesia	1995
Bezymianny	Russia	1995
Ruapehu	New Zealand	1995
Manam	Papua New Guinea	1996
Soputan	Celebes, Indonesia	1996
Karangetang	Sangihe, Indonesia	1995
Pinatubo	Luzon, Phillipines	1995
Akita Komaga-take	Honshu, Japan	1996
Aso	Kyushu, Japan	1995
Bulusan	Luzon, Phillipines	1995
Karymsky	Russia	1996

Volcanoes -- Active Since 1995 in Asia-Oceana, Continued

Volcano	Location	Most Recent Eruption
Unzen	Kyushu, Japan	1996
Sakura-jima	Kyushu, Japan	1996
Langila	Papua New Guinea	1996
Krakatau	Indonesia	1995
Suwanose-jima	Kyushu, Japan	1996
Rabaul	Papua New Guinea	1996
White Island	New Zealand	1995

Volcanoes -- Active Since 1995 in the Mid-Atlantic & Mid-Pacific

Volcano	Location	Most Recent Eruption
Kilauea	Hawaii, HI	1996

Volcanoes -- Active Since 1995 in Cent. America & the Caribbean

Volcano	Location	Most Recent Eruption
Pacaya	Guatemala	1995
Rincón de la Vieja	Costa Rica	1995
Arenal	Costa Rica	1996

Volcanoes -- Active Since 1995 in Europe

Volcano	Location	Most Recent Eruption
Etna	Italy	1996
Stromboli	Italy	1996

Volcanoes -- Active Since 1995 in North & South America

Volcano	Location	Most Recent Eruption
Popocatépetl	Mexico	1996
Shishaldin	Aleutian Isl., AK	1995
Veniaminof	Alaska	1995
Láscar	Chile	1995
Sangay	Ecuador	1996
Llaima	Chile	1995
Fernandina	Galapagos Isls., Ecuador	1995

Forests

32% of the Earth's land area is tree-covered.

In the Trees
Countries with the Most Forestland

Country	Forest Area in Acres	Country	Forest Area in Acres
Russia	1,892,607,000	Australia	358,302,000
Canada	1,220,699,000	China	322,462,000
Brazil	1,205,872,000	Indonesia	276,199,000
United States	731,406,000	Peru	209,545,000
Zaire	429,468,000	India	169,267,000
		World Total	10,225,227,000

Americans in the Woods
Largest U.S. National Forests

About 29% of America's land area is forestland.

Forest	Acres	Location
Tongass National Forest	16,719,874	Sitka, AK
Chugach National Forest	5,404,414	Anchorage, AK
Toiyabe National Forest	3,212,229	Sparks, NV
Tonto National Forest	2,874,593	Phoenix, AZ
Boise National Forest	2,647,740	Boise, ID
Humboldt National Forest	2,478,102	Elko, NV
Challis National Forest	2,464,524	Challis, ID
Shoshone National Forest	2,436,834	Cody, WY
Flathead National Forest	2,354,511	Kalispell, MT
Payette National Forest	2,323,232	McCall, ID

World's Most Forested Countries
by Percent of Land Area

1.	Suraname	92%
2.	Papua New Guinea	91%
3.	Solomon Islands	85%
4.	French Guiana	81%
5.	Guyana	77%
6.	Gabon	74%
7.	Finland	69%
8.	Bhutan	66%
9.	Japan	66%
10.	North Korea	65%

The tallest known trees in the United States are the Coast Douglas Firs found in Coos County, Oregon, which reach 329 feet, and the Coast Redwoods growing in Humboldt Redwoods State Park, California to heights of 313 feet.

There are three types of forest fires. Ground fires burn the humus layer of the forest floor but do not damage much above the surface. Surface fires burn forest undergrowth and surface litter. Crown fires spread through the tops of trees. Most forest fires are caused by human carelessness, but some result from lightning. Some fires are nature's way of maintaining its ecosystem, so complete fire suppression might allow too much fuel to accumulate, perhaps increasing the chances of catastrophic fires.

Deserts

Aswan, Egypt, at the Sahara's edge, reports an annual average of 0.02 inches of rainfall, making it the world's driest inhabited place.

Sand & More Sand
Largest Deserts in the World

Desert	Size	Location
Arabian (Eastern)	70,000 sq. mi.	Egypt, Sudan
Atacama	600-mi. long	N Chile
Chihuahuan	140,000 sq. mi.	TX, NM, AZ, Mexico
Dasht-e Kauir	300 mi. long	N Central Iran
Dasht-e Lut	20,000 sq. mi.	E Iran
Death Valley	3,300 sq. mi.	California and Nevada
Gibson	120,000 sq. mi.	W Australia
Gobi	500,000 sq. mi.	Mongolia and China
Great Sandy	150,000 sq. mi.	W Australia
Great Victoria	150,000 sq. mi.	SW Australia
Kalahari	225,000 sq. mi.	S Africa
Kara Kum	120,000 sq. mi.	Turkmenistan
Kyzyl Kum	100,000 sq. mi.	Kazakstan and Uzbekistan
Libyan	450,000 sq. mi.	In the Sahara, Libya, SW Egypt, Sudan
Mojave	15,000 sq. mi.	S California
Namib	800 mi. long	SW coast of Africa
Nubian	100,000 sq. mi.	In the Sahara in NE Sudan
Patagonia	300,000 sq. mi.	S Argentina
Painted Desert	150 mi. long	N Arizona
Rub al-Khali	250,000 sq. mi.	Arabian Peninsula
Sahara	3,500,000 sq. mi.	N Africa
Sonoran	70,000 sq. mi.	SW AZ, SE CA, Mexico
Syrian	100,000 sq.-mi.	N Saudi Arabia, E Jordan, S Syria, and W Iraq
Taklimakan	140,000 sq. mi.	Xinjiang Prov., China
Thar	100,000 sq.-mi.	India-Pakistan border

Animals

There are hundreds of breeds of dogs but only eight originated in America. They are the Alaskan Malamute, American Foxhound, American Staffordshire Terrier, Basset Hound, Black and Tan Coonhound, Boston Terrier, Chesapeake Bay Retriever, and Siberian Husky.
Source: Dog Facts

Cats are the most common pets in America (we own about 66 million), followed by dogs (58 million) and parakeets (14 million).

Most Common Dog Breeds

1. Labrador Retriever
2. Rottweiler
3. German Shepherd
4. Golden Retriever
5. Beagle
6. Poodle
7. Dachshund
8. Cocker Spaniel
9. Yorkshire Terrier
10. Pomeranian

Source: The American Kennel Club

Most Common Cat Breeds

1. Persian
2. Maine Coon
3. Siamese
4. Abyssinian
5. Exotic
6. Scottish Fold
7. Oriental Shorthair
8. Am. Shorthair
9. Birman
10. Burmese

Source: Cat Fanciers Association

Most Common Female Dog Names

1. Princess
2. Lady
3. Sandy
4. Sheba
5. Ginger
6. Brandy
7. Samantha
8. Daisy
9. Missy
10. Misty

Most Common Male Dog Names

1. Max
2. Rocky
3. Lucky
4. Duke
5. King
6. Rusty
7. Prince
8. Buddy
9. Buster
10. Blacky

Source: New York City Department of Health, 1996

Most Common Female Cat Names

1. Samantha
2. Misty
3. Patches
4. Cali/Calico
5. Muffn
6. Angel/Angela
7. Ginger
8. Tiger/Tigger
9. Princess
10. Punkin/Pumpkin

Most Common Male Cat Names

1. Tiger/Tigger
2. Smokey
3. Pepper
4. Max/Maxwell
5. Simon
6. Snoopy
7. Morris
8. Mickey
9. Rusty/Rusti
10. Boots/Bootsie

Source: <u>Famous Names for Your Pampered Pet</u>

Heaviest Sea Animals
in Tons

1. Blue whale   143.3
2. Fin whale   49.6
3. Right whale   44.1
4. Sperm whale   39.7
5. Gray whale   36.0

Fastest Swimming Fish
in Miles per Hour

1. Sailfish   68
2. Marlin   50
3. Bluefin tuna   46
4. Yellowfin tuna   44
5. Blue shark   43

Longest Snakes
in Feet

1. Royal python   35
2. Anaconda   28
3. Indian python   25
4. Diamond python   21
5. King cobra   19
6. Boa constrictor   16
7. Bushmaster   12
8. Giant brn. snake   11
9. Diamondback Rattlesnake   9
10. Indigo or gopher snake   8

Largest Flightless Birds
in Pounds

1. Ostrich   345
2. Emu   88
3. Cassowary   73
4. Rhea   55
5. Emperor penguin   64

Fastest Flying Birds
in Miles per Hour

1. Spine-tailed Swift   106
2. Frigate bird   95
3. Spur-winged Goose   88
4. Red-breasted Merganser   80
5. White-rumped Swift   77

Most Common Birds in America

1. Red-winged blackbird
2. House sparrow
3. Mourning dove
4. European starling
5. American robin

Heaviest Land Animals *in Pounds*		
1.	African elephant	14,432
2.	White rhinoceros	7,937
3.	Hippopotamus	5,512
4.	Giraffe	2,527
5.	Amerian bison	2,205

Longest Land Animals *in Feet*		
1.	Royal python	35
2.	Tapeworm	33
3.	African elephant	24
4.	Crocodile	19
5.	Giraffe	19

Running Like the Wind
Speeds of Land Animals, in Miles per Hour

Animal	Speed	Animal	Speed
Cheetah	70	Reindeer	32
Pronghorn antelope	61	Giraffe	32
Wildebeest	50	White-tailed deer	30
Lion	50	Wart hog	30
Thomson's gazelle	50	Grizzly bear	30
Quarterhorse	47.5	Cat (domestic)	30
Elk	45	Human	27.89
Cape hunting dog	45	Elephant	25
Coyote	43	Black mamba snake	20
Gray fox	42	Six-lined race runner	18
Hyena	40	Wild turkey	15
Zebra	40	Squirrel	12
Mongolian wild ass	40	Pig (domestic)	11
Greyhound	39.35	Chicken	9
Whippet	35.5	Spider (Tegenaria atrica)	1.17
Rabbit (domestic)	35	Giant tortoise	0.17
Mule deer	35	Three-toed sloth	0.15
Jackal	35	Garden snail	0.03

Source: U.S. Fish and Wildlife Service

Selected Endangered Species

Armadillo, giant
Bat, gray
Bison, wood
Bobcat
Camel, Bactrian
Caribou, woodland
Cheetah
Chimpanzee, pygmy
Condor, California
Cougar, eastern
Crane, hooded
Crane, whooping
Crocodile, American
Curlew, Eskimo
Dolphin, Chinese river
Elephant, Asian
Falcon, American
    peregrine
Fox, northern swift
Frog, Israel painted
Gorilla
Hawk, Hawaiian
Hyena, brown
Kangaroo, Tasmanian
Leopard
Lion, Asiatic
Macaw, indigo
Manatee, West Indian
Ocelot
Ostrich, West African

Otter, marine
Panda, giant
Panther, Florida
Parakeet, golden
Parrot, imperial
Python, Indian
Rhinoceros, black
Rhinoceros, northern
    white
Salamander, Chinese
    giant
Sea turtle, leatherback
Squirrel, Carolina
    northern
Stork, Oriental white
Tiger
Tortoise, Galapagos
Turtle, Plymouth red-
    bellied
Whale, gray
Whale, humpback
Wolf, red
Woodpecker, ivory-billed
Yak, wild
Zebra, mountain

Dwindling Wildlife
Number of U.S. Endangered & Threatened Species

Group	Endangered		Threatened	
	U.S.	Foreign	U.S.	Foreign
Mammals	55	252	9	19
Birds	76	178	16	6
Reptiles	14	65	19	15
Amphibians	7	8	6	1
Fishes	65	11	40	0
Snails	15	1	7	0
Clams	51	2	6	0
Crustaceans	14	0	3	0
Insects	20	4	9	0
Arachnids	5	0	0	0
Animal total	*320*	*521*	*115*	*41*
Flowering plants	403	1	92	0
Conifers	2	0	0	2
Ferns, others	26	0	2	0
Plant total	*431*	*1*	*94*	*2*
Grand total	*751*	*522*	*209*	*43*

World's Most Endangered Species
Number Remaining

1. Tasmanian wolf — ?
2. Halcon fruit bat — ?
3. Ghana fat mouse — ?
4. Javan rhinocerous — 50
5. Iromote cat — 60

America's Most Endangered Birds

1. Golden-cheeked warbler
2. Kirtland's warbler
3. Bachman's warbler
4. Black-capped vireo
5. Cerulean warbler
6. Colima warbler
7. Golden-winged warbler
8. Black swift
9. Baird's sparrow
10. Cassin's sparrow

Pollution

Getting Easier to Breathe

Number of Days Air Quality Failed to Meet EPA Standards

MSA	1986	1988	1990	1992	1994	1995
Atlanta, GA	18	21	17	5	4	19
Bakersfield, CA	54	85	48	16	45	45
Baltimore, MD	23	43	12	5	17	14
Boston, MA	2	15	1	1	1	1
Chicago, IL	9	22	3	7	8	4
Dallas, TX	9	14	8	3	1	13
Denver, CO	49	19	9	7	2	2
Detroit, MI	5	17	3	0	8	11
El Paso, TX	43	16	27	13	10	4
Fresno, CA	37	29	22	27	11	19
Hartford, CT	7	27	7	9	10	9
Houston, TX	55	61	61	31	29	54
Las Vegas, NV	40	30	21	5	12	7
Los Angeles/ Long Beach, CA	226	239	178	185	136	103
Miami, FL	4	5	1	0	0	0
Minneapolis/ St. Paul, MN/WI	13	1	1	1	3	3
New Haven/Meriden, CT	7	16	10	3	8	8
New York, NY	58	46	18	4	8	8
Orange County, CA	66	65	47	43	14	6
Phoenix/Mesa, AZ	88	26	9	9	7	13
Pittsburgh, PA	8	25	11	2	2	7
Riverside/ San Bernardino, CA	170	180	143	150	122	110
San Diego, CA	70	84	60	37	16	14
Sacramento, CA	69	76	43	21	11	16
Salt Lake City, UT	36	11	6	10	10	1
San Francisco, CA	4	2	1	0	0	1
Seattle/Bellevue/ Everett, WA	13	20	5	1	0	0
St. Louis, MO/IL	13	18	8	3	11	14
Ventura, CA	84	83	36	25	24	30
Washington, DC	12	37	5	2	7	8

Source: U.S. Environmental Protection Agency

*Ozone -- the main component of smog -- is
formed when sunlight acts on emissions of
nitrogen oxides and volatile organic compounds.*

A Little Less Smog

Emissions of Pollutants, in Thousands of Short Tons

Source	1988	1990	1992	1994	1995
Carbon monoxide	115,849	100,650	94,043	98,017	92,099
Lead	6.5	5.7	4.9	5.0	5.0
Nitrogen oxides	23,618	23,038	22,847	23,615	21,779
Volatile organic compounds	25,720	23,600	22,422	23,174	22,865
Particulate matter	3,067	2,704	2,725	2,688	2,547
Sulfur oxides	22,647	22,433	21,836	21,118	18,319
Total	190,907	172,430	163,877	168,617	157,614

Dangerous Places

U.S. Hazardous Waste Sites, 1996

State	General	Federal	Proposed	Total
Alabama	9	3	1	13
Alaska	2	6	0	8
Arizona	7	3	0	10
Arkansas	12	0	0	12
California	69	23	3	96
Colorado	13	3	2	18
Connecticut	14	1	0	15
Delaware	18	1	0	19
DC	0	0	0	0
Florida	46	5	2	53
Georgia	11	2	1	14
Hawaii	1	3	0	4
Idaho	6	2	2	10
Illinois	33	4	1	38
Indiana	32	0	1	33
Iowa	15	1	1	17

U.S. Hazardous Waste Sites, Continued

State	General	Federal	Proposed	Total
Kansas	8	1	2	11
Kentucky	16	1	0	17
Louisiana	13	1	3	17
Maine	8	3	1	12
Maryland	8	5	1	14
Massachusetts	22	8	0	30
Michigan	71	0	4	75
Minnesota	31	3	0	34
Mississippi	1	0	2	3
Missouri	19	3	0	22
Montana	8	0	1	9
Nebraska	8	1	1	10
Nevada	1	0	0	1
New Hampshire	16	1	0	17
New Jersey	99	6	2	107
New Mexico	8	2	1	11
New York	74	4	1	79
North Carolina	21	2	0	23
North Dakota	2	0	0	2
Ohio	31	3	4	38
Oklahoma	9	1	1	11
Oregon	9	2	1	12
Pennsylvania	95	6	2	103
Rhode Island	10	2	0	12
South Carolina	23	2	0	25
South Dakota	2	1	1	4
Tennessee	11	3	1	15
Texas	23	4	0	27
Utah	8	4	4	16
Vermont	8	0	0	8
Virginia	18	6	1	25
Washington	35	17	0	52
West Virginia	4	2	1	7
Wisconsin	40	0	1	41
Wyoming	2	1	0	3
Total	1,074	153	49	1,276

15. Weather

See also 'The Environment' and 'Nations of the World.'

Clouds & Storms

Temperatures & Precipitation

Clouds & Storms

A Cloud, by Any Other Name . . .
Types of Clouds, and Their Altitudes

Family	Altitude	CloudType
Low	Surface - 6,500 feet	Cumulus
		Stratocumulus
		Stratus
Middle	6,500 - 23,000 feet	Altocumulus
		Altostratus
		Nimbostratus
High	16,500 - 45,000 feet	Cirrus
		Cirrocumulus
		Cirrostratus
Clouds with Extensive Vertical Development	Bases from 1,000 to 10,000 feet; tops can exceed 60,000 feet	Towering Cumulus
		Cumulonimbus

Stratus (or flat) clouds form in stable air, while cumulus clouds form in unstable (rising) air. They have flat bottoms and dome-shaped tops. Widely spaced cumulus clouds that develop in mostly clear skies are called fair weather cumulus. Towering cumulus clouds are similar, but much taller clouds. They form in thick layers of unstable air and can contain heavy turbulence. Cumulonimbus clouds are the most powerful, dangerous clouds. They represent danger of thunderstorms, which can spawn hail, heavy winds, and tornadoes. The suffix 'nimbus' associated with any type of cloud indicates that it might produce rain.

Stormy Weather
Types of Storms and Their Characteristics

Storm	Winds	Characteristics
Severe Thunderstorm	58 m.p.h. +	Thunder, lightning, can cause hail, tornadoes
Tornado	Up to 300 m.p.h.	Counter-clockwise rotating column
Blizzard	35 m.p.h. +	Blowing snow restricts visibility to 1/4 mile or less
Tropical Storm	39 - 73 m.p.h.	Begins over water
Hurricane	74 m.p.h. +	Begins over water

The Power of Wind
Beaufort Scale

B#	Wind m.p.h.	Effect on Land	B#	Wind m.p.h.	Effect on Land
0	> 1	Calm	7	32-38	Walking is difficult
1	1-3	Rising smoke reveals wind	8	39-46	Cars run off roads
2	4-7	Leaves rustle	9	47-54	Roof slates may blow away
3	8-12	Flags extended	10	55-63	Trees uprooted
4	13-18	Sm. branches move	11	64-72	Widespread damage
5	19-24	Small trees sway	12	73+	Widespread damage
6	25-31	Lg. branches move			

Hurricane Force
Saffir-Simpson Scale

Category	Wind m.p.h.	Severity	Surge (feet)
1	74-95	Weak	4-5
2	96-110	Moderate	6-8
3	111-130	Strong	9-12
4	131-155	Very Strong	13-18
5	>155	Devastating	> 18

The National Weather Service issues a 'watch' when threatening weather is likely. A 'warning' means severe weather is already in progress.

Temperatures & Precipitation

The Chill Is in the Air

Wind Chill, in °F
(Wind, in Miles per Hour)

	Temperature						
	35	30	25	20	15	10	5
Wind							
5	33	27	21	16	12	7	0
10	22	16	10	3	-3	-9	-15
15	16	9	2	-5	-11	-18	-25
20	12	4	-3	-10	-17	-24	-31
25	8	1	-7	-15	-22	-29	-36
30	6	-2	-10	-18	-25	-33	-41
35	4	-4	-12	-20	-27	-35	-43
40	3	-5	-13	-21	-29	-37	-45
45	2	-6	-14	-22	-30	-38	-46

	Temperature						
	0	-5	-10	-15	-20	-25	-30
Wind							
5	-5	-10	-15	-21	-26	-31	-36
10	-22	-27	-34	-40	-46	-52	-58
15	-31	-38	-45	-51	-58	-65	-72
20	-39	-46	-53	-60	-67	-74	-81
25	-44	-51	-59	-66	-74	-81	-88
30	-49	-56	-64	-71	-79	-86	-93
35	-52	-58	-67	-74	-82	-89	-97
40	-53	-60	-69	-76	-84	-92	-100
45	-54	-62	-70	-78	-85	-93	-102

Source: National Weather Service

How Hot Does It Feel?

Heat Index, in °F

	Temperature				
	70	**75**	**80**	**85**	**90**
Humidity					
0%	64	69	73	78	83
10%	65	70	75	80	85
20%	66	72	77	82	87
30%	67	73	78	84	90
40%	68	74	79	86	93
50%	69	75	81	88	96
60%	70	76	82	90	100
70%	70	77	85	93	106
80%	71	78	86	97	113
90%	71	79	88	102	122
100%	72	80	91	108	

	Temperature					
	95	**100**	**105**	**110**	**115**	**120**
Humidity						
0%	87	91	95	99	103	107
10%	90	95	100	105	111	116
20%	93	99	105	112	120	130
30%	96	104	113	123	135	148
40%	101	110	123	137	151	
50%	107	120	135	150		
60%	114	132	149			
70%	124	144				
80%	136					
90%						

Source: National Weather Service

How's the Weather?

Average Recorded Temperatures, 1961-1990

		January		July	
State	**Station**	**High**	**Low**	**High**	**Low**
Alabama	Mobile	60	40	91	73
Alaska	Anchorage	21	8	65	52
Alaska	Barrow	-7	-19	45	34
Arizona	Phoenix	66	41	106	81
Arkansas	Little Rock	49	29	92	72
California	Los Angeles	68	49	84	65
California	San Diego	66	49	76	66
California	San Francisco	56	42	72	54
Colorado	Denver	43	16	88	59
Connecticut	Hartford	33	16	85	62
Delaware	Wilmington	39	22	86	67
D.C.	Washington	42	27	89	71
Florida	Jacksonville	64	41	91	72
Florida	Miami	75	59	89	76
Georgia	Atlanta	50	32	88	70
Georgia	Savannah	60	38	91	72
Hawaii	Honolulu	80	66	88	74
Idaho	Boise	36	22	90	58
Illinois	Chicago	29	13	84	63
Illinois	Moline	28	11	86	65
Indiana	Indianapolis	34	17	86	65
Iowa	Des Moines	28	11	87	67
Kentucky	Lexington	39	22	86	66
Kentucky	Louisville	40	23	87	67
Louisiana	New Orleans	61	42	91	73
Maine	Caribou	19	-2	77	55
Maine	Portland	30	11	79	58
Maryland	Baltimore	40	23	87	67
Mass.	Boston	36	22	82	65
Michigan	Detroit	30	16	83	61
Michigan	Sault Ste. Marie	21	5	76	51
Minnesota	Duluth	16	-2	77	55
Minnesota	Minn.-St. Paul	21	3	84	63
Mississippi	Jackson	56	33	92	71
Missouri	Kansas City	35	17	89	68

Average Recorded Temperatures, 1961-1990, Continued

State	Station	January High	January Low	July High	July Low
Missouri	St. Louis	38	21	89	70
Montana	Helena	30	10	85	53
Nebraska	Omaha	31	11	88	66
Nebraska	Scottsbluff	38	12	90	59
Nevada	Reno	45	21	92	51
New Jersey	Atlantic City	40	21	85	65
New Mexico	Albuquerque	47	22	93	64
New York	Albany	30	11	84	60
New York	Buffalo	30	17	80	62
New York	New York	37	26	84	69
N. Carolina	Asheville	47	25	83	62
N. Carolina	Raleigh	49	29	88	68
N. Dakota	Bismarck	20	-2	84	56
Ohio	Cleveland	32	18	82	61
Ohio	Columbus	34	19	84	63
Oregon	Portland	45	34	80	57
Pennsylvania	Philadelphia	38	23	86	67
Pennsylvania	Pittsburgh	34	19	83	62
Rhode Island	Providence	37	19	82	63
S. Carolina	Charleston	58	38	90	73
S. Dakota	Huron	24	2	87	62
S. Dakota	Rapid City	34	11	86	58
Tennessee	Memphis	49	31	92	73
Tennessee	Nashville	46	27	90	69
Texas	Galveston	58	47	87	79
Texas	Houston	61	40	93	72
Utah	Salt Lake City	36	19	92	64
Vermont	Burlington	25	8	81	60
Virginia	Norfolk	47	31	86	70
Virginia	Richmond	46	26	88	68
Washington	Seattle-Tacoma	45	35	75	55
Washington	Spokane	33	21	83	54
Wisconsin	Milwaukee	26	12	80	62
Wyoming	Lander	31	8	86	56

Source: National Weather Service

It's a Record!

Record High & Low Temperatures, in °F, Through 1996

State	Low	High	State	Low	High
Alabama	-27	112	Montana	-70	117
Alaska	-80	100	Nebraska	-47	118
Arizona	-40	128	Nevada	-50	125
Arkansas	-29	120	New Hampshire	-46	106
California	-45	134	New Jersey	-34	110
Colorado	-61	118	New Mexico	-50	122
Connecticut	-32	106	New York	-52	108
Delaware	-17	110	North Carolina	-34	110
Florida	-2	109	North Dakota	-60	121
Georgia	-17	112	Ohio	-39	113
Hawaii	12	100	Oklahoma	-27	120
Idaho	-60	118	Oregon	-54	119
Illinois	-35	117	Pennsylvania	-42	111
Indiana	-36	116	Rhode Island	-25	104
Iowa	-47	118	South Carolina	-19	111
Kansas	-40	121	South Dakota	-58	120
Kentucky	-37	114	Tennessee	-32	113
Louisiana	-16	114	Texas	-23	120
Maine	-48	105	Utah	-69	117
Maryland	-40	109	Vermont	-50	105
Massachusetts	-35	107	Virginia	-30	110
Michigan	-51	112	Washington	-48	118
Minnesota	-60	114	West Virginia	-37	112
Mississippi	-19	115	Wisconsin	-54	114
Missouri	-40	118	Wyoming	-66	114

Source: National Weather Service   **ww.ncdc.noaa.gov**

America's Hottest Cities
Average Annual Temperature

1. Key West, FL   77.8 °F
2. Miami, FL   75.9 °F
3. W. Palm Beach, FL   74.7 °F
4. Fort Myers, FL   74.4 °F
5. Yuma, AZ   74.2 °F

Pack Your Umbrella

Average Annual Precipitation, in Inches, 1961-1990

State	Station	Precipitation
Alabama	Mobile	63.96
Alaska	Anchorage	15.91
Alaska	Barrow	4.49
Arizona	Phoenix	7.66
Arkansas	Little Rock	72.10
California	Los Angeles	14.77
California	San Diego	9.90
California	San Francisco	19.70
Colorado	Denver	15.40
Connecticut	Hartford	44.14
Delaware	Wilmington	40.84
D.C.	Washington	38.63
Florida	Jacksonville	51.32
Florida	Miami	55.91
Georgia	Atlanta	50.77
Georgia	Savannah	49.22
Hawaii	Honolulu	22.02
Idaho	Boise	12.11
Illinois	Chicago	35.82
Illinois	Moline	39.08
Indiana	Indianapolis	39.94
Iowa	Des Moines	33.12
Kentucky	Lexington	44.55
Kentucky	Louisville	44.39
Louisiana	New Orleans	61.88
Maine	Caribou	36.60
Maine	Portland	44.34
Maryland	Baltimore	40.76
Mass.	Boston	41.51
Michigan	Detroit	32.62
Michigan	Sault Ste. Marie	34.23
Minnesota	Duluth	30.00
Minnesota	Minn.-St. Paul	28.32
Mississippi	Jackson	55.37
Missouri	Kansas City	37.62

Average Annual Precipitation, in Inches, Continued

State	Station	Precipitation
Missouri	St. Louis	37.51
Montana	Helena	11.60
Nebraska	Omaha	29.86
Nebraska	Scottsbluff	15.27
Nevada	Reno	7.53
New Jersey	Atlantic City	40.29
New Mexico	Albuquerque	8.88
New York	Albany	36.17
New York	Buffalo	38.58
New York	New York	42.12
N. Carolina	Asheville	47.59
N. Carolina	Raleigh	41.43
N. Dakota	Bismarck	15.47
Ohio	Cleveland	36.63
Ohio	Columbus	38.09
Oregon	Portland	36.30
Pennsylvania	Philadelphia	41.41
Pennsylvania	Pittsburgh	36.85
Rhode Island	Providence	45.53
S. Carolina	Charleston	51.53
S. Dakota	Huron	20.08
S. Dakota	Rapid City	16.64
Tennessee	Memphis	52.10
Tennessee	Nashville	47.30
Texas	Galveston	42.28
Texas	Houston	46.07
Utah	Salt Lake City	16.18
Vermont	Burlington	34.47
Virginia	Norfolk	44.64
Virginia	Richmond	43.16
Washington	Seattle-Tacoma	37.19
Washington	Spokane	16.49
Wisconsin	Milwaukee	32.93
Wyoming	Lander	13.01

Temperatures for Travelers

*Average International Temperatures,
1961-1990*

Station	January High	January Low	July High	July Low
Algiers, Algeria	61.7	42.6	87.1	65.3
Athens, Greece	56.1	44.6	88.9	73.0
Auckland, New Zealand	74.8	61.2	58.5	46.4
Bangkok, Thailand	89.6	69.8	90.9	77.0
Berlin, Germany	35.2	26.8	73.6	55.2
Bogotá, Colombia	67.3	41.7	64.6	45.5
Bombay (Mumbai), India	85.3	66.7	86.2	77.5
Bucharest, Romania	34.7	22.1	83.8	60.1
Budapest, Hungary	34.2	24.8	79.7	59.7
Buenos Aires, Argentina	85.8	67.3	59.7	45.7
Cairo, Egypt	65.8	48.2	93.9	71.1
Cape Town, South Africa	79.0	60.3	63.3	44.6
Caracas, Venezuela	79.9	60.8	81.3	66.0
Casablanca, Morocco	62.8	47.1	77.7	66.7
Copenhagen, Denmark	35.6	28.4	68.9	55.0
Damascus, Syria	54.3	32.9	97.2	61.9
Dublin, Ireland	45.7	36.5	66.0	52.5
Geneva, Switzerland	38.3	27.9	76.3	53.2
Havana, Cuba	78.4	65.5	88.3	74.8
Hong Kong	65.5	56.5	88.7	79.9
Istanbul, Turkey	47.8	37.2	82.8	65.3
Jerusalem, Israel	53.4	39.4	83.8	63.0
Lagos, Nigeria	90.0	72.3	82.8	72.1
Lima, Peru	79.0	66.9	66.4	59.4
London, England	44.1	32.7	71.1	52.3
Manila, Philippines	85.8	74.8	89.1	76.8
Mexico City, Mexico	70.3	43.7	73.8	53.2
Montreal, Canada	21.6	5.2	79.2	59.7
Nairobi, Kenya	77.9	50.9	71.6	48.6
Paris, France	42.8	33.6	75.2	55.2
Prague, Czech Republic	32.7	22.5	73.9	53.2

Average International Temperatures, 1961-1990, Cont'd.

Station	January		July	
	High	Low	High	Low
Reykjavik, Iceland	35.4	26.6	55.9	46.9
Rome, Italy	53.8	35.4	88.2	62.1
San Salvador, El Salvador	86.5	61.3	86.2	66.4
Sao Paolo, Brazil	81.1	65.7	71.2	53.1
Shanghai, China	45.9	32.9	88.9	76.6
Singapore	85.8	73.6	87.4	75.6
Stockholm, Sweden	30.7	23.0	71.4	56.1
Sydney, Australia	79.5	65.5	62.4	43.9
Tehran, Iran	45.0	30.0	98.2	75.2
Tokyo, Japan	49.1	34.2	83.8	72.1
Toronto, Canada	27.5	12.0	80.2	57.6

The World's Driest Inhabited Places
Average Annual Inches of Rainfall

1. Aswan, Egypt   0.02
2. Luxor, Egypt   0.03
3. Arica, Chile   0.04
4. Ica, Peru   0.09
5. Antofagasta, Chile   0.19

The World's Wettest Inhabited Places
Average Annual Inches of Rainfall

1. Buenaventura, Columbia   265.47
2. Monrovia, Liberia   202.01
3. Pago Pago, American Samoa   196.46
4. Mulmein, Myanmar, Burma   191.02
5. Lae, Papua New Guinea   182.87

16. Time Zones & Area Codes

Time Zones

U.S. Area Codes

International Dialing Codes

Time Zones

Pacific   Mountain   Central   Eastern

What's the Time Where You Are?
Standard Time at 12 Noon Eastern Standard Time

City	Time	City	Time
Akron, OH	12 Noon	Des Moines, IA	11 AM
Albuquerque, NM	10 AM	Detroit, MI	12 Noon
Atlanta, GA	12 Noon	Duluth, MN	11 AM
Austin, TX	11 AM	El Paso, TX	10 AM
Baltimore, MD	12 Noon	Erie, PA	12 Noon
Birmingham, AL	11 AM	Evansville, IN	11 AM
Bismarck, ND	11 AM	Fairbanks, AK	8 AM
Boise, ID	10 AM	Flint, MI	12 Noon
Boston, MA	12 Noon	Fort Wayne, IN [1]	12 Noon
Buffalo, NY	12 Noon	Fort Worth, TX	11 AM
Butte, MT	10 AM	Frankfort, KY	12 Noon
Charleston, SC	12 Noon	Galveston, TX	11 AM
Charleston, WV	12 Noon	Grand Rapids, MI	12 Noon
Charlotte, NC	12 Noon	Halifax, NS	1 PM
Chattanooga, TN	12 Noon	Hartford, CT	12 Noon
Cheyenne, WY	10 AM	Helena, MT	10 AM
Chicago, IL	11 AM	Honolulu, HI [1]	7 AM
Cleveland, OH	12 Noon	Houston, TX	11 AM
Colorado Spr., CO	10 AM	Indianapolis, IN [1]	12 Noon
Columbus, OH	12 Noon	Jacksonville, FL	12 Noon
Dallas, TX	11 AM	Juneau, AK	8 AM
Dayton, OH	12 Noon	Kansas City, MO	11 AM
Denver, CO	10 AM	Knoxville, TN	12 Noon

374

Standard Time at 12 Noon Eastern Standard Time, Cont'd.

City	Time	City	Time
Lexington, KY	12 Noon	Providence, RI	12 Noon
Lincoln, NE	11 AM	Reno, NV	9 AM
Little Rock, AR	11 AM	Richmond, VA	12 Noon
Los Angeles, CA	9 AM	Rochester, NY	12 Noon
Louisville, KY	12 Noon	Sacramento, CA	9 AM
Memphis, TN	11 AM	St. Louis, MO	11 AM
Miami, FL	12 Noon	St. Paul, MN	11 AM
Milwaukee, WI	11 AM	Salt Lake City, UT	10 AM
Minneapolis, MN	11 AM	San Antonio, TX	11 AM
Mobile, AL	11 AM	San Diego, CA	9 AM
Nashville, TN	11 AM	San Francisco, CA	9 AM
New Haven, CT	12 Noon	Santa Fe, NM	10 AM
New Orleans, LA	11 AM	Savannah, GA	12 Noon
New York, NY	12 Noon	Seattle, WA	9 AM
Nome, AK	8 AM	Shreveport, LA	11 AM
Norfolk, VA	12 Noon	Sioux Falls, SD	11 AM
Oklahoma City, OK	11 AM	Spokane, WA	9 AM
Omaha, NE	11 AM	Tampa, FL	12 Noon
Peoria, IL	11 AM	Toledo, OH	12 Noon
Philadelphia, PA	12 Noon	Topeka, KS	11 AM
Phoenix, AZ [1]	10 AM	Tucson, AZ [1]	10 AM
Pierre, SD	11 AM	Tulsa, OK	11 AM
Pittsburgh, PA	12 Noon	Washington, DC	12 Noon
Portland, ME	12 Noon	Wichita, KS	11 AM
Portland, OR	9 AM	Wilmington, DE	12 Noon

[1] *Does not observe Daylight Saving Time.*

Daylight Saving Time begins when we advance our clocks one hour at 2 am on the first Sunday in April . It ends when we turn our clocks back one hour at 2 am on the last Sunday in October. Arizona, Hawaii, the eastern time zone portion of Indiana, Puerto Rico, the U.S. Virgin Islands, and American Samoa do not observe Daylight Saving Time.

What Time Should I Call Sydney?

Time at World Cities at 12:00 Noon Eastern Standard Time

City	Time		City	Time	
Addis Ababa	20	0	Geneva	18	0
Alexandria	19	0	Havana	12	0
Amsterdam	18	0	Helsinki	19	0
Athens	19	0	Ho Chi Minh City [1]	0	0
Auckland [1]	5	0	Hong Kong [1]	1	0
Baghdad	20	0	Istanbul	19	0
Bangkok [1]	0	0	Jakarta [1]	0	0
Beijing [1]	1	0	Jerusalem	19	0
Belfast	17	0	Johannesburg	19	0
Berlin	18	0	Karachi	22	0
Bogotá	12	0	Le Havre	18	0
Bombay	22	30	Lima	12	0
Bremen	18	0	Lisbon	17	0
Brussels	18	0	Liverpool	17	0
Bucharest	19	0	London	17	0
Budapest	18	0	Madrid	18	0
Buenos Aires	14	0	Manila [1]	1	0
Cairo	19	0	Mecca (Saudi Arabia)	20	0
Calcutta	22	30	Melbourne [1]	3	0
Cape Town	19	0	Mexico City	11	0
Caracas	13	0	Montevideo	14	0
Casablanca	17	0	Moscow	20	0
Copenhagen	18	0	Nagasaki [1]	2	0
Delhi	22	30	Oslo	18	0
Dhaka	23	0	Paris	18	0
Dublin	17	0	Prague	18	0
Gdánsk	18	0	Rio de Janeiro	14	0
			Rome	18	0
			St. Petersburg	20	0
			Santiago (Chile)	13	0
			Seoul [1]	2	0
			Shanghai [1]	1	0
			Singapore [1]	1	0

Time at World Cities at 12:00 Noon E.S.T., Continued

City	Time		City	Time	
Stockholm	18	0	Vladivostok [1]	3	0
Sydney (Australia) [1]	3	0	Vienna	18	0
Tashkent	23	0	Warsaw	18	0
Tehran	20	30	Wellington (NZ) [1]	5	0
Tel Aviv	19	0	Yangon (Rangoon)	23	30
Tokyo [1]	2	0	Yokohama [1]	2	0
Valparaíso	13	0	Zürich	18	0

[1] *Morning of the following day*

Each of the world's 24 time zones is 15 ° of longitude in width, and sets its clocks one hour earlier than the zone immediately to its east.

Canada and Mexico observe Daylight Savings Time during the same period as the United States (from the first Sunday in April to the last Sunday in October). Member nations of the European Union begin their 'Summer-time period' one week earlier (the last Sunday of March).

The International Date Line is a zig-zag line that follows the 180th meridian -- halfway around the world from the Prime (or first) Meridian at Greenwhich, England, from which time is calculated. The Date Line separates the calendar dates. If you cross the date line gong west, advance the date one day; when crossing going east, set it back one day.

U.S. Area Codes

Calling Around America

U.S. Area Codes by State for Places of 50,000 or More

Place	Code	Place	Code	Place	Code
Alabama		Bakersfield	805	Fremont	510
Birmingham	205	Baldwin Park	626	Fresno	209
Dothan	334	Bellflower	323	Fullerton	714
Huntsville	205	Berkeley	510	Garden Grove	714
Montgomery	334	Buena Park	714	Glendale	818
Tuscaloosa	205	Burbank	818		323
		Camarillo	805		626
Alaska		Carlsbad	760	Hacienda Hgts	626
Anchorage	907	Carson	310	Hayward	510
		Cerritos	562	Hesperia	760
Arizona		Chino	909	Huntington Bch.	714
Apache Jnct.	602	Chula Vista	619	Huntington Pk.	323
Chandler	602	Citrus Hghts	916	Inglewood	213
Glendale	602	Clovis	209		310
Mesa	602	Compton	925		323
Phoenix	602	Concord	510	Irvine	714
Scottsdale	602	Corona	909		949
Tempe	602	Costa Mesa	714	La Habra	562
Tucson	520		949		949
Yuma	520	Daly City	415	La Mesa	619
			650	Lancaster	805
Arkansas		Diamond Bar	909	Livermore	925
Fort Smith	501	Downey	562	Lodi	209
Little Rock	501	E. Los Angeles	323	Long Beach	310
N. Little Rock	501		562		562
Pine Bluff	870	El Cajon	619	Loomis	916
		El Monte	626	Los Angeles	818
California		El Toro	949		213
Alameda	510	Escondido	760		310
Alhambra	323	Fairfield	707		323
	626	Florence-Graham		Lynwood	213
Anaheim	714		323		310
Antioch	925	Fontana	909		323
Arden-Arcade	916	Fountain Vlly	714	Merced	209

378

U.S. Area Codes, Cont'd.

Place	Code
Milpitas	408
Mission Viejo	949
Modesto	209
Montebello	323
Monterey Prk.	818
	323
	626
Moreno Valley	909
Mountain View	650
Napa	707
National City	619
Newport Bch	949
Norwalk	562
Oakland	510
Oceanside	760
Ontario	909
Orange	714
Oxnard	805
Palmdale	805
Palo Alto	650
Pasadena	323
	626
	818
Pico Rivera	562
Pleasanton	925
Pomona	909
Rch.Cucamonga	909
Redding	530
Redlands	909
Redondo Bch	310
Redwood City	650
Richmond	510
Riverside	909
Rosemead	626
Sacramento	916

Place	Code
Salinas	831
San Bernardino	909
San Buenaventura	
(Ventura)	805
San Diego	619
San Francisco	415
San Jose	408
San Leandro	510
San Mateo	650
Santa Ana	714
	949
Santa Barbara	805
Santa Clara	408
Santa Clarita	805
Santa Cruz	831
Santa Maria	805
Santa Monica	310
Santa Rosa	707
Santee	619
Simi Valley	805
South Gate	323
	562
South San	
Francisco	650
Spring Valley	619
Stockton	209
Sunnyvale	408
Thousand Oaks	805
Torrance	310
Tracy	209
Tustin	714
	949
Union City	510
Upland	909
Vacaville	707

Place	Code
Vallejo	707
Visalia	209
Walnut Creek	925
West Covina	626
Westminster	714
Whittier	562
Yorba Linda	714
Colorado	
Air Force Acdmy	719
Arvada	303
Aurora	303
Boulder	303
Colorado Spr.	719
Denver	303
Derby	303
Fort Collins	970
Greeley	970
Lakewood	303
Longmont	303
Pueblo	719
Thornton	303
Westminster	303
Connecticut	
Bridgeport	203
Bristol	860
Danbury	203
Darien	203
East Hartford	860
Fairfield	203
Greenwich	203
Hamden	203
Hartford	860
Meriden	203

U.S. Area Codes, Cont'd.

Place	Code	Place	Code	Place	Code
Middlebury	203	Orlando	407	Cicero	708
New Britain	860	Palm Bay	407	Decatur	217
New Haven	203	Palm Harbor	813	Des Plaines	847
Newington	860	Pembroke Pines	954	Elgin	847
Norwalk	203	Pensacola	850	Evanston	847
Stamford	203	Plantation	954	Joliet	815
West Haven	203	Pompano Bch	954	Mt. Prospect	847
		Port St. Lucie	561	Naperville	630
Delaware	302	St. Petersburg	813	Oak Lawn	708
		Sarasota	941	Oak Park	708
District of		Sunrise	954	Peoria	309
Columbia	202	Tallahassee	850	Rockford	815
		Tampa	813	Schaumburg	847
Florida		Town 'n' Country	813	Skokie	847
Boca Raton	561	W. Palm Bch.	561	Springfield	217
Brandon	813			Waukegan	847
Cape Coral	941	*Georgia*		Wheaton	630
Carol City	305	Albany	912		
Clearwater	813	Atlanta	404	*Indiana*	
Coral Springs	954	Columbus	706	Anderson	765
Daytona Bch.	904	Macon	912	Bloomington	812
Deltona	407	Savannah	912	Evansville	812
Ft. Lauderdale	954	S. Augusta	706	Fort Wayne	219
Gainesville	352			Gary	219
Hialeah	305	*Hawaii*	808	Hammond	219
Hollywood	954			Indianapolis	317
Homestead	305	*Idaho*	208	Muncie	765
Jacksonville	904			South Bend	219
Kendall	305	*Illinois*		Terre Haute	812
Lakeland	941	Arlington Hgts.	847		
Melbourne	407	Aurora	630	*Iowa*	
Miami	305	Bloomington	309	Cedar Rapids	319
Miami Beach	305	Champaign	217	Council Bluffs	712
Miami Grdns.	954	Chicago	312	Davenport	319
North Miami	305		773	Des Moines	515

U.S. Area Codes, Cont'd.

Place	Code	Place	Code	Place	Code
Dubuque	319	Columbia	410	Dearborn	313
Iowa City	319		301	Dearborn Hgts.	313
Sioux City	712	Dundalk	410	Detroit	313
Waterloo	319	Silver Spring	301	East Lansing	517
		Wheaton-		Farmington Hls.	248
Kansas		Glenmont	301	Flint	810
Kansas City	913			Grand Rapids	616
Lawrence	785	**Massachusetts**		Kalamazoo	616
Olathe	913	Boston	617	Lansing	517
Overland Prk.	913	Brockton	508	Livonia	734
Topeka	785	Brookline	617	Pontiac	248
Wichita	316	Cambridge	617	Redford	313
		Chicopee	413	Rochester Hls.	248
Kentucky		Fall River	508	Roseville	810
Lexington	606	Framingham	508	Royal Oak	248
Louisville	502	Haverhill	508	Saginaw	517
Owensboro	502	Lawrence	508	St. Clair Shrs.	313
		Lowell	508	Southfield	248
Louisiana		Lynn	617	Sterling Hgts.	810
Baton Rouge	504	Malden	617	Taylor	313
Bossier City	318	Medford	617		734
Kenner	504	New Bedford	508	Warren	810
Lafayette	318	Newton	617	Waterford	248
Lake Charles	318	Quincy	617	W. Bloomfield	248
Metairie	504	Somerville	617	Westland	313
Monroe	318	Springfield	413		734
New Orleans	504	Waltham	617	Wyoming	616
Shreveport	318	Weymouth	617		
		Worcester	508	**Minnesota**	
Maine	207			Bloomington	612
		Michigan		Brooklyn Pk.	612
Maryland		Ann Arbor	734	Burnsville	612
Baltimore	410	Battle Creek	616	Coon Rapids	612
Bethesda	301	Canton	734	Duluth	218
		Clinton	517	Minneapolis	612

U.S. Area Codes, Cont'd.

Place	Code
Plymouth	612
Rochester	507
Saint Paul	612
Mississippi	601
Missouri	
Columbia	573
Florissant	314
Independence	816
Kansas City	816
Saint Charles	314
Springfield	417
Montana	406
Nebraska	
Lincoln	402
Omaha	402
Nevada	702
New Hampshire	
	603
New Jersey	
Bayonne	201
Brick Twp.	732
Camden	609
Cherry Hill Twp.	609
Clifton	973
Edison Twp.	908
	732
Elizabeth	908
Hamilton Twp.	609

Place	Code
Irvington	973
Jersey City	201
Middletown Twp.	732
Newark	973
Old Bridge Twp.	732
Passaic	973
Paterson	973
Trenton	609
Union Twp.	908
Union City	201
Vineland	609
Woodbridge Township	732
New Mexico	505
New York	
Albany	518
Amherst	716
Binghamton	607
Buffalo	716
Cheektowaga	716
Irondequoit	716
Levittown	516
Mount Vernon	914
New Rochelle	914
New York	212
	718
Niagara Falls	716
Rochester	716
Schenectady	518
Syracuse	315
Tonawanda	716
Troy	518
Utica	315

Place	Code
Yonkers	914
North Carolina	
Asheville	704
Charlotte	704
Durham	919
Fayetteville	910
Gastonia	704
Greensboro	919
High Point	910
Wilmington	910
Winston-Salem	910
N. Dakota	701
Ohio	
Akron	330
Canton	330
Cincinnati	513
Cleveland	216
Columbus	614
Dayton	937
Elyria	440
Euclid	216
Hamilton	513
Kettering	937
Lakewood	216
Lorain	440
Mansfield	419
Parma	216
	440
Toledo	419
Warren	330
Youngstown	330

U.S. Area Codes, Cont'd.

Place	Code	Place	Code	Place	Code
Oklahoma		**Tennessee**		Mesquite	972
Broken Arrow	918	Chattanooga	423	Midland	915
Edmond	405	Clarksville	615	Odessa	915
Lawton	405	Knoxville	423	Pasadena	713
Oklahoma City	405	Memphis	901		281
Tulsa	918	Nashville	615	Plano	972
				Port Arthur	409
Oregon		**Texas**		Richardson	972
Beaverton	503	Abilene	915	San Angelo	915
Eugene	541	Amarillo	806	San Antonio	210
Gresham	503	Arlington	817	Tyler	903
Portland	503	Austin	512	Victoria	512
Salem	503	Baytown	281	Waco	254
		Beaumont	409	Wichita Falls	940
Pennsylvania		Brownsville	956		
Allentown	610	Bryan	409	**Utah**	
Altoona	814	Carrolton	972	Ogden	801
Bethlehem	610	College St.	409	Provo	801
Erie	814	Corpus Christi	512	Salt Lake City	801
Lancaster	717	Dallas	214	W. Valley City	801
Levittown	215		972		
Philadelphia	215	Denton	940	**Vermont**	802
Pittsburgh	412	El Paso	915		
Reading	610	Fort Worth	817	**Virginia**	
Scranton	717	Galveston	409	Alexandria	703
		Garland	972	Annandale	540
Rhode Isl.	401	Grand Prairie	972	Arlington	703
		Houston	713	Burke	703
South Carolina			281	Chesapeake	757
Charleston	803	Irving	972	Danville	804
Columbia	803	Killeen	254	Hampton	757
Greenville	864	Laredo	956	Lynchburg	804
		Longview	903	Newport News	757
S. Dakota	605	Lubbock	806	Norfolk	757
		McAllen	956	Portsmouth	757

International Dialing Codes

U.S. Area Codes, Cont'd.

Place	Code
Richmond	804
Roanoke	540
Suffolk	757
Virginia Bch.	757

Washington

Place	Code
Bellevue	426
Bellingham	360
Everett	425
Federal Way	253
Lakewood	253
Seattle	206
	425
Spokane	509
Tacoma	253
Yakima	509

W. Virginia	304

Wisconsin

Place	Code
Appleton	920
Eau Claire	715
Green Bay	920
Janesville	608
Kenosha	414
La Crosse	608
Madison	608
Milwaukee	414
Oshkosh	920
Waukesha	414
West Allis	414

Wyoming	307

To place an international call, dial: 01 + country code (listed in the table below) + city code (if needed) + local number.

International Calls
International Telephone Codes

Place	Code	Place	Code
Afghanistan	93	Bermuda	441 [1]
Albania	355	Bhutan	975
Algeria	213	Bolivia	591
Am. Samoa	684	Bosnia &	
Andorra	376	Herzegovina	387
Angola	244	Botswana	267
Anguilla	264 [1]	Brazil	55
Antarctica	64240	Brunei	673
Antigua & Barbuda		Bulgaria	359
	268 [1]	Burkina Faso	226
Argentina	54	Burundi	257
Armenia	374	Cambodia	855
Aruba	297	Cameroon	237
Ascension Isl.	247	Canada	
Australia	61	Alberta	403 [1]
Austria	43	Br. Columbia	250 [1]
Azerbaijan	994	Vancouver	604 [1]
Bahamas	242 [1]	Manitoba	204 [1]
Bahrain	973	N. Brunswick	506 [1]
Bangladesh	880	Newfoundland	709 [1]
Barbados	246 [1]	Nova Scotia	902 [1]
Belarus	375	Ontario	
Belgium	32	London	519 [1]
Belize	501	North Bay	705 [1]
Benin	229	Ottawa	613 [1]

International Telephone Codes, *Continued*

Place	Code	Place	Code	Place	Code
Thunder Bay	807 [1]	Equatorial Guinea		Iran	98
Toronto Metro	416 [1]		240	Iraq	964
Toronto Vicinity	905 [1]	Eritrea	291	Ireland	353
Prince Edward Isl.		Estonia	372	Israel	972
	902 [1]	Ethiopia	251	Italy	39
Quebec		Falkland Isl.	500	Jamaica	876 [1]
Montreal	514 [1]	Fiji	679	Japan	81
Quebec City	418 [1]	Finland	358	Jordan	962
Sherbrooke	819 [1]	France	33	Kazakstan	7
Saskatchewan	306 [1]	Fr. Antilles	596	Kenya	254
Cape Verde	238	Fr. Guiana	594	Kiribati	686
Cayman Isl.	345 [1]	Fr. Polynesia	689	Korea, North	850
Cent. African Rep.		Gabon	241	Korea, South	82
	236	Gambia	220	Kuwait	965
Chad	235	Georgia	995	Kyrgyzstan	7
Chile	56	Germany	49	Laos	856
China	86	Ghana	233	Latvia	371
Colombia	57	Gibraltar	350	Lebanon	961
Comoros	269	Greece	30	Lesotho	266
Congo	242	Greenland	299	Liberia	231
Costa Rica	506	Grenada	809 [1]	Libya	218
Côte d'Ivoire	225	Guadeloupe	590	Liechtenstein	4175
Croatia	385	Guam	671 [1]	Lithuania	370
Cuba	53	Guantanamo Bay	5399	Luxembourg	352
Cyprus	357	Guatemala	502	Macau	853
Czech Rep.	42	Guinea	224	Macedonia	389
Denmark	45	Guinea-Bissau	245	Madagascar	261
Djibouti	253	Guyana	592	Malawi	265
Dominica	767 [1]	Haiti	509	Malaysia	60
Dominican		Honduras	504	Maldives	960
Republic	809 [1]	Hong Kong	852	Mali	223
Ecuador	593	Hungary	36	Malta	356
Egypt	20	Iceland	354	Marshall Isl.	692
El Salvador	503	India	91	Martinique	596
		Indonesia	62	Mauritania	222

International Telephone Codes, Continued

Place	Code	Place	Code	Place	Code
Mauritius	230	Romania	40	Tonga	676
Mexico	52	Russia	7	Trinidad & Tobago	
Micronesia	691	Rwanda	250		868 [1]
Moldova	373	St. Kitts & Nevis		Tunisia	216
Monaco	377		869 [1]	Turkey	90
Mongolia	976	St. Lucia	758 [1]	Turkmenistan	7
Montserrat	664 [1]	St. Vincent & the		Turks & Caicos	
Morocco	212	Grenadines	809 [1]	Islands	809 [1]
Mozambique	258	San Marino	378	Tuvalu	688
Myanmar	95	São Tomé &		Uganda	256
Namibia	264	Príncipe	239	Ukraine	380
Nauru	674	Saudi Arabia	966	United Arab	
Nepal	977	Senegal	221	Emirates	971
Netherlands	31	Seychelles	248	United Kingdom	44
New Caledonia	687	Sierra Leone	232	Uruguay	598
New Zealand	64	Singapore	65	Uzbekistan	7
Nicaragua	505	Slovakia	42	Vanuatu	678
Niger	227	Slovenia	386	Vatican City	39
Nigeria	234	Solomon Isl.	677	Venezuela	58
N. Mariana Isl.	670 [1]	Somalia	252	Vietnam	84
Norway	47	South Africa	27	Virgin Isl.	809 [1]
Oman	968	Spain	34	W. Samoa	685
Pakistan	92	Sri Lanka	94	Yemen	967
Palau	680	Sudan	249	Yugoslavia	381
Panama	507	Suriname	597	Zaire	243
Papua New		Swaziland	268	Zambia	260
Guinea	675	Sweden	46	Zimbabwe	263
Paraguay	595	Switzerland	41		
Peru	51	Syria	963		
Philippines	63	Taiwan	886		
Poland	48	Tajikistan	7		
Portugal	351	Tanzania	255		
Puerto Rico	787 [1]	Thailand	66		
Qatar	974	Togo	228		

[1] *Area Codes, rather than Country Codes. Dial: 1 + area code + local number.*

17. Holidays, Measurements & Miscellaneous

Holidays

It's a Holiday!
Legal or Public Holidays

Date	Holiday
Jan. 1	New Year's Day
3rd Mon. in Jan.	Martin Luther King Jr. Day
3rd Mon. in Feb.	Presidents' Day
Last Mon. in May	Memorial Day
July 4	Independence Day
1st Mon. in Sept.	Labor Day
Nov. 11	Veterans Day
4th Thurs. in Nov.	Thanksgiving
Dec. 25	Christmas Day

Taking the Day Off?
Other Often Recognized Holidays

Date	Holiday
Feb. 2	Ground Hog Day
Feb. 14	St. Valentine's Day
Apr. 1	April Fool's Day
3rd Mon. in Apr.	Patriot's Day
Last Friday in Apr.	Arbor Day
Mar. 17	St. Patrick's Day
May 1	May Day
1st Thurs. in May	National Day of Prayer
2nd Sun. in May	Mother's Day
3rd Sat. in May	Armed Forces Day
Jun. 14	Flag Day
2nd Sun. in Jun.	Children's Day
3rd Sun. in Jun.	Father's Day
1st Sun. After Labor Day	National Grandparent's Day
Sept. 17	Citizenship Day
Oct. 24	United Nations Day
Oct. 31	Halloween
1st Sat. in Nov.	Sadie Hawkins Day
Dec. 26 - Jan. 1	Kawanzaa

Anniversaries

It's Your Anniversary
Traditional Anniversary Gifts

Anni-versary	Gift
1	Paper, Clocks
2	Cotton, China
3	Leather, Crystal
4	Linnen, Appliances
5	Wood, Silverware
6	Iron, Wood
7	Wool, Desk Sets
8	Bronze, Linnens
9	Pottery, Leather
10	Tin, Diamond
11	Steel, Jewelry
12	Silk, Pearls
13	Lace, Textiles
14	Ivory, Gold
15	Crystal, Watches
20	China, Platinum
25	Silver
30	Pearl, Diamond
35	Coral, Jade
40	Ruby
45	Sapphire
50	Gold
55	Emerald
60	Diamond

For information on how to obtain birth, marriage or death records, call the U.S. Government Printing Office Superintendent of Documents at (202) 512-1800 or fax (202) 512-2250, and request the bro-chure *Where to Write for Vital Records: Births, Deaths, Marriages, and Divorces* (Stock number 017-022-01196-4).

Birthdays & Signs of the Zodiac

Happy Birthday
Birthstones and Flowers

Anniversary	Birthstone	Flower
January	Garnet	Carnation
February	Amethyst	Primrose
March	Aquamarine	Violet
April	Diamond	Daisy of Lily
May	Emerald	Lily-of-the-Valley
June	Pearl	Rose
July	Ruby	Sweet Pea
August	Peridot	Gladiolus
September	Sapphire	Aster
October	Opal	Dahlia
November	Topaz	Chrysanthemum
December	Turquoise	Poinsettia

What's Your Sign?
Signs of the Zodiac

Date of Birth	Sign	Symbol
December 22 - January 19	Capricorn	Goat
January 20 - February 18	Aquarius	Water Bearer
February 19 - March 20	Pisces	Fish
March 21 - April 19	Aries	Ram
April 20 - May 20	Taurus	Bull
May 21 - June 20	Gemini	Twins
June 21 - July 22	Cancer	Crab
July 23 - August 22	Leo	Lion
August 23 - September 22	Virgo	Virgin
September 23 - October 22	Libra	Scales
October 23 - November 21	Scorpio	Scorpion
November 22 - December 21	Sagittarius	Centaur

Chinese Calendar Cycles

Chinese Zodiac, by Birth Year

Rat	Ox	Tiger	Rabbit	Dragon	Snake
1876	1877	1878	1879	1880	1881
1888	1889	1890	1891	1892	1893
1900	1901	1902	1903	1904	1905
1912	1913	1914	1915	1916	1917
1924	1925	1926	1927	1928	1929
1936	1937	1938	1939	1940	1941
1948	1949	1950	1951	1952	1953
1960	1961	1962	1963	1964	1965
1972	1973	1974	1975	1976	1977
1984	1985	1986	1987	1988	1989
1996	1997	1998	1999	2000	2001
2008	2009	2010	2011	2012	2013

Horse	Sheep	Monkey	Rooster	Dog	Pig
1882	1883	1884	1885	1886	1887
1894	1895	1896	1897	1898	1899
1906	1907	1908	1909	1910	1911
1918	1919	1920	1921	1922	1923
1930	1931	1932	1933	1934	1935
1942	1943	1944	1945	1946	1947
1954	1955	1956	1957	1958	1959
1966	1967	1968	1969	1970	1971
1978	1979	1980	1981	1982	1983
1990	1991	1992	1993	1994	1995
2002	2003	2004	2005	2006	2007
2014	2015	2016	2017	2018	2019

U.S. & Metric Measures

U.S. Customary Measurements
U.S. Weight

Unit of Weight	Equivalent
1 dram (dr)	27 11/32 grains
1 ounce (oz)	16 drams
	437-1/2 grains
1 pound (lb)	16 ounces
	256 drams
	7,000 grains
1 hundredweight (cwt)	100 pounds
1 ton (t)	20 hundredweights
	2,000 pounds
1 gross/long hundredweight	112 pounds
1 gross or long ton	20 gross or long hundredweights
	2,240 pounds

The U.S. standard ounce and pound have their origins in early pharmacological units, refered to as avoirdupois (avdp) measures. Metric units, however, are the current standard for medical measures.

U.S. Volume -- Liquid

Unit of Volume	Equivalent
1 tablespoon (T)	3 teaspoons
1 ounce (oz)	2 tablespoons
1 gill	4 ounces
	1/2 cup
1 cup	8 ounces
	16 tablespoons
1 pint (pt)	2 cups
	16 ounces
	4 gills (gi)
1 quart (qt)	2 pints
1 gallon (gal)	4 quarts
	8 pints

U.S. Volume -- Dry

Unit of Volume	Equivalent
1 quart (qt)	2 pints (pt)
	67.2006 cubic inches
1 peck (pk)	8 quarts
	537.605 cubic inches
	16 pints
1 bushel (bu)	4 pecks
	2,150.42 cubic inches
	32 quarts

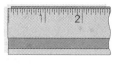 *The inch was first defined in statute by King Edward II of England as the length of three barley grains laid end to end.*

U.S. Length

Unit of Length	Equivalent
1 foot (ft)	12 inches (in)
1 yard (yd)	3 feet
1 rod (rd), pole, or perch	5 ½ yards
1 furlong (fur)	40 rods
	220 yards
	660 feet
1 statute mile (mi)	8 furlongs
	1,760 yards
	5,280 feet
1 league	3 miles
1 nautical mile	6076.11549 feet

The ancient Greek measure of a 'Cubit' is equivalent to 18.3 inches, while a Roman 'Cubit' equals 17.5 inches, by today's standards. The Greek 'Stadion' and Roman "Stadium" were similar to today's furlong, measuring 622 feet and 606 feet, respectively.

Metric System

Metric Length

Unit of Length	Equivalent
1 centimeter (cm)	10 millimeters
1 decimeter (dm)	10 centimeters
	100 millimeters
1 meter (m)	10 decimeters
	1,000 millimeters
1 dekameter (dam)	10 meters
1 hectometer (hm)	10 dekameters
	100 meters
1 kilometer (km)	10 hectometers
	1,000 meters

Metric Weights

Unit of Weight	Equivalent
1 centigram (cg)	10 milligrams
1 decigram (dg)	10 centigrams
	10 decigrams
1 gram (g)	1,000 milligrams
1 dekagram (dag)	10 grams
1 hectogram (hg)	10 dekagrams
1 kilogram (kg)	10 hectograms
	1,000 grams
1 metric ton (t)	1,000 kilograms

Metric Volume

Unit of Volume	Equivalent
1 centiliter (cL)	10 milliliters
1 deciliter (dL)	10 centiliters
	100 milliliters
1 liter (L)	10 deciliters
	1,000 milliliters
1 dekaliter (daL)	10 liters
1 hectoliter (hL)	10 dekaliters
1 kiloliter (kL)	10 hectoliters
	1,000 liters

How Many Liters in a Gallon?

Metric - U.S. Standard Conversions

Metric	U.S. Standard
1 gram	0.035274 ounce
1 kilogram	2.204623 pounds
1 metric ton	1.102 tons
	2,204.623 pounds
1 milliliter	0.271 fluid dram
1 liter	1.056688 quarts
1 dekaliter	2.642 gallons
1 hectoliter	26.418 gallons
1 millimeter	0.03937 inch
1 centimeter	0.3937 inch
1 decimeter	3.937 inches
1 meter	39.37 inches
	1.094 yards
1 dekameter	32.808 feet
1 kilometer	0.621 mile

U.S. Standard - Metric Conversions

U.S. Standard	Metric
1 ounce, liquid	29.574 milliliters
1 ounce, dry	28.34952 grams
1 pound	0.453592 kilogram
1 ton	0.90718474 metric ton
1 pint, dry	0.551 liter
1 pint, liquid	0.473 liter
1 quart, dry	1.101 liters
1 quart, liquid	0.946 liter
1 gallon	3.785 liters
1 inch	2.54 centimeters
1 foot	0.3048 meter
1 yard	0.9144 meter
1 mile	1.609 kilometers

How Fast Are You Driving?
Speed in Miles per Hour & Kilometers per Hour

m.p.h.	k.p.h.	m.p.h.	k.p.h.
5	8	50	80
10	16	55	88
15	24	60	97
20	32	65	105
25	40	70	113
30	48	75	121
35	56	80	129
40	64	90	145
45	72	100	161

How Much Does It Weigh?
Weight in Pounds & Kilograms

lbs.	kg.	lbs.	kg.	lbs.	kg.
1	0.4	50	23	180	82
2	0.9	60	27	200	91
3	1.4	70	32	210	95
4	1.8	80	36	220	100
5	2.3	90	41	230	104
6	2.7	100	45	240	108
7	3.2	110	50	250	113
8	3.6	120	54	260	118
9	4.0	130	59	270	122
10	4.5	140	64	280	127
20	9.1	150	68	290	132
30	14	160	73	300	136
40	18	170	77	310	141

Clothing Sizes

Men's Clothing & Shoe Sizes
U.S., U.K., & European Size Equivalents for Men

U.S.	U.K.	European
Men's Suits & Overcoats		
36	36	46
38	38	48
40	40	50
42	42	52
44	44	54
46	46	56
Men's Shirts		
14	14	36
14½	14½	37
15	15	38
15½	15½	39
16	16	41
16½	16½	42
17	17	43
Men's Shoes		
7	6½	39
7½	7	40½
8	7½	41
8½	8	42
9½	9	43
10½	10	44½
11½	11	46
Men's Socks		
9½	9½	39
10	10	40
10½	10½	41
11	11	42
11½	11½	43
12	12	44

Women's Clothing & Shoe Sizes

U.S., U.K., & European Size Equivalents for Women

U.S.	U.K.	European
Women's Suits & Dresses		
8	30	36
10	32	38
12	34	40
14	36	42
16	38	44
18	40	46
20	42	48
Women's Shoes		
6	4½	36½
6½	5	37
7	5½	37½
7½	6	38
8	6½	38½
8½	7	39
9	7½	40

Children's Clothing Sizes

U.S., U.K., & European Size Equivalents for Children

	U.K.		European	
U.S.	Height	Age	Height	Age
Children's Clothes				
4	43"	4-5	125cm	7
6	48"	6-7	135cm	9
8	55"	9-10	150cm	12
10	58"	11	155cm	13
12	60"	12	160cm	14
14	62"	13	165cm	15

More Ways to Measure

*The ancient Greek 'Mina'
is equal to 0.9463 of
today's pounds, while a
Roman 'Libra,' or
'Pondus' would weigh in
at 0.71864 pound.*

Other Measurements of Weight
Weight Equivalents

Unit of Weight	Equivalent
1 assay ton	29.167 grams
1 bale (cotton measure)	500 pounds in U.S.
	750 pounds in Egypt
1 carat	200 milligrams
	3.086 grains
1 gamma	1 microgram
	0.035 ounce avdp
1 grain	0.002286 ounces avdp
	64.79891 milligrams
1 metric ton	1.102311 short tons
	0.984207 long tons
	1,000 kilograms
1 ounce troy	1.097143 ounces avdp
	480 grains
	31.10348 grams
1 pennyweight	1.555 grams
1 pound troy	12 ounces troy
	13.16571 avdp
	0.373242 kilograms

Other Volume Measures

Volume Equivalents

Unit of Volume	Equivalent
1 barrel, liquid	31 to 42 gallons
1 barrel, fruits, vegetables	7,056 cubic inches
	105 dry quarts
	3.281 bushels
1 board foot	foot-square board 1 inch thick
1 bushel, U.S.	2,150.42 cubic inches
	35.239 liters
1 bushel, heaped, U.S.	2,747.715 cubic inches
	1.278 bushels
1 bushel, British Imperial	1.032 U.S. bushels
	2,219.36 cubic inches
1 cord, firewood	128 cubic feet
1 drachm, fluid, British	0.961 U.S. fluid dram
	0.217 cubic inch
	3.552 milliliters
1 dram, fluid	0.125 ounces avdp
1 gallon, British Imperial	277.42 cubic inches
	1.201 U.S. gallons
	4.546 liters
	160 British fluid ounces
1 ounce, fluid, British	0.961 U.S. fluid ounce
	1.734 cubic inches
	28.412 milliliters
1 peck	8.810 liters

The size of a barrel varies according to its use.
Federal taxes on fermented liquors are based on
barrels of 31 gallons; for proof spirits, the standard is
a 40 gallon barrel. Crude oil and petroleum products
are shipped in barrels of 42 gallons. Many state laws
recognize the 42 gallon barrel for all liquids, while
others use a barrel of 31-1/2 gallons.

Other Ways to Measure Length

Length Equivalents

Unit of Length	Equivalent
1 angstrom	0.1 nanometer
	0.000 000 1 millimeter
	0.000 000 004 inch
1 cable's length	120 fathoms
	720 feet
	219 meters
1 chain, surveyor's	66 feet
	20.1168 meters
1 chain, engineer's	100 feet
	30.48 meters
1 degree (geographical)	364,566.929 feet
° of latitude	68.708 miles at equator
	69.403 miles at poles
° of longitude	69.171 miles at equator
1 fathom	6 feet
	1.8288 meters
1 furlong	10 chains (surveyors)
	660 feet
	201.168 meters
1 hand (height for horses)	4 inches
1 league (land)	3 statute miles
	4.828 kilometers
1 link (engineer's)	1 foot
1 micrometer	0.001 millimeter
	0.000 039 37 inch
1 mil	0.001 inch
	0.025 4 millimeter
1 nautical mile	1.852 kilometers
	1.150779 miles
	6,076.11549 feet
1 nanometer	0.001 micrometer
1 pica (typography)	12 points
1 point (typography)	0.013 837 inch
	0.351 millimeter

Ships measure speed in knots, or nautical miles per hour.

Temperature Conversions

To convert temperature in degrees Fahrenheit to degrees Celsius, subtract 32 degrees and divide by 1.8; to convert Celsius to Fahrenheit, multiply by 1.8 and add 32 degrees.

Reading Thermometers
Temperature Conversions

Fahrenheit =	Celsius	Celsius =	Fahrenheit
-100	-73.3	-100	-148
-50	-45.6	-50	-58
-40	-40	-40	-40
-30	-34.4	-30	-22
-20	-28.9	-20	-4
-10	-23.3	-10	14
0	-17.8	*0*	*32*
10	-12.2	10	50
20	-6.67	20	68
30	-1.11	30	86
40	4.44	40	104
50	10	50	122
60	15.6	60	140
70	21.1	70	158
80	26.7	80	176
90	32.2	90	194
100	37.8	*100*	*212*
110	43	110	230
120	49	120	248
130	54	130	266
140	60	140	284
150	66	150	302
200	93	200	392
250	121	250	482
300	149	300	572

Numbers & Language

When in Rome
Roman Numerals

Arabic	Roman
1	I
2	II
3	III
4	IV
5	V
6	VI
7	VII
8	VIII
9	IX
10	X
11	XI
12	XII
13	XIII
14	XIV
15	XV
16	XVI
17	XVII
18	XVIII
19	XIX
20	XX
25	XXV
30	XXX
40	XL
50	L
60	LX
70	LXX
80	LXXX
90	XC
100	C
150	CL

Arabic	Roman
200	CC
300	CCC
400	CD
500	D
600	DC
700	DCC
800	DCCC
900	CM
1,000	M
1,500	MD
1,900	MCM or MDCCCC
1,910	MCMX
1,920	MCMXX
1,930	MCMXXX
1,940	MCMXL
1,950	MCML
1,960	MCMLX
1,970	MCMLXX
1,980	MCMLXXX
1,990	MCMXC
2,000	MM
3,000	MMM
4,000	MMMM or M$\overline{\text{V}}$
5,000	$\overline{\text{V}}$
10,000	$\overline{\text{X}}$
50,000	$\overline{\text{L}}$
100,000	$\overline{\text{C}}$
1,000,000	$\overline{\text{M}}$

What All those Letters Mean
Common Abbreviated Titles Following Names

Abbreviation	Meaning
B.A.	bachelor of arts
B.D.	bachelor of divinity
B.S.	bachelor of science
D.B.	bachelor of divinity *(divinitatis baccalaureus)*
D.C.	doctor of chiroprictic
D.D.	doctor of divinity *(divinitatis doctor)*
D.D.S.	doctor of dental surgery
D.O.	doctor of osteopathy
D.S.O	Distinguishesd Service Order
D.V.M.	doctor of veterinary medicine
F.N.P.	family nurse practitioner
J.D.	doctor of law *(juris doctor)*
J.P.	justice of the peace
L.H.D.	doctor of humanities *(litterarum humaniorum doctor)*
Litt.D.	doctor of letters *(litterarum doctor)*
LL.B.	*legum baccalaureus,* or bachelor of law
M.A.	master of arts
M.B.A.	master of business administration
M.D.	doctor of medicine *(medicinae doctor)*
M.P.	member of Parliament
M.S.	master of science
M.S.W.	master of social work
Ph.B.	bachelor of philosophy *(philosophiae baccalaureus)*
Ph. D.	doctor of philosophy *(philosophiae doctor)*
Ph. G.	graduate in pharmacy
Psy. D.	doctor of phychology
R.N.	registered nurse

Where Our Words Come From
Common Greek Prefixes & Suffixes

Greek Prefix	Meaning	Greek Suffix	Meaning
a	not	aglia	pain
aero	air, gas	androus	man
an	not	archy	government
anti	against	biosis	life
aster	star	chrome	color
auto	self	cracy, crat	government
biblio	book	dendron	tree
bronchio	throat	derm	skin
cardio	heart	emia	blood
chrono	time	gamy	marriage
cryo	cold	gnomy	knowledge
crypto	hidden	graph	writing
ex	out	hedron	side, sided
geo	earth, land	iasis	disease
geronto	old age	iatrics, iatry	medical
gynec	woman		treatment
helio	sun	itis	inflammation
homeo	similar	kinesis	movement
homo	same	lepsy	seizure
hydro	water	lith	stone
hypno	sleep	lyte	dissolving
macro	large	mania	craving
meta	changed	meter	measure
mono	single	nomy	science of
neo	new	opia	eye
osteo	bone	pathy	disease
pedo	child	phobia	fear
phono	sound	phony	sound
pneumo	lung	plasia	growth
poly	many	plast	cell
psuedo	false	plegia	paralysis
tele	distant	scope	observation
toxico	poison	sperm	seed

More Word Origins
Common Latin Prefixes & Suffixes

Latin Prefix	Meaning	Latin Prefix	Meaning
a	from	nati	birth
alti	high	nocti	night
ambi	both	oculo	eye
ante	before	oleo	oil
aqui	water	oro	mouth
arbori	tree	ossi	bone
audio	hearing	pari	equal
avi	bird	pisci	fish
centi	hundred	plano	flat
cerebro	brain	pluvio	rain
co	with	post	after
contra	arainst	pre	before
cruci	cross	preter	beyond
de	not, down	primi	first
deci	tenth	pulmo	lung
demi	half	quadri	four
denti	tooth	re	again
digit	finger	reni	kidney
extra	outside	retro	backward
ferri	iron	sangui	blood
fluvio	river	spiro	breath
igni	fire	stelli	star
inter	between	terri	land
intra	inside	trans	through
juxta	beside	uni	one
labio	lip	vario	different
lacto	milk		
luni	moon	**Latin Suffix**	**Meaning**
magni	great	cidal	kill
mal	bad	fugal	run away
multi	many	grade	walking
naso	nose	vorous	eating

Commonly Misspelled Words

accept/except	fascinate	omitted
accessory	fatigue	parallel
accidentally	forth/fourth	parliament
accommodate	freight	phenomenon
accompany	government	potatoes
accrue	grammar	precede/
acquaintance	guarantee	proceed
acquire	guess	privilege
address	guest	probably
all right	harass	quiet/quite
argument	height	receipt
athletic	hygiene	receive
bargain	independence	recommend
beginning	indict	reference
bizarre	indispensable	rendezvous
bookkeeper	its/it's	ridiculous
calendar	judgment	sandwich
capital/capitol	khaki	scissors
cinnamon	league	seize
cough	license	separately
debt	literature	similar
dependent	lying	special
disappear	maintenance	succeed
disappoint	maneuver	success
dissatisfied	mosquitoes	suit/suite
effect/affect	necessary	they're/there/
eighth	neighbor	their
embarrass	noticeable	Tuesday
environment	obedience	usually
exaggerate	occur	vacuum
exceed	occurred	Wednesday
existence	offence	weird

Stain Removal

Generally, stains can be categorized as greasy, non-greasy, or combination. To remove a greasy stain from washable fabrics, rub detergent into the stain, let stand for several hours and then wash. If the stain remains, sponge with a grease solvent. For non-greasy stains, begin by sponging with cool water or soaking for 30 minutes or more in cool water. If the stain persists, rub with detergent and rinse, or use bleach. Treat combination stains the same as non-greasy stains. If, after treatment, a greasy stain remains, use a grease solvent. If a colored stain remains, use bleach.

Stain Removal Guide
Types of Stains -- Follow Instructions Above

Greasy	Non-greasy	Combination
Butter/margarine	Blood	Candy
Furniture polish	Scorching	Chocolate
Car grease	Coffee, tea (black)	Coffee, tea
Lard	Urine	(with cream)
Mineral oil	Cocoa	Gravy/meat juice
Vegetable oil	Alcohol/perfume	Ice cream
Linseed oil	Eggs	Mayonnaise
Fish-liver oil	Catsup	Salad dressing
Tar	Ink	Sauces
Floor wax	Milk	Soups
Car wax	Soft drinks	Cream
Machine oil	Vegetables	Syrup

More About Stubborn Stains
Stain Removal Tips for Washable Fabrics

Stain	Removal Tip
Acids	Rinse immediately. Apply ammonia. Rinse again.
Adhesive tape, chewing gum	Scrape gently from fabric. Sponge with grease solvent.
Carbon paper	Rub detergent into stain. Rinse well. If stain persists, apply a few drops of ammonia and repeat treatment.
Cosmetics	Apply detergent. Rub until suds form. Continue working until outline of stain is gone, rinse well. Repeat if necessary.
Fruit, fruit juices	Sponge immediately with cool water. Use non-greasy stain treatment, or pour boiling water over stain (if safe for fabric)
Grass, flowers, tobacco	Work detergent into stain, the rinse. sponge with alcohol (if safe for fabric). Dilute alcohol with 2 parts water for use on acetate. If stain remains, use bleach.
Metals (tarnish)	Apply vinegar, lemon juice, acetic acid, or oxalic acid.
Mildew	Wash thououghly. Dry in the sun. If stain remains, treat with bleach.
Mustard	Rub detergent into stain. Rinse. If stain persists, soak in hot detergent solution for several hours, or use bleach.
Nail polish	Sponge with acetone or amyl acetate, or nail polish remover. Test first on fabric for safety.
Paint	If wet, rub detergent into stain and wash. If dried, sponge with turpentine, then rub with detergent and soak in hot water overnight. Wash. Repeat if necessary.
Pencil	Use soft eraser.
Perspiration	Sponge with detergent and warm water. Apply ammonia to fresh stains and vinegar to old stains. Rinse.

Tipping

Tips on Tipping
How Much to Tip for Services Adequately Rendered

Location	Person	Tip Amount
Restaurant	Waiter	15% of bill
	Maitre d'	None, unless special services provided, then $5
	Wine steward	15% of wine bill
	Bartender	15% of bar bill
	Busboy	None
	Coat check att'd.	$1
	Restroom att'd.	$1
	Car park att'd.	$1
Hotel	Chambermaid	None for one-night stay; $1 - $2 a night for longer stays
	Room service	15% of bill
	Bellhop	$1 per bag
Train	Waiter	15% of bill
	Bar stewards	15% of bar bill
	Red caps	Posted rate plus 50 cents
Airports	Skycaps	$1 or more for baggage cart
	In-flight att'd.	None
Cruise ship	Cabin steward	2.5% - 4% of total fare
	Dining rm. steward	2.5% - 4% of total fare
	Cabin boy, bath steward, bar steward, wine steward	5% - 7% of total fare, divided among them, paid weekly
Taxi	Driver	15% of fare
Barbershop	Haircutter	15% of bill
Beatyshop	Operator	15% of bill
	Manicurist	$1 - $2, or more, depending on cost
Sports arena	Usher	50 cents to $1 if shown to seat

Index